PENGUIN BOOKS

The Rise of the Player Manager

Philip Augar was a Player Manager in investment banking for twenty years. His first book, *The Death of Gentlemanly Capitalism*, was published by Penguin in 2000 and he now writes, broadcasts and lectures on financial services and related issues. He has a doctorate in History and is a Visiting Fellow at Cranfield School of Management.

Joy Palmer has run Interactives in the UK and US for over fifteen years while serving as a coach and advisor to Global 500 companies. She co-authored her first book, *Delivering Exceptional Performance*, published by FT Management, in 1996 and has taught and written extensively about new forms of organization and work.

The authors can be contacted at www.player-manager.com

The Rise of the Player Manager

Philip Augar and Joy Palmer

PENGUIN BOOKS

PENGUIN BOOKS

Published by the Penguin Group
Penguin Books Ltd, 80 Strand, London WC2R ORL, England
Penguin Putnam Inc., 375 Hudson Street, New York, New York 10014, USA
Penguin Books Australia Ltd, 250 Camberwell Road, Camberwell, Victoria 3124, Australia
Penguin Books Canada Ltd, 10 Alcorn Avenue, Toronto, Ontario, Canada M4V 3B2
Penguin Books India (P) Ltd, 11, Community Centre, Panchsheel Park, New Delhi – 110 017, India
Penguin Books (NZ) Ltd, Cnr Rosedale and Airborne Roads, Albany, Auckland, New Zealand
Penguin Books (South Africa) (Pty) Ltd, 24 Sturdee Avenue, Rosebank 2196, South Africa

Penguin Books Ltd, Registered Offices: 80 Strand, London WC2R ORL, England

www.penguin.com

First published 2002
1

Copyright © Philip Augar and Joy Palmer, 2002

Grateful acknowledgement is given to Faber and Faber Ltd for
permission to reprint three lines from 'Macavity: The Mystery Cat'
from Old Possum's Book of Practical Cats by T. S. Eliot

Set in Sabon and TheSans
Typeset by Rowland Phototypesetting Ltd, Bury St Edmunds, Suffolk
Printed in England by Clays Ltd, St Ives plc

ISBN 0-140-28665-9

To Elliott, Harrison, Ian
and
Sally

Contents

Methodology

The book is in three parts. Part One, 'The Rise of the Player Manager', defines our subject and traces its origins.

Part Two, 'Player Managers at Work', tells stories about different types of Player Manager and their organization climate.

Part Three, 'Double Jeopardy', is a single chapter that looks at the future of work for Player Managers.

The book is based on fieldwork with over five hundred people in the private and public sectors in the UK and US over the last four years. This comprised interviews, shadowing, training, coaching and 360 degree assessments. We have combined the results with our own experiences of player managing but we have not carried out an academic study.

We have changed personal details, amalgamated certain characters, conversations and events and created new settings. As a consequence of this methodology few events occurred exactly as described, and the people, publications and corporate entities that feature in Part Two do not, as far as we are aware, exist. Any resemblance to real people, places and entities is unintentional.

The use of stories is not common in business literature. Our approach is intended to inform without being prescriptive. We have been involved in management for too long and have made too many mistakes of our own to believe that we have any right to tell readers what to do or how to do it, but we hope that Player Managers everywhere will find something of interest in what we tell.

Acknowledgements

We first used the term Player Manager at a Schroders conference following encouragement from Sue Cox and Nick Ferguson. We would like to acknowledge their support together with the work of Judith Hesketh, Peter Cole, Lea Blackham, David Perry and Lynne Smitham, our faculty colleagues. Joy developed her ideas in this field after working with Janice Light, Gwen Ventris, Bill Halbert, Ed Lee and Charles Doyle, and with the help of Michelle Keeley. We are grateful for the research of Deana Plummer and Catherine Black and for the invaluable critical input of George Pearson, Sir Keith Peters, Professor Richard Taffler and, at Penguin, Stuart Proffitt and Daniel Hind.

Our work has brought us into contact with many Player Managers. Most spoke to us on a confidential basis, and in the interests of balance we have decided not to name any of those who helped with our fieldwork. However, we are deeply grateful to all of these men and women.

Finally, thanks go to our respective families, Denise, William and Rachel in England, and Ian, Harrison and Elliott in the USA. All of them had to put up with us, and sometimes with each other, as we travelled back and forth across the Atlantic to write this book.

Joy's Preface

To avoid the troublesome business of sorting out my own problems I threw myself into making a living from coaching and developing others. This involved working with people who were juggling professional work and management, but the first time I heard the term Player Manager in business was in 1998. Schroders, the London investment bank, approached me with an idea to run a programme to develop the management skills of around eighty of the firm's highest potential producers.

Each year these high flyers were brought together in a programme called 'Synergy'. To date its primary objective had been cross-divisional networking. This year the sponsor was to be Philip Augar, one of the Group Managing Directors. People I knew described Philip to me as a man with some very interesting ideas and with an intellectual depth that was unusual in the City. They felt that Philip and I would hit it off and have many interesting discussions together.

We have indeed had many interesting discussions together since that initial meeting. As for hitting it off when we met, well, nothing could have been wider of the mark.

Management skills were never a highly praised attribute in the City of London, kudos going instead to star producers. I was warned that it would be difficult to tackle too openly the 'soft' people-related skills of management, even though these were considerably underdeveloped. 'You have to appreciate that many of the top people in the City closed down emotionally as boys in boarding school,' a colleague told me. 'The idea of opening up again makes them squirm.' However, the firm formally engaged me and I began to develop a structure and faculty team for the programme, but beyond that there was not much more I could do to tailor it without meeting the conference sponsor and chairman. It was time to meet Philip Augar.

In a week that I was delivering management training to a diverse group of international business managers on a programme at Ashridge Management College, I travelled into London for a lunchtime meeting with Philip. My assumptions were that he had read my proposal, been briefed as to my background and been party to the decision to hire me. I was wrong.

Although I was greeted cordially and calmly, something quietly penetrating in Philip's gaze told me I was about to undergo the same kind of thorough scrutiny that a father reserves for a daughter just home from a first date.

'You do understand the difference between two types of consultancy, don't you?' Philip asked in a disquieting tone. 'The first type is when a consultant is hired to do a specific job and the second type is more open ended, when the consultant comes in for longer to help with change. This assignment is the first type.'

I said that I understood the boundaries of the assignment, adding that it was like distinguishing between safe and unsafe sex. Although I felt he was less than reassured we moved on – but not much further. After giving an outline of my past successes with similar projects his quietly penetrating gaze returned, accompanied by a question that left me nonplussed.

'Have we hired you?' Philip asked pointedly.

'Yes,' I replied, but as I said it I knew that this was not the answer he had wanted. What is going on, I wondered, and why was everyone so confident that I would strike a rapport with this man? As the meeting closed I was no longer sure I wanted the job, and I felt safe in assuming that Philip wasn't sure he wanted me either. So much for my initial assumptions!

The only glimmer of hope for any meeting of minds was the concept of the Player Manager or 'Player Coach' as it is usually called in the US. Like many female professionals I was used to forcing a smile when listening to military and sports analogies of business, especially described by delusional male counterparts. Yet as I sat listening to Philip telling me how he had taken the idea from sport, the concept caught my attention and made immediate sense. As a management coach, I knew that one of the most difficult career transitions for any individual was to combine existing technical work with new management responsibilities. I had worked on models for dealing with this in my early career at Texas Instruments and subsequently in my consulting work and writing. I was used to the need for professionals to develop on a dual axis – adding greater breadth of business and relationship skills to complement their deep, but often narrow, technical skills. Frameworks of this kind that aided the professionals' progression to management were always in demand.

First impressions count. But in the case of my first meeting with Philip they were not fatal. Despite initial discomfort on both sides Philip and I were able to work around our differences, coming together with a zeal for the Player Manager. It became the unifying theme of the conference at Schroders. Beyond that, we have worked together to understand the relevance of the concept to the changing world of management and organizations. In the process I have even learned something about sport.

Soon after the Synergy conference, my business and family moved to the US. I began working on Wall Street and for other American professional services firms. I was struck by the fact that most of the executives I was working with were Player Managers. I coached women and men who were striving to be better managers and leaders while continuing to deliver personal results. I remember calling Philip to discuss this, and we came up with the idea of writing this book.

Work, like any adventure, can never be completely safe. Player Managers cannot take refuge in the status quo, accepting the limitations of their personal skills or the position of the team they are managing. Player Managers must move the game on, recognizing the need to continually redefine their expertise if they are to succeed in a dynamic, competitive environment.

This book explores the socio-economic forces that have contrived to make many of us Player Managers and discusses the challenges that this role brings. While the stories that we tell are not completely factual, they are not completely fictional either.

Joy Palmer
Austin, Texas, 2002

Philip's Preface

I spent much of my early life in a fantasy world where my day job was an unwelcome but temporary intrusion into my true calling as a professional sportsman. As I realized that dreams do not always come true and that I lacked the talent to become a professional sportsman, I drew some comfort from the similarities between the skills needed to succeed in their world – technical ability, positive thinking and tactical acumen – and in mine.

The management skills needed to run a successful team are very similar in sport and work. Factors such as time management, motivation, improving the skills of the players, strategic direction and discipline are as relevant to the head coach of a sports team as to a business leader. The purpose for which these skills are deployed might be different, the language of working and sporting activity might be dissimilar, the culture and characteristics of the participants will almost certainly diverge, but the basic management task of getting a group of people to work together successfully for the organization's common aims is identical.

I understood this when, being new to management, I heard an interview with a recently appointed football coach. One of his players had missed an easy chance to win a match, and the coach recounted how initially he had joined in with the crowd's groan and begun to berate the unfortunate player. Then it occurred to him: that's really my responsibility, not his. He asked himself, 'Was I right to have selected him, to play him in that position, and if so, how could I have prepared him better to take that chance?'

I had faced an identical situation at work when a member of my team had made a major error of judgement. As the individual's manager, my initial reaction of irritation quickly gave way to a feeling of responsibility. I considered whether it was fair to have exposed the person in that way and if so, how I could have helped them improve their performance.

The connection between sport and work resurfaced for me when I was given a new job that required me to manage a team whilst continuing to be a producer within it. At around this time Liverpool Football Club gave one of its star players, Kenny Dalglish, the additional responsibility of managing the team. Dalglish was very successful, winning trophies and maintaining high standards as a player. My initial experience was less good – no trophies and a decline in my personal performance. However, it struck me that the challenges facing us in learning the art of management whilst also striving to maintain the highest levels of playing performance were similar. I wondered how many other people were struggling to combine these two roles. Unable to find much specialist training literature addressed to Player Managers I, like many other managers looking for help, devised my own way of coping: a mixture of common sense, theories devised on the job and humbling mistakes. In short, just plain old muddling through.

In 1998, Schroders, the investment bank for whom I worked, asked me to run the group's annual offsite weekend for its most promising people. These included some of the firm's best producers who had either just become, or were about to be, team leaders. I chose The Player Manager as the theme, believing this would capture the management challenge they faced. In the summer of that year, 1998, the firm hired a consultant, Joy Palmer, to work with us to develop a programme for an offsite meeting to be held in September.

Initially, preparations did not go well. Joy came to see me, having already been engaged by the firm to work on the job; I was expecting to meet someone who was at the top of the shortlist but who had not yet been hired. I had just been through a couple of bad experiences with consultants and had envisaged having some influence over the final selection. Like most people, my view of the future was heavily influenced by the immediate past. Some previous consultants had blinded me with science, or 'management speak' as I called it, and had not been reliable at delivering on time or in detailed implementation. My first impression of Joy was coloured by this: she seemed to use a lot of jargon and was not someone I felt I could trust to deliver a programme of this magnitude. Her ideas seemed wacky, she threw a lot of concepts at me and, to begin with, my doubts about consultants were confirmed. However, the contract had been signed and I felt that I had no choice but to press on. Joy began to develop an outline programme, briefing me on progress every couple of weeks during the summer of 1998.

She built a theoretical framework around my Player Manager idea and a curriculum to cover the key skills. Substance was added to what had previously been a concept without a core. Equally important to me, as I was very busy trying to cope with managing my own business on a day-to-day basis, Joy demonstrated a grip on detail and commitment to delivery that won my confidence. I became fully engaged in the process of transforming a hazy outline of how to develop Player Managers into a rigorous programme.

The theme struck a chord with those attending the conference. Many of them had been thrown in at the deep end in their first managerial jobs, and they were grateful for the practical training as well as the opportunity to discuss their problems in open forum. Their feedback and enthusiasm encouraged us to persist further with the Player Manager. This book is the result.

Philip Augar
Cambridge, England, 2002

PART ONE

The Rise of the Player Manager

I

Managing While You Work

As a model for management, the Player Manager isn't exactly new. From the time that prehistoric tribes sustained themselves by eating what they killed until the time that postmodern teams sustained themselves by, well, by eating what they killed, Player Managers have always been around.

A Player Manager, as the name suggests, is someone who combines the roles of producing and managing. Numerous business and public service professionals, foremen in industry and construction, farmers, shopkeepers and many more small independent business owners combine working in an organization with managing.

Think of any profession or any business today and the chances are that you will find Player Managers at the core. In healthcare, sisters on the ward and senior doctors who combine patient care with management responsibility are good examples. In education, department heads who have budgets to control, programmes to plan and people to manage in addition to doing their own research and teaching are Player Managers. So too are senior partners of law firms, running the business whilst also handling cases, the investment bankers, accountants and management consultants who juggle client interface with team management, and the millions of people in business and industry who routinely balance managing while they work.

Historically, there were two reasons for the existence of Player Managers. The first is economic, in that many enterprises relied on Player Managers because they could not afford full time managers. They found it more cost effective to have senior producers double up as managers than to employ two people in separate roles. The second is the prevalent culture in many professions that has always valued 'playing' above 'managing'. Over the years interplay in ideas about progress and production has at different times both increased and decreased the emphasis on management.

The Golden Age of Management.   Management's apotheosis was in the middle of the twentieth century when it became recognized as both a profession in its own right and an integral part of modern business. Large national and multinational organizations reasserted themselves in the period after the Great Depression of the thirties. Military success in World War Two reinforced hierarchical, authority-based structures and confirmed the importance of management as a function. By the 1950s and 1960s, full time managers and the corporations that employed them were regarded as the mainstays of production and the pillars of society.

The hegemony of management was such that people believed it could compensate for leadership.[1] The business manager – 'not a "theorist" but a practical man' according to Galbraith in *The Affluent Society*[2] – who could oversee how to get things done, was considered necessary at every supervisory level. People were appointed to run teams, factories and offices free of the burden of production responsibilities. Badges of rank like a separate office, a secretary, and different working clothes, dining facilities and salary structures distinguished the manager from the worker and other specialist players.

Player Managers still existed at this time, particularly in the old professions and small enterprises that could not afford a layer of full time management. But in larger organizations, the rise of full time middle management minimized the role of 'Player Managing', often pushing it down onto the shop floor in the form of supervisory responsibilities for senior operatives.

Even in the Golden Age, management had its critics. Writers like C. Wright Mills raised concerns about bureaucracy crushing individualism, and in 1959 Vance Packard's book *The Status Seekers* linked hierarchical management with emerging class divisions in society. The institutions that made management came under attack from several sources. Ralph Nader's crusade against corporate irresponsibility started in 1964, and capitalism itself and the growing power of multinationals were targets for the student protesters of the 1960s.[3]

But these criticisms were not yet mainstream. Although the economic problems caused by the oil crises of the early 1970s might have shaken faith in the established order, there seemed little alternative to the prevailing system of management. Indeed, at the end of the third quarter of the twentieth century, full time management as a profession was still apparently safe, secure, and more prestigious than pure producing.[4]

Management had become a highly prestigious career. To be a rising young executive was to have arrived and, as competition for such jobs increased, so did the range and number of qualifications that were offered by professional bodies and educational institutions. The enlargement of MBA programmes and the creation of an academic discipline around management theory further added to its legitimacy. However, this apparent security was about to be seriously threatened as the profitable growth that had followed World War Two began to taper off in the face of rising inflation and competition from the East. In the last quarter of the century, this brought about an end to the Golden Age of Management and ushered in changes in the way that organizations were managed, leading to a bigger role for Player Managers.

'Why can't we?' If we were to pinpoint a moment in history when the Golden Age of Management was significantly challenged, we might pick 24 June 1980; it was then that viewers in the United States watched an NBC programme entitled 'If Japan Can . . . Why Can't We?'[5] This revealed that the Japanese award for quality was named after an American, William Edwards Deming, who was virtually unknown in his own country. A revolution would soon break around the idea of 'quality' as a mantra for restoring productivity in the West, on the back of which the conventional wisdom of management crumbled.

Competition from Japan stimulated great interest in the management techniques that were proving to be so effective there. Traditionally-managed firms studied Japanese competitors and implemented their methods. Ford in 1980 applied a programme of labour relations known simply as 'AJ' (After Japan): 'Instead of the rigid job classifications and tight managerial control which were characteristic of Fordism, the Japanese system relied on teams of workers capable of carrying out a variety of different tasks and committed to a constant drive for better quality and higher productivity.'[6] These Japanese work practices and the culture of 'quality' that encouraged teamwork and employee involvement created the right environment for Player Managers to flourish.

What started as a hunger for quality soon became a more general appetite for change and transformation and spread beyond the US. In the UK, where managerial incompetence was fast gaining public attention, several enquiries were launched, leading to proposals to improve leadership and management skills through more systematic approaches to management development.[7]

The imposition of codes of conduct drawn up by so-called 'experts' and bureaucrats provoked vocal resistance from sections of the private and public sectors, but the idea slowly and surely took hold that someone's ability to manage others productively should be more formally developed. It came to predominate over the view that managing, like home improvement, could be mastered by amateur DIY. As a result, the templates that emerged for managing in these years increasingly included not only 'hard' competencies such as 'efficiency orientation' and 'commercial acumen' but also 'soft' competencies such as 'influencing and developing others', many of which were tools to help achieve the new focus of management thinking at this time, namely 'empowerment'.

The concept of empowerment was explained by Peter Drucker, later cited as the guru's guru, as 'the assumption of managerial responsibility by the individual employee, the work team, and the employee group alike'.[8] A seminal paper published in the US in 1983 by Yankelovich and Immerwahr entitled *Putting the Work Ethic to Work*[9] drew attention to what they termed 'discretionary effort', in effect the difference between someone's best possible work and the minimum they have to do to not get fired. The challenge for management was straightforward: how to engender a climate where everybody was motivated to give consistently their best, not least, possible effort.

The key question was what sort of climate that might be. For a post Kennedy, post beat, post Vietnam generation comprising an increasingly white-collar and well-educated workforce, the only palatable method would need to be more democratic than what had prevailed in the old 'command and control' model. Empowerment, the process by which authority as well as work was handed on to others, soon became the preferred method for creating a positive work climate. It would create an environment, it was believed, that would secure the 'discretionary effort' from which high performance would follow.

The idea that people worked better if they felt fulfilled and that involvement was the key to fulfilment, gained ground. Theories developed by psychologists such as Maslow[10] and Herzberg[11] through the 1960s were increasingly applied and developed into full-blown treatises by academics, notably the Harvard professor Rosabeth Moss Kanter in *The Change Masters*.[12] Theories of empowerment reached into hierarchical models and led to the devolution of responsibility to grades that were previously non-managerial. These were Player Managers.

Practice Meets Theory. Against this background of developing theory and the example of Japan, three factors in the last quarter of the twentieth century increased the importance of Player Managing. The first factor was tied to the elevation of shareholder value above other considerations in the private sector in the 1980s. Organizations had to meet more demanding financial targets, which involved more management, whilst at the same time cutting costs, which implied employing fewer people. One solution to these apparently conflicting forces was to cut out middle management and create Player Managers out of producers.

The second factor in the rise of the Player Manager was the massive change occurring in the public and private professional services sectors from the 1980s onwards. The spread of ideas about 'managing for value' into public sector professions such as health and education meant adjusting to cultures of performance. Traditionally hostile to 'management' and previously glorifying the value of almost pure playing, the public sector simultaneously expanded professional administration and also turned many specialists – for example teachers, academics and doctors – into Player Managers by imposing market economy considerations. Likewise expansion and consolidation in the private sector service economy led to the need for more management in firms traditionally reluctant to manage. The implications of complexity and scale led to the global professional services firm, the emergence of publicly owned 'professional partnerships' such as Goldman Sachs and Accenture, and the spread of managerial practice. This created more full time managers and increased Player Managing as the professionals in these firms faced the demands of working in more complex and more managed businesses.

The third factor giving rise to the Player Manager was the growth of the information economy, particularly the 'New Economy', alongside manufacturing and services. Business advantage was being redefined away from tangible assets to intellectual capital. As Microsoft rather than General Motors and US Steel became the model of a modern corporation, 'knowledge workers' with an expectation of being decision makers replaced less skilled workers accustomed to command and control as the driving force in Western economies. As the importance of the industrial organization declined, so too did the power of the pure manager. After all, if Microsoft's growth relied on coders rather than on professional managers, then management as a full time discipline seemed somewhat less essential.

These three factors converged to challenge three accepted truths. First, that command and control hierarchies were the best way to structure and organize work productively; second, that the corresponding 'top down' authority structures of large organizations were an effective way to motivate people and manage business decisions; and third, that top-heavy cadres of full time managers separated from other types of workers were the best custodians of the organization's performance. In their place came not only more developed ideas about empowerment but also a further wave of management thinking, emphasizing the importance of human[13] and intellectual assets[14] and requiring 'adaptive'[15] leaders and 'flexible'[16] approaches to managing business complexity. All of this came together to create the rise of the Player Manager.

Missed Connections. Curiously, although much of the new management literature has acknowledged that producing and managing are increasingly hard to separate, there has been little recognition of Player Managers *as a group*. The 'responsible worker' was at the heart of the ideas of Drucker and others that led to empowerment and post-industrial emergence, but the interests of Player Managers as a group were not much discussed. A huge body of management literature including good answers to direct questions like 'What is happening to middle management?'[17] has missed the point that, for many people, playing and managing are inextricably entwined. Many excellent studies of the changing nature of management in the professions,[18] in the public sector[19] and in industry[20] have acknowledged the increasing involvement of producers in management but have stopped short of defining the Player Manager as a distinct and important category of management. Similarly, comments about the creation of new kinds of jobs such as 'knowledge workers'[21] and 'customer managers'[22] in the post-industrial economy have perceived how specialist producers now have more involvement in managing. Yet few discuss the peculiar problems that result from combining the two activities.

Some observers come close. An article published in 1987 referred to 'the producing manager: a person responsible for both management activities and generation of client services'.[23] The term 'producer manager' is used in some professional services firms such as Goldman Sachs and Merrill Lynch but has not become mainstream. In organizations and in the literature there are many references to 'producer' and even more references to 'manager', but very little that joins them together.

British academic Harry Scarbrough recognized how changes in the structure of organizations spread management across different groups. His 1998 paper 'The Unmaking of Management' contrasted the outcome for British managers with the path predicted in the 1980s by, amongst others, Charles Handy in his report 'The Making of Managers'. Scarbrough observed that: 'Although the flatter hierarchy of JIT/TQC suggests that the controlling function of middle management has completely disappeared, we would argue that, rather than being dispensed with, it has simply been incorporated into the consciousness of the members themselves'.[24] He had noticed what our research bears out. Managing was not reduced during the period of restructuring in the West but instead reallocated across a wider spectrum, away from what was known as middle management and into the hands of producers.

Occasional references apart,[25] Player Managers as a category have largely been overlooked and unrecognized. Yet it is a complex role, made more so by the demands of shareholders to get more from less and the ever intensifying pace of work. For Player Managers this means a dual workload, competing demands, the need to learn new skills and, in many cases, an employer who is either ignorant of, or indifferent to, the challenges. Not surprisingly given this background, during the course of our research we found many Player Managers who were performing below their potential and others who were turning away from the stresses that the role brings. This has serious implications, for it is usually the most ambitious and valuable people, the very ones that companies can least afford to lose to disillusionment, burnout or competitors, that are asked to combine production and management responsibilities.

If, as seems likely, the Player Manager remains at the core of twenty-first century work, the model can evolve in one of two ways. The adoption of more democratic and adaptive work cultures, with higher levels of autonomy, offers the potential of improved job satisfaction along with improved results. If, on the other hand, employers persist with a mechanized emphasis on short-term results, then more work, more stress and less fulfilment are likely. This could ultimately jeopardize the organization's success. Neither outcome is by any means guaranteed.

2
Step Up the Player Manager

In this chapter we discuss the three major influences that gave rise to the Player Manager over the last quarter of a century. These are the elevation of shareholder value as a business rationale, the growth of the professional services sector and the emergence of the New Economy.

1. Managing for Value
'Winning the right to manage'

It often takes a crisis to bring about change and there was enough going wrong in Western economies in the 1970s to cause a break with the past. The oil crisis had provided a major shock to the stock market and increased industry's raw material costs. Double-digit inflation became a fact of life defying various Governments' attempts to 'Whip Inflation Now' (WIN: Gerald Ford's campaign slogan in 1976).

Corporate America found itself facing competitive decline in an emerging global economy. The Japanese in particular were challenging the supremacy of the American way, and US manufacturers were losing market share to higher-quality Japanese consumer goods. National confidence was broken and there was a search for solutions. The UK was experiencing similar problems of high inflation and a lack of competitiveness compounded by industrial relations strife. The circumstances were ripe for political change. New politicians with a different message took power as Mrs Thatcher formed her first Government in 1979 and Ronald Reagan was elected President in 1980. New economic policies built around monetarism in the UK, supply-side economics in the US and a belief nearly everywhere in the virtues of open market competition and deregulation, transformed the environ-ment for business.

Inflation became public enemy number one in the US and UK, and labour costs became a favourite weapon with which to beat it. Pro-ductivity gains replaced price rises as the most acceptable way to increase profits. It was easier to cut costs than to increase volume in the search for productivity. In the UK in particular, where the emasculation of the trade unions under Mrs Thatcher's government tilted the balance between employer and employee, downsizing became not merely acceptable but a virility symbol for senior management. We moved to a world where redundancies were more likely to be described as 'jobs saved' than 'jobs lost' and where managers exulted in the re-establishment of their managerial prerogative. 'For the first time in my career', one of them told us, 'we had won the right to manage.'

The Elevation of Shareholder Value

The belief that markets were best placed to make business judgements fitted in well with the emerging concept of shareholder value that came to dominate all others as the rationale for business: 'The notion of shareholder value as the guiding ethic of business . . . began to get a serious hearing in the 1970s as a new breed of investment bankers saw in these theories a way to make a lot of money quickly'.[1] Respectability was conferred by the work of Alfred Rappaport of Northwestern University Business School.[2] Business people fell eagerly on these ideas, believing that everything could be justified as long as it was in the interests of the shareholders. In the drive to grow earnings per share, ruthless cost cutting, financial engineering and a wave of mergers and acquisitions characterized the business landscape of the 1980s.[3]

Fear became a factor in corporate decision-making. In a series of high profile takeover battles in the 1980s, corporate raiders used innovative financing techniques to buy shares that had fallen far below asset value. The title of the definitive study of Kohlberg, Kravis, and Roberts's bid for RJR-Nabisco in 1988 – *Barbarians at the Gate* – summarized the fear that corporate America had at this time, a fear that motivated managements into programmes of massive cost cutting.

What we have described reflected a trend right across the developed world. The one hundred largest companies in the US shed a quarter of their workforce between 1980 and 1995, a total of four million jobs. GE under Jack Welch was one of the first companies to respond, cutting all businesses not capable of superior performance and buying new ones that offered the potential for more value. One analysis showed that almost one third of the hundred largest market capitalization companies in the United States followed the direction of GE. GM, IBM, Dow Chemical, Pepsico, Procter & Gamble, 3M and many others downsized, reduced real spending on R&D, disposed of various parts of their business while buying others and invested heavily in stock buy-back programmes.[4]

In the UK, aggressive conglomerates like Hanson Industries, BTR and Williams applied similar principles. They bought badly run companies, improved the bottom line by closing intractable loss makers and imposed better cost control on the parts they retained. The message quickly spread throughout industry as management learned that if they too did not introduce 'best practice', their companies and their jobs would be gone. 'A new generation of corporate predators came on the scene and even the largest companies were not immune to the threat of takeover.'[5] Shareholders wanted value, not loyalty. Soon the about-to-be privatized public utilities like BT (British Telecom), BG (British Gas) and the electricity and water companies were subjected to the same treatment as staffing levels were slashed in a frenzy of preparations for 'free market competition'. At BT for example, a company in 1984 with a quarter of a million employees and a reputation for never having imposed redundancy, staff numbers were first managed down in 1985 ahead of privatization and by 1999 had fallen to just half of 1984's total.

In mainland Europe neoconservatism had not ascended so quickly. Some countries still had socialist governments and a more robust system of labour representation. The corporate culture on the Continent was different, with a greater degree of ownership by the founding families and with the big banks, especially in Germany, using their substantial stakes and board representation to encourage longer term considerations. This 'Rhine Model' also prevailed in Switzerland and Holland and gave some protection against the pressures of shareholders' short-termism, but the ripple effect spread to the Continent where 20% of all jobs in manufacturing industry were cut in the eighties and early nineties. Certain industries were affected especially

seriously. Old ones like textiles and leather experienced massive consolidation: the number of firms in these activities in Germany more
than halved in the final quarter of the last century. In France, where
the corporate culture was poised midway between the Rhine and
American models, the defence industry lost 90,000 jobs out of a total
of 270,000 between 1982 and 1993.[6]

New technology combined with the pursuit of shareholder value
had a massive impact on many industries. For example in Banking,
after computers speeded up data handling and improved accuracy, the
banks required fewer people and so reassessed their branch networks.
Analysts eagerly watched cost to income ratios as shareholder value
was elevated above customer service and loyalty to staff as the benchmark of success. In the UK, Barclays and NatWest for example each
shed a third of their staff in the 1990s, cutting 40,000 and 30,000
jobs respectively. A senior manager at another British bank, Lloyds,
described the new culture there as 'results-driven, ruthless in pursuit
of excellence and performance', and a leading commentator summed
it up as 'a culture in which the bank is run as a business for shareholder
value with minimal priority on people.'[7]

A similar pattern occurred in the US in the 1990s. Driven by
opportunities arising from new technology and a wave of mergers,
banks such as Chase, First Union, US Bancorp and NationsBank were
able to achieve massive staff savings between themselves and their
partners. By the mid 1990s, US banks' average costs had fallen to just
56% of their revenues, the lowest since 1960.[8]

As the pursuit of shareholder value opened up industry to market
forces, many industries found new ways to survive whether by cost
cutting, hunting for niche markets, demerging non-core divisions or
seeking foreign investment. In Britain the financial results were dramatic in sectors as diverse as Paper, Textiles, Engineering, Aerospace
and Airlines.[9] Apparently intractable loss makers were turned round.
British Steel, a company that had lost £1.8 billion in 1979–80, was
successfully privatized in 1988 with 52,000 employees compared to
142,000 at the start of the decade. There was a period of sustained
growth in the economy between 1982 and 1989, when manufacturing
output grew by 29% during these eight years. Output per head grew
every year from 1982 into the 1990s, faltering but not falling even
during the Major–Lamont recession of 1990–91.[10]

The US also experienced a dramatic and sustained surge in pro-ductivity. After the recession early in the 1990s it rebounded with the longest running expansion in the nation's history. From 1992 GDP grew every year throughout the remainder of the decade. Output per hour in non-farm business grew by a third, and manufacturing corporations trebled their profits in the eighties and nineties.[11] Com-mentators are in no doubt about what was responsible for these results: 'The power of institutional investors increased and companies came under greater pressure to maximize shareholder value'.[12]

Making Managers Into Shareholders

For those at the top, fear of the consequences of not managing for value was accompanied by greed for the rewards of success as a result of the increased importance of share options. This began in the US where proponents such as Bennett Stewart, co-founder of the con-sultancy Stern Stewart & Co, advocated 'making managers into owners' to create shareholder value.[13] Options made millionaires out of many top managers, most famously Walt Disney Co's Michael D. Eisner who collected $569.8m in fiscal 1998.[14] The importance of options rose from being under 10% of the total compensation of American chief executive officers in the 1980s to 50% in the mid nineties and 63% by the turn of the century.[15] In the UK in 1984, the Conservative Government introduced measures to encourage share options. This had an immediate effect: in 1981 only 24% of British organizations had an incentive scheme of any kind for directors, but by 1985 this figure had grown to two thirds.

With more and more of management's future earnings becoming tied to stock options, managing for value became paramount. While shareholders and a few very senior managers benefited, there was an equally significant and much less positive effect on the great bulk of the work force. As *The Economist* noted, with share options to protect, 'many bosses have responded, entirely rationally, by trying to sweat as much return in as short a period of time as they can manage.'[16]

In most cases, managing for value involved downsizing. To begin with it was nearly always the work force that bore the brunt, but gradually restructuring worked through to management. As we show below, many middle managers lost their jobs, others had their roles redefined and, as a vacuum appeared where the middle managers had once been, producers were asked to take on management functions along with their operational duties. They were being asked to become Player Managers, though few were yet aware of it.

Enter the Player Manager

The radical changes underway in economic policy and business in the West coincided with the new wave of management theory discussed in Chapter One. The proponents of shareholder value, including influential top managers, found ways to adapt these new ideas in their drive to cut costs. The concept of 'reengineering'[17] was developed beyond its original meaning of using information technology to improve business processes into a broader and more brutal framework for improving efficiency.

Managers at this time – the early 1980s – remember how an initially exciting period turned harsh as restructuring kicked in: 'Empowerment started out as a well meaning movement in a way that was good for business as well as good for people. But it was hijacked by shareholder value and thereafter ceased to be authentic. The quality movement and work teams brought team leaders into decision making as we went through quality training and Tom Peters excellence training. Single status broadened, we held attitude surveys, 360-degree appraisals and opened up team communications. Then the pressure mounted. Quality teams became more than an enlightened management technique, they became a weapon of survival.'[18]

In most parts of the world a cycle emerged. The early days of restructuring saw relatively easy pickings. Powerful trade unions and benign governments had protected employees for a long time. Business had grown fat, and once the signal was given from the government dramatic results were achieved for shareholders. Beyond the first wave, however, it got harder. After units that were clearly unprofitable had been closed and the most obvious abuses of overmanning had been cleaned up, where else could productivity gains be made? The answer was in middle management, no longer the mainstay of industrial corporations and professional organizations, but instead a juicy target for cost reductions.

In the US as elsewhere, after manual labour had been downsized the managers were next in the firing line. One US businessman recalls how: 'Like most businesses, we'd gotten rid of middle management in the 1980s, partly because we couldn't afford it any more and partly because we didn't need it. In the old days middle managers provided us with the information we relied on to run the business but computers eliminated that function. Meanwhile our margins were getting squeezed by competition. Something had to go. It turned out to be middle management.'[19]

The UK's Labour Force Survey shows that the number of managers in the country fell from 2.3 million in 1984 to 2.1 million in 1985, reflecting the first wave of downsizing. We remember a middle ranking British executive bitterly recalling the stress he suffered when he laid off dozens of loyal workers and the local unpopularity and abuse he endured, only to be called in and fired himself. The spectre of unemployed middle managers with too much time to spend at the golf club or leaving the neat new estates of executive homes to pretend to work at the offices of the outplacement agencies became vivid in the public mind. In France, 'the weekend seminars aimed at developing teamwork and creating soldiers of management suddenly ended. They were replaced by a campaign to eliminate these same employees by such means as outsourcing their functions and early retirement.'[20]

The next stage in the cycle was the discovery that downsizing in middle management had gone too far. Managers were either re-hired or, more commonly, senior producers were asked to become Player Managers by taking on supervisory work in addition to their line duties. The experience of one American firm turned out like that of many others: middle management might have been deemed less essential than it was, but it had been performing a useful function. Who would take over that role? The answer provides another part of the explanation for the rise of the Player Manager: 'Then came the labor shortage. We found ourselves hiring more people with less work experience and fewer job skills. To maintain our productivity, we had some of the more experienced and capable employees take on managerial duties. The role evolved and suddenly we realized we had a new group of middle managers in the company. There's an important difference this time around however. The middle managers we used to have were strictly support people. They never dreamed of doing the jobs they were overseeing. In many cases they didn't know how. Our new middle managers are proficient in the work they supervise. If we're short handed, they can step in and cover for other workers and they often do. So they're better managers. They know what to expect. They don't make unreasonable demands of people and they don't accept lame excuses. They can get more out of a department because they have the respect of the people they work with.'[21]

The restoration of management including the creation of Player Managers was reflected in official statistics. Apart from a dip around the recession of the early nineties, the number of people classified as 'manager' in the UK grew steadily from the lows of the mid eighties as organizations sought to fill the perceived void. A million new managerial positions were created in ten years, many of these apparently combining production and managerial duties. Management numbers in the US grew by a third in the nineties[22] as organizations filled the middle management void with Player Managers. In small and medium sized enterprises the Player Managers had never been away; in big business they were being mobilized. The rise of the Player Manager was underway.

2. The Bandwagon of Change

Many of the forces that were reshaping industry during the last quarter of the century also affected the public and private sector professions. Always the heartland of Player Managing, the professions in this period rode a bandwagon of change that reinforced, even as it challenged, the Player Manager model.

Squeezing the Public Sector

As changes in industry spilled into the public sector, professionals in health, education and government service faced new competitive pressures. These required more management, which came from two sources: the recruitment of more administrators and the creation of Player Managers out of the professional staff. Change was particularly dramatic in the UK, but it was the US that supplied both the theory and the role model.

There in the early 1980s, 'a new cadre of economically oriented health care policy makers and researchers argued that competitive mechanisms were the only way to control medical costs'.[23] Legislation encouraged 'managed care' and Health Management Organizations (HMOs) were established, introducing competition into the selection and provision of healthcare.

By this time, inspired by the improved financial results in business, Margaret Thatcher had decided that the UK's public sector would benefit from exposure to the now coupled principles of managerialism and the open market. She observed that in the Civil Service, 'certain attitudes and work habits had crept in that were an obstacle to good administration' and that there was 'a long way to go before all the resources of the Health Service would be used efficiently for the benefit of patients.'[24]

In 1985, one of the people behind the managed care programme in the US, Professor Alain Enthoven, published a paper, 'Reflections on the Management of the NHS', and the internal market it proposed was introduced in 1990. Hospitals and GPs would have the opportunity to hold their own NHS budgets,[25] and trusts were set up on behalf of the patients to seek better 'value for money'. Medical staff became in Enthoven's words, 'resource managers'.[26]

The entire British public sector was also encouraged to operate as though it was a business in a competitive market place. In education, the universities were shaken up and the 1988 Education Reform Act linked the funding of schools to performance, applying the principle of market forces to this sector. As Mrs Thatcher explained: 'By exerting financial pressure we had increased administrative efficiency and pro-voked overdue rationalization.'[27]

Under the old system, Player Managers in the form of senior pro-fessional staff did much of the management with relatively few full time managers and administrators. Two things now happened: more full time managers and administrators were created and everyone had to consider the financial aspects of their work as well as quality of service. The addition of this extra management changed the role of many doctors, nurses, teachers, academics and civil servants from pure professional specialist into Player Manager. The term 'hybrid professional-manager' has been coined in academic writing to describe this role in the public sector.[28]

Enthoven had observed 'a fetish surrounding the NHS about not spending money on management. As a result the service is seriously under managed.'[29] He had put his finger on the anti-managerial culture that was common throughout the public and private sector professions, a culture that prized playing above managing. Just as the reforms in the public sector challenged this head on, so too did developments in the private sector professions.

Transformation and All That Jazz

The transformation in Western corporations at the end of the 1970s stimulated the demand for professional services. After the relatively stable and prosperous post-war period, traditional management needed help to meet competition. They turned to the professional services firms, who invented and then sold to top executives the tools associated with restructuring and downsizing.

An unprecedented market for external advice developed. The firms that could meet this demand in areas such as the law, accountancy, management consulting, investment banking, information technology and e-commerce, and advertising and public relations became the fastest growing sectors of employment in the developed world.

Historically these sectors were run by good senior players. As demand for service offerings grew and the size and ambition of their firms expanded, this ad hoc and amateur approach to management began to change. More full time administrators were appointed, but people who combined managing and producing remained central. As the number of Player Managers in professional services rose, so too did the importance of the Player Manager as a model for management.

The Growth of the Professional Services Economy

It is difficult to separate cause from effect when it comes to the professional services sector and the industrial restructuring of the late twentieth century. Did the investment bankers and management consultants create the need for change or did they respond to industry's cry for help? Either way, within Western economies that were already moving fast from manufacturing to servicing, the professional services sector became increasingly important. In the UK for example, auditing and consulting combined generate as much of national income – about

2% – as industries that are generally considered to be more significant such as Chemicals and Pharmaceuticals.[30]

In *financial services*, investment banking was the hottest of many hot spots. Demand for initial public offerings, merger and acquisition work, private equity and new financing techniques was strong, and the investment banks, as leading proponents of the shareholder value movement, whipped it along. The numbers working in the securities industry on Wall Street alone doubled in the eighties and nineties to 300,000. The value of mergers and acquisitions in the US in the second half of the eighties was more than double what it had been in the first half of the decade. Remuneration for practitioners soared, such that seven figure packages became common in both New York and London. Globalism and scale, which the investment bankers advocated to their clients, came to apply equally to their own industry and previously substantial independents such as Morgan Stanley and Dean Witter merged. In London, Europe and the US, the medium sized investment banks almost without exception decided to seek bigger parents. By the end of the century investment banks and asset managers featured amongst the world's largest employers; twenty years before they had been cottage industries.

Management consulting worked with investment banking on promoting the idea of shareholder value, and the sector also grew rapidly in the last quarter of the twentieth century. Annual revenue growth regularly exceeded 10 per cent and global industry revenues pushed well through $100 billion in 2000, despite recessionary fears and a decline in the important technology, media and telecoms industries. The scale of the leading firms is striking. Shortly after its split from Andersen, Accenture had over 70,000 employees and revenues in excess of $10 billion.

Business restructuring also created more *auditing* and *legal* work and required both professions to reorganize to meet changing client needs. Through two decades of growth and consolidation in auditing, 'global' replaced 'international' as the qualifying standard and the eight dominant firms of the 1980s were whittled down to what became known as the 'Big Five' with names, for example Pricewaterhouse-Coopers, that said it all. They became financial services superstores offering audit services, information technology advice, back office outsourcing and, controversially, consulting.

For a long time the *legal profession* remained fragmented as a result of the historical importance of relationships and, in the US, of local laws. However, the globalization of business created demand for cross-border advice in key areas such as mergers and acquisitions, capital markets transactions, and tax and anti-trust issues. This triggered consolidation in the profession, and in 2000 there was a series of mergers between East and West Coast practices in the US. The year 2001 began with the merger of London's Clifford Chance and New York's Rogers & Wells, setting the agenda for aspiring global law practices amidst evidence that the bigger firms are gaining at the expense of the smaller outfits as the profession scales up.[31]

Newer categories in the professional services sector also grew rapidly. *Advertising* became a global industry estimated to be worth around $450 billion. As multinationals spread so did the Full Service Agency, handling all aspects of corporate life from planning to placement, and often communication and public relations. Scale became important in this sector, and WPP Group became the world's largest advertising group in 2000 following its $4.7 billion acquisition of Young & Rubicam.

The most recent symbol of the establishment of the professional services firm as a global business is *PR*. The need for 'business image management' has been growing for fifty years and this accelerated towards the end of the century as business leaders, formerly 'practical men in gray suits', became heroes of revitalized productivity. Advertising understood this, and by 1999 thirteen of the fifteen largest public relations companies worldwide were owned by advertising agencies. A top firm such as Burson-Marsteller, the PR arm of Young & Rubicam, earns billions of dollars in fees per annum. 'Spin' is a respectable profession at last, and there are 150 college courses on the subject of public relations in the US alone.

'I am a trader and I hate meetings'

When the senior partner of a leading investment bank started off a staff notice with this apology for management, he knew exactly what note to strike with his colleagues. Like Enthoven's health workers and most other professionals, the investment bankers at this firm valued production more highly than pure management. The real heroes in the business were the deal makers, the hotshot traders, the star analysts and the 'big swinging dicks' on the sales desk. Management, according to conventional wisdom in the professions, was something the real heroes didn't do, or if they did it was in their 'spare' time after normal business hours. Management was regarded as tedious administration best left to the bureaucrats or those who had not quite made it in the front office.

A clue to the origins of this culture lies in the names of many professional services firms. The custom of naming a firm after its founding and first managing partners has a long tradition. The tendency to keep all these names following acquisitions, even after the founders have long moved on, highlights a primary difference between those who run professional practices and those who head up the world's corporations. We are speaking of the private partnership as opposed to the public corporation, and of the different beliefs about decision making and influence between these two types of organization. Unlike corporate hierarchies, professional partnerships typically remained relatively small and flat; anyone who joined a private partnership as a professional could aspire to join the partner ranks. In theory, if you were a top contributor you could have a voice in the affairs of the firm. Player Managing was not only sanctioned, it was lionized. Practitioners brought in large fees and were rewarded accordingly. The opportunity cost of not having them producing was considered too great to bear, so they became Player Managers, doing their managing in between attending to clients.

Academics applied a framework to describe the different managerial form of professional services firms. An early analysis of this was in 1979 when Mintzberg found that 'professional bureaucracies have a small strategic apex and few middle managers or supervisors as the professional workers exercise self-management'.[32] Ten years later, Greenwood et al's study of professional partnership[33] confirmed that in traditional professional organizations the professionals were still not only the operators but also the owners and the managers.

The growth of the professional services sector that we have outlined above had two effects on Player Managing. Firstly, more people were exposed to the model in that they worked for Player Managers and took on Player Managing themselves. Secondly, as the businesses grew in size and scale to become multi-site, multi-functional and multinational and accountability for performance became more intense, the model came under pressure. It evolved into what has been termed the Managed Professional Business[34] as full time management from the centre increased.

Managed Professionals

Research revealed that 'increasingly competitive markets have induced professional bureaucracies to adopt more corporate and managerial modes'.[35] Encouraged also by the new corporate governance environment that grew up in the 1990s, professional organizations strengthened and formalized their management. More full time managerial positions were created, particularly in the areas of Operations, Finance, IT and HR as these functions were expanded to meet the growing complexity of the firms. Administrators and executives from outside the professions were appointed to roles such as 'Practice Manager', 'Marketing Director', 'Chief Operating Officer' and occasionally 'Chief Executive', and the incorporation of partnerships became more widespread.

The arrival of the 'managed professional business',[36] however, has not neutered the Player Manager nor done much to dent the status of those who 'contribute'. In most professional services firms, team leaders and even business unit and division heads still combine client interface with team management, and now they have to interact with the central management framework as well. They are still Player Managers, operating in a culture where it is their performance as players rather than position in the management structure that wins the respect of the people they are managing.

Management professionals, in what are disparagingly known as the 'functions', 'support areas', or 'administration', who do no fee-based playing find it hard to establish credibility and voice. Many who have moved into professional services from multinationals are often surprised at how little value their expertise is expected to add, how unsophisticated the metrics are for measuring management contribution and how hard it is to break into the producer networks. Player Managers still hold power and resources and make the critical decisions about running the business. Large service firms may need more managing, but there is still resistance to accepting management as an equal profession in its own right.

A good illustration of this comes from the advertising sector in the story of WPP and its founder, Sir Martin Sorrell. Between 1977 and 1986, Sorrell was finance director at Saatchi & Saatchi during the London agency's phenomenal worldwide growth. He then became one of the firm's rivals, building up WPP into a formidable global force through acquisitions including J. Walter Thompson, the Ogilvy Group and Young & Rubicam. Sorrell is unusual in the professional services sector in that he owned up to his interest in management: 'I am someone who is very interested in the detail of running a business. I take it as a compliment to be described as a micro-manager.' An industry that valued playing above managing unfairly dismissed him 'as an odious little jerk' and accused him of never having 'written an ad in his life', a judgement that says more about its own anti-managerial cultures than about Sorrell himself.

A more typical leader in the professional services sector was Sir Win Bischoff, chairman of Schroders until its investment bank was sold to Citigroup in 2000. Bischoff was accountable to shareholders for the results and to the regulators for the operational control of a business that employed 6,000 globally. Yet he retained a significant involvement in client business, frequently appearing in pitches for new business, advising Schroders' senior executives on aspects of deals in progress and being consulted regularly by clients on key matters. A strong, full time managerial force in operational areas supported Bischoff, but there at the head of one of Britain's largest quoted professional services companies at the beginning of the twenty-first century stood a Player Manager. This model of a Player Manager supported by full time administrators and a whole raft of other Player Managers throughout the organization remains widespread in professional services areas, not just in finance but also in the law, advertising and consultancy right through to health and education.

3. The New Economy's Dubious Sum

In the late eighties and early nineties, the transformation of Western economies and the creation of shareholder value through restructuring, was given added impetus by a revolution in information technology. Until the high tech crash of 2000–1, stock markets powered ahead, business prospered and a new era of inflation-free limitless growth was acclaimed. Fears abated that capitalism had become 'a zero sum game'.[37] The New Economy had arrived and boosted Player Managing in two ways.

First, radical change was in the air. When a company like IBM was wrong footed by Microsoft, not long since a back room start-up, and another industrial age stalwart AT&T sold off its core local phone businesses, it was clear that the present was no guide to the future. A *New Order* was afoot, as we discuss below, and the quest for even greater agility and speed further weakened the role of full time middle management.

Second, as post-industrial work became more knowledge based, *The New Workplace* appeared. Manufacturing and services were transformed by new technologies, becoming more and more dependent on knowledge and information work. 'Human capital', known euphemistically in these years as 'talent', grew to be as important as tangible capital and fixed assets.[38]

Knowledge and networking became the motors of productivity in the New Economy just as raw materials and mechanization had been in the Old. Sectors such as software, biotechnology and other forms of research and development employed more and more people. Many others working in telecoms, banking, insurance, advertising and public services also became involved in information handling, and the term 'knowledge worker' became widespread. Whether in New Economy businesses such as Amazon or AOL or in Old Economy organizations whose operations were revolutionized by IT, more people became Player Managers, being called on to make and manage an expert technical contribution and also share in the overall managing of the project team.

New Economy: Fact or Fiction?

The New Economy stemmed from deregulation and technological change, notably the convergence of computing and communications, the ubiquity of desktop processing, and mobile communications and the commercial use of the Internet.

It spread world-wide from the US, where its effects are most evident. In a decade US corporations spent $2.2 trillion, a third of total capital expenditure, on information technology.[39] By 2000 IT was the biggest single component of the US economy, accounting for 11% of GDP. The whole economy benefited from this investment,[40] but those sectors most closely involved accelerated their productivity gains by 50%.

The New Economy affected the pattern of employment. At the beginning of the twentieth century, two thirds of working US citizens earned a living by making things; at the beginning of the twenty-first century two thirds earned theirs by making decisions. One in six new jobs were in the New Economy,[41] and smaller[42] younger companies with shorter life cycles[43] became a common source of employment for many Americans.

In the nineties the number of Initial Public Offerings in the US doubled over the levels seen in the eighties. With over 5,000 companies listed on Nasdaq, the New Economy sectors of Computers and Data Processing Services, Communications Equipment, Electronic Components and Telecommunications and Biotech accounted for over half of the market capitalization. Venture Capital funding rose from $3.5 billion in 1990 to $104 billion in 2000. The Fortune E50 was established, and in the UK the FTSE index of leading shares was transformed one day in March 2000 when nine old economy companies were removed to make way for newcomers such as Freeserve and Psion.[44] New Internet-related sectors were formed and older sectors like financial services were changed by the sudden growth of e-trading businesses such as Charles Schwab and Ameritrade. The New Economy apparently created a virtuous circle, fuelling its own growth with demand for more IT and creating new markets for the already booming consulting sector.

New Order

Hayseeds with Know-how.   Realization that the IT revolution was creating a New Economy was precipitated by a series of spectacular corporate transformations. IBM, described by Bill Gates as 'awesome by every measure capitalism knows' in the 1980s, was replaced as the powerhouse of the IT revolution by Microsoft in the 1990s. Microsoft was the archetypal New Economy company. Founded in a garage by maverick entrepreneurs with little regard for traditional protocols and authority, it offered a new business model involving small teams, little management and plenty of freedom to encourage talent to break through.

Yesterday's giants had to change or perish. In 1984 AT&T spun off its local telephone operations, recognizing 'a vision of the future being the information age, and that the future of communications is the melding of computers and communications.'[45] When Ma Bell, symbol of modern America, acted so radically, few could doubt that the world was changing.

The metamorphosis of the old and the birth of the new shook people. As old companies struggled, new ones emerged such as Compaq, which sold $100 million worth of PCs in its first year, and Dell, founded in 1984 with the unprecedented idea of selling custom-made PCs directly to end users. By 1988 when Dell went public, sales had reached $159 million and Michael Dell, who quit college before graduating with just $1,000 of start-up money, soon became the youngest CEO of a Fortune 500 company.[46]

What was most disturbing about the new order was its continuous wave of change. Only a decade after the first new companies formed, their markets matured and another round of start-ups, this time Internet-based, moved into play. Microsoft, only recently a start-up itself but now with all the advantages of a modern corporation, was initially wrong footed by Netscape which came with only Marc Andreessen, a team of designers, and a breakthrough idea. Netscape set about making it easy to put business on line, built a browser that everyone could use and Andreessen became an Internet hero, 'the hayseed with the know-how' as he was dubbed.

These challengers emerged so fast that business leaders had to rethink the accepted wisdom of competitive strategy. New rules and new business models for the New Economy[47] became influential. In turn, this gave shape to the New Workplace, one suited to New Economy business ideas.

Player Managers in the New Workplace

Work Styles. The New Economy's break with the past was symbolized in a hip look – 'business casual'. The 'cool' image of the Californian high tech start-up became more desirable than the gravitas of 'suits', so to emulate the feel of the start-up the old economy dressed down.

In professional services, law firms received image consulting and discounts from upscale casual retailers like Ralph Lauren and even Wall Street got rid of its suits. There were specific instructions for the spontaneous look: 'DON'T wear short sleeves unless it's summer, and only on button-down shirts. DO wear this uniform. Buttoned cuffs are optional. DON'T don cargo shorts, surfer shorts, biking shorts. Get it? No shorts. DO buy many pairs of khakis; you'll be wearing them every day! DO wear socks. Old Navy argyles are okay, but bare toes are certainly not! DON'T wear shirts without collars. Sweaters are okay for Silicon Alley, but not Wall Street. DO wear pants. But we think this linen drawstring pair might be a bit too California. DON'T put on sandals. Even with nice clean socks.'[48]

Everyone agreed that the New Economy meant smart casual and better coffee, but did it mean anything else? Some pundits mocked the 'organized spontaneity' of the dress down look and wrote off the rest of the New Economy's influence on the workplace as being equally artificial. But there is evidence that deeper changes are trickling down to affect everyone's working lives.

Redefining Leadership.   The nature of managing was redefined by the New Economy. As old economy corporate collapse became more common and businesses learned first hand the competitive meaning of Internet speed, the concept of leadership was revitalized. The steady state implications of management and administration no longer seemed sufficient. Handling the unexpected and unpredictable appeared more vital than staying in control.

This redefinition of leadership accelerated progress on empowerment and the rise of Player Managers. In the belief that inspiring others was more important than instructing them, business leaders focused more on the performance climate than on performance per se.[49] Enabling talent became the way to avoid being vanquished, and the 'shift away from directly managing and controlling the performance of others towards a more inspirational and guiding role'[50] became associated with the New Economy.

E-Leaders.   As the spirit of the new workplace took hold a new kind of business hero emerged, the 'E-Leader'. Often, like Martha Lane Fox, 27 years old when lastminute.com floated in London in March

2000, they were young, dynamic and members of a recognizable group. 'They're transforming staid, autocratic organizations into power-houses that hum with innovation. They have a global mind-set that recognizes that the Internet is opening new markets and recharging existing ones. They don't bother fighting mere battles with competitors because they're too busy creating businesses that will surround and destroy them. At heart, they're entrepreneurs, and they spread that enthusiasm for new ideas throughout their enterprises.'[51]

This Player Manager is typified in the stereotype of the MBA or Stanford College graduate operating out of a workroom, a garage, or, in the well-known case of Michael Dell, a car. These Player Managers were simultaneously developing a technical product or service and building the commercial and managerial support system that would ensure its take-off. As their companies grew, these e-leaders such as Jerry Yang and Dave Filo, founders of Yahoo, often remained as Player Managers, filling resource gaps with hands-on work in sales, customer management, deal doing and fund raising. By the late 1990s, this type of Player Manager role was being filled by well-respected managers jumping into the New Economy from the old. Meg Whitman's move to eBay from Hasbro and Tim Coogle's to Yahoo from Motorola are examples. Not even Bill Gates could keep out of producing, announcing in the late 1990s that he would become more involved as a 'software architect' in addition to leading Microsoft.

New Wine in Old Bottles.   In the early days the old business heroes felt left in the cold. They weren't part of the buzz. Many senior executives, who had for years been proud of their lack of 'tech savvy' and boasted about never switching on the PCs in their office, were caught short. If they didn't have one already a dotcom was a must, together with a strategy for e-commerce. They even had to learn to type and send e-mails.

Increasingly afraid of losing out to newcomers, many corporations and top services firms adopted features of the New Economy model. They built web sites to present a modern face to customers and worked out how to conduct business on line. They created start-ups and funded growing networks to form extended business alliances.

As established companies adapted their management, old economy heroes adjusted. Restructuring had made success stories of the likes of

Jack Welch and Lou Gerstner, and now, using new technologies and techniques, they cut, pasted and modernized the operations and cultures of GE and IBM.

Eventually the New Economy affected everyone as people in all professions found themselves in flatter, more connected organizations. More people in the nineties – 3 million in the US and 1 million in the UK – were described as 'managers'. Some of these were old style full time middle managers, as companies expanded in the conventional way. Others were Player Managers working in positions that we have just described.[52]

Great Babbling Bazaars.   In addition to creating the technology that powered the New Economy, the software industry also pioneered new methods of business organization. Linux, a community of software developers who made their designs free to all under the Open Source model[53] and who were only loosely grouped into self-organizing teams, represented the extreme of New Order thinking.

When, in the 1998 browser war with Microsoft, Netscape announced that it was to give away its Linux-driven web browser, Navigator, and release the source code, the influence of Open Source thinking was clear.[54] Netscape's CEO, Jim Barksdale, inspired by Eric Raymond's *The Cathedral and the Bazaar*, invited Raymond to help plan the release.[55]

The Bazaar style, typified by the Linux community, was characterized by Raymond as 'a great babbling bazaar of different agendas and approaches.'[56] Far from bringing about failure through confusion, Linux's chaotic self-organization resulted in faster development speeds than Cathedral builders – 'small bands of mages working in splendid isolation, with no beta to be released before its time' – could achieve. As Microsoft failed to lock down the server market in the same way they did the desktop, it was hard to ignore the implications of what the Linux community had achieved.[57]

The Open Software Movement was controversial – 'utopian balderdash' according to the journalist Bob Metcalfe, in his 'From the Ether' column on 19 June 1999 – but others saw the self-organizing character of Open Source as the future of software development.[58] The self-organizing 'bazaar' does more than devolve management to Player Managers, it dissolves management entirely. Although still rare, except, perhaps, in New Economy industries, self-management influences many of the ideas about 'new management'[59] which companies such as BP, Shell, Xerox and Monsanto have pioneered.[60]

Too Good to be True?

If something sounds too good to be true it usually is, and the New Economy was no exception. Enthusiasm spilled over into speculative excess in 1999 and alarm bells soon rang as many start-ups failed to find the revenue streams that their business models had been based on.[61] The market crashed, the dotcoms scaled back their businesses and many disappeared as capital became harder to find. For example, online grocer Webvan 'consumed $1.2 billion before flaming out'[62] and Theglobe.com closed all its web operations in mid 2001, laying off 50% of its workforce, after never once turning in a profit.[63]

The downturn was so fierce that articles started to appear advising employers to be vigilant about 'layoff rage'[64] and the smart 20–30 something dotcommers discovered business reality: 'We were excited to work for these grown-up sounding companies. We didn't understand stock options or pension plans, but it didn't matter. We were too busy shooting around whatever company promised beer on Fridays.' Adjusting to the sudden stop of start-ups left many blind-sided. 'And just like that it was over. Last paycheck in hand, shoe imprint still visible on the behind, I was suddenly given all the freedom in the world.'[65] One telling sign of the times was the new meaning of the parlance B2C and B2B (business to consumer and business to business). On graduate campuses in the US at least, it now stood for 'back to consulting' and 'back to banking'.[66]

The collapse of the high tech boom put an end to irrational exuberance and led to aspersions being cast on the validity of the New Economy. Some business academics, analysts and investors abandoned the faith, rewriting the history of the period as a bubble rather than a boom. Thoughts about the New Workplace were hastily revised: 'Some corporate leaders are abandoning talk of empowerment and decentralization and centerless companies and pushing for a return to the good old days of command and control.'[67]

Yet few believe that the New Economy's influence is over. As Alan Greenspan has noted, 'we are only partway through a technological expansion'[68] and further change will bring more management challenges, not less. Collaborative chaos has not become the new order, but few practitioners are advocating the re-establishment of layers of full time middle management in the Player Manager's place.

Conclusion

In this chapter we have described the rise of the Player Manager over a 25 year period in large organizations in the public and private sectors, in firms of varying sizes engaged in professional services and in the New Economy. The survival of the role through so many social and economic changes suggests that it has merit. For shareholders and other types of owner it is cost-effective, because production capability is not lost to full time management. For the Player Managers themselves, it has cultural attractions for well-qualified professionals who do not want to put their training to waste by switching into full time management. It also provides comfort for those who feel insecure unless they are involved in production.

As downsizing, delayering and decentralizing produced smaller and flatter organizations, developments in modern management theory supported the model. Old command and control structures were challenged by newer concepts, involving empowerment, networking and emergence. Belief grew that people work better if they are given responsibility and choices rather than instruction and discipline. In the economic upswing anything less seemed to be a threat to survival, and Player Managers stepped forward.

However, for these newly empowered Player Managers in a period of increased competition and pressure for short-term returns, a drop in their producer responsibilities has not been an option. Many are overworked, overstressed and unhappy.

In the first wave of downsizing, many survivors described themselves as being 'in a hell hole' after cuts that left their companies too weak to compete and people too shellshocked to care.[69] Managers expressed pain and difficulty in implementing downsizing, concern about their new workloads, which had not decreased following reorganization and difficulty in adapting to new kinds of organization structures.

In the second wave of downsizing, as the return to business fundamentals peeled away the New Economy's casual feel, people felt the real impact of information technology. For the many millions engaged in knowledge jobs, it has increased and intensified work rather than reducing it. The forty-hour week of the twentieth century – a product of industrialism's physical workspaces such as the office, the warehouse and the factory – has gone. The basic workweek is more likely to be fifty to sixty hours as New Economy communications devices help keep people on line, '24/7/52'.

Paradoxically, the most durable and widespread of managerial models saves the organization money, but the individual on whom its resurgence depends may pay a price. This human cost, which we explore in the next chapter, is offset in many cases only by chequebook management. At the end of a quarter of a century that started and ended with downsizing, we wonder what has really changed and what lessons have been learned.

3
No End of Work

A Wolf in Sheep's Clothing

The development of more participatory approaches to management in parallel with the drive to save costs and run businesses more efficiently was a strange juxtaposition: the menacing snarl of the cost cutter and the 'come walk with me' smile of the team builder, a veritable wolf in sheep's clothing. But in an environment where financial capital was readily available and communications were so fast that first mover advantage did not last for very long, business was now reliant on a different competitive advantage. With nearly three quarters of the workforce and a similar proportion of GDP in service industries, 'human capital, defined as the skill, dexterity, and the knowledge of the population' was identified as the critical input.[1] Once the value of human capital was acknowledged, an appreciation that creating a climate in which everyone was able and motivated to contribute came to lie at the centre of managerial work.[2]

Empowerment, the process by which authority as well as work was handed on to others, soon became the preferred method for creating this climate. The term has received a mixed press, frequently being treated with derision and its advocates being regarded as disingenuous. Releasing the reins of authority and control was (and remains) risky for people on both sides of the empowerment coin, especially given mixed messages about how earnestly it should be applied. But while finding the will or skill to develop and empower others proved difficult, it has nevertheless become established as one of the 'must have' features of a high performance climate. It is also one of the strongest influences on Player Managers and their work.

It was to them – newly empowered by restructuring, the move to shareholder value, the rise of the professions and the impact of the New Economy – that responsibility fell. How would they do? While few Player Managers ever experience trouble raising their playing game, once they are asked to do the managing part as well, their continued success becomes less assured. In a context where they face no end of work, they discover that managing the performance of others is tricky, rarely coming naturally to people recruited for this task from a pool of all-stars. Even when it does come naturally, the sheer volume of work and conflicting demands of both producing personally and managing the production of others can prove overwhelming.

This has created a potential Aunt Sally. Widespread acceptance that sustained success in the post-industrial age requires effective use of human capital sets expectations amongst managers and the managed. But delivering against these expectations via effective management remains elusive, so creating the potential for frustration, stress and disappointment. Twenty years into the movement, it should be coming clear whether the longer-term gains in human and financial capital that were anticipated from empowerment are in fact being achieved. Or are these gains being put at risk by misapplied theory and mismanaged practice as Player Managers struggle to replace the full time managers that went before them?

Stories from the Field

In the absence of much specific comment in traditional management theory about how Player Managers were coping with the combination of producing and managing, we set off to discover for ourselves the answer to these questions. We drew from our experience as managers and educators and also went out to observe real life Player Managers. As our original idea for the model came from sport, it was there that we started our fieldwork. We wanted to find out how the most successful Player Managers in sport coped with the problems of managing and playing in the public eye, and whether there were any lessons to be drawn from their experience.

We started by looking into the career of Gianluca Vialli, who was appointed player manager of Chelsea Football Club in 1998. It was a stunning appointment. Born to a wealthy Italian family, he had been one of the team's highest profile players and was synonymous with Italian chic and West London style. He took over from Ruud Gullit, one of the highest profile people in soccer, in controversial circumstances. With no experience of management, little grounding in the culture of English football and still with an important role to play on the pitch, he seemed certain to fail. The Italian press was incredulous at the apparent folly and likened it to giving the keys of a Ferrari to an eighteen year old.

However within a couple of years the team under Vialli's leadership had won trophies in England and Europe with style, flair and glamour. Things did eventually come unstuck for Vialli, as they do for most football managers, but in his heyday he seemed to have this Player Manager business taped. He told his biographer: 'Admittedly the figure of a player-manager is a delicate one and all at once I had a thousand different responsibilities as well as a thousand different preoccupations. In my entire life I have only met one other player-manager, Toninho Cerezo at Sampdoria, who seemed capable of being a player-manager but after a trial period I found a way to organize myself.'

This was a promising beginning to our enquiry: without leaving our desks we appeared to have found the model Player Manager, a person who had the juggling act sorted. However, our excitement was short lived for the next paragraph of Vialli's biography had a more familiar ring to it: 'He quickly accepted the multitude of extra responsibilities, abandoned much of his golf, returned to smoking, departed from his childhood sweetheart (who returned to Italy) and underwent fits of depression before, during and after every game.'[3]

Disappointed, but not surprised, that the best Player Managers in sport were not invincible after all, we began digging deeper into the field. Not unexpectedly the messages we heard were mixed. Some of the Player Managers that we met were enthusiastic about their jobs and what they were accomplishing within them. These Player Managers were clearly believers and we outline their credo under the heading 'I'm a Believer' below. Others were less convinced. Overworked and unclear about how to improve things, they were much less enthusiastic and sometimes deeply unhappy. These Player Managers were clearly 'Under Pressure' and we have grouped them together under that heading.

The cases that follow in the rest of this book are based on the real experiences of over 500 Player Managers. However, to respect their privacy we have concealed their identities by changing their personal details and merging certain events, characters and conversations.

I'm a Believer

Those Player Managers who were enjoying what they were doing, achieving the results they felt were expected of them and were fulfilled by this, fell into four categories. The categories are based round what Player Managers said about their reasons for being happy at work.

In the first category we found a will to win and a belief that in today's tough business climate only those with a killer instinct would come through. We have covered this under *Winner Takes All*. In the second category, *The Good Life*, we met people who shared the desire to achieve but whose pursuit of excellence was guided by an overriding dedication to a certain set of values. These values could be those of an institution or a chosen profession or they could flow from a personal ideal. All were sufficient for the Player Managers involved to tolerate the strains that came with the role and to strive for the ideal. A third category, much less about conviction, comprised more practically focused people who displayed neither the killer instinct nor great devotion to a cause. At the office, they simply had a job to do. Their pragmatic and phlegmatic view of work is summed up by our title to this section, *Getting On With It*. Our fourth and final category of believers consists of Player Managers who couldn't bring themselves to take it all too seriously. Yes, they had a job to do, but work was only the backdrop to what was really going on. People in this group are *Seizing The Day*, living life as it comes and learning from, and enjoying, the experience.

Winner Takes All

Unsurprisingly, we met a lot of people who enjoyed competing, usually those with the abilities and the resources to come out on top. Not wanting to be amongst life's losers, the proponents of the philosophy that winner takes all shared a common love of being the best. These Player Managers united their teams to do battle against the common enemy, regardless of who they were – competitors, regulators, suppliers or even other teams in the business in different divisions, regions or product areas.

We discovered that teams with common enemies can thrive on the belief that there is a prize worth going for, that their wits are pitted in competition for this prize and that losing just isn't a respectable option. We met Player Managers who enjoyed being stretched by meeting a challenge and passing this challenge on to their teams. They were unfazed by having to compete in difficult circumstances and they took most of the constraints of their work environment confidently in their stride.

One of these is Richard, an account director in an advertising agency, who told us with enthusiasm: 'I want to win. I want us to win and I want to win personally. I want us to be the best in the industry. That means being the most profitable, having the highest share price, hiring the best talent, winning the industry awards. I do my managing at the end of the day and my paperwork, dull as it is, at home at weekends. Of course it can be tough, tough on me, tough on Julia and the kids. But it funds a great lifestyle and, you know, life's not a rehearsal! This way I get to do two things at once and I welcome the challenge.'

When we asked Richard what kind of climate had developed in his team, he replied that he had never thought about it: 'I just want to run the best account team in the company. I want us to be the absolute best. I want my boss to know it, his boss to know it and I want clients to be the ones who are telling them. Everyone in my team has to be thinking about how we are going to outsmart everyone else. That way we will stand out. We need to have the best ideas and to be the A team that wins the account. I don't have a management formula. I suppose I lead by example. I like to keep the adrenalin pumping.'

For the many people like Richard, business success and personal success were tied. Happiness came from knowing where they stood relative to others and by expectations of the material rewards that would follow from stealing a lead. If work had got tougher and competition had got stiffer in the last few years, then they were not complaining.

Others we met had decided to win on their own terms. Selina, the Founder and Managing Director of a start-up dotcom, was as upbeat as Richard and as equally determined to succeed. She told us that she worked from 7 am until 7 pm, was responsible for closing all of the firm's big sponsorship deals and for dealing with shareholders, as well as being Head of HR, and of Operations.

'Why am I in it? One, to make money. Two, to give people a buzz at work. Three, to give customers something they want. And four, to realize a good idea. I'm living out my fantasy and I couldn't be more excited.'

We asked her how she gave people a buzz at work.

'By giving them a chance to shine. By loading them with more work than they think they can handle and then letting them surprise themselves by handling it. People like to be stretched and to know I am counting on them to come through. Plus it is a jungle out there. We never stop thinking about the competition, about the big dotcom graveyard and that the only difference between us and them will be our smarts and our determination to win.'

We wondered if people like Richard and Selina ever felt exhausted by being permanently on the high wire. What would happen if they slipped? We soon discovered that for this group exhaustion, like losing, just wasn't an option. Take the case of David.

'I run the technology sector for our M&A division. You can imagine that for the last few years we have been speeding down the fast lane at over 100 miles per hour. Suddenly there is a pile up. Carnage every-where. Now I have to steer a course through it while making sure we don't join the pile. I can't hit the brakes. If anything, I need to hit the accelerator even harder. And when I do there will be no tolerance for nervous or screaming passengers. There is no margin for error. We need nerves of steel. It will be the eject button for those that crumble.'

It struck us that David, like many star performers, was relishing this difficult challenge and was mentally preparing himself for difficult days ahead. But as David bound his anxiety in steely resolve and focus, we couldn't help but notice that his attitude towards others in his team was hardening. We could see that more than twenty years of staying lean and mean to compete on an increasingly competitive stage had opened the way for the ascendance of Darwinian values in the work-place. Talk of involvement and the espousal of 'sharing for all' cultures was just that: talk. We could also see that for a large group of people this was just as it should be. There was no alternative: winning was best.

Such values could undoubtedly generate climates of involvement and high performance where people were motivated to give their best – while the going was good at least. However, if people needed warmth, comfort, support and reassurance that they would be looked after, 'winner takes all' climates might not be best. As one very senior partner in a consulting firm told us: 'The easiest way for me to motivate my people is fear. For example we have a new principal who has been here about six months. Came in with a fanfare of publicity and all sorts of new ideas about how to manage the team for the long term and how the short term would look after itself. I called him up to my office just before he went on holiday last week and asked him when things were going to happen, we were getting curious. It's nothing heavy, but if we have to motivate people quickly and get a bright self-starting individual to go in a direction that might not sound too appealing to them at first, then fear, however terrible it sounds, is still the thing that works best.' It struck us that in a climate of winner takes all not only would the weak fail to survive, so would the strong if their values differed from those of the organization.

The Good Life

For Aristotle, happiness was tied to virtue, to leading a good life. While all Player Managers aspire to a good life in the modern sense of material rewards and comfort, we found that some also hold an aspiration to a good life in more philosophical or idealistic terms. For them, achieving this ideal is at least as important as any other kind of success at work.

One example is Alistair, who held a senior position at a large academic publisher. He was the Publishing Director of the Scientific Division, 'not the largest of the four that go to make up our total stable', he told us, 'but probably the most complicated. You try dealing with scientists who have double the average IQ, but about as much idea of delivering on time as the second class mail.' He had a wide-ranging brief that included responsibility for the division's financial results, all staffing matters, technical production, editing and the over-all shape of the publishing list. Far from being overcome by all of this, Alistair assured us that he loved the role.

'In fact,' he said after a moment's reflection, 'I feel honoured to hold the position. We are into our second century of academic publishing, we have published some of the most important books ever to appear in the history of science and I have no doubt that some of our current and future lists will be equally important. I see myself as the temporary custodian of a great office and my duty is to ensure that standards do not slip. Of course it is difficult to square that up with the financial demands of our Board of Trustees, so we have a balance of repeat earners that I call "the gravy train" to go along with ground-breaking books that might win the author a Nobel Prize yet will sell only a few hundred copies.

'I regard it as a matter of principle to be working on several titles myself alongside the full time editors. I believe that it improves my credibility with them, it enables me to keep my hand in and also I enjoy it. It makes for a relief from the people management, which I do find gruelling. But if I get that wrong I would end up editing all of the books myself, and that would be no fun either!'

We asked Alistair about the hours he worked.

'Too many, my wife tells me, but I couldn't get the job done if I worked a standard 9 till 6 day. The hours are worth it for the sake of science and literature.'

It was unusual to meet an idealist like Alistair, but several other Player Managers we came across were equally committed to their institution and calling. John, the Medical Director of a specialist hospital, told us that 'although the whole business of managing a financial budget can get in the way of patient care, we have to accept that we live in the real world. I operate on at least two days of the week so that I stay fresh and so that I don't forget that this whole activity is about making people well again. But in all honesty, I enjoy the managing equally. After so many years working all day with patients, the administration and financial management is a welcome relief. But I would hate to do it all the time.'

On reflection, it did not seem unusual to find Player Managers working to fulfil an ideal or a set of values, given the old idea of the professions as a vocation. But would an idealistic commitment to art, science and healthcare be matched in the commercial world by any kind of commitment to the values of business? We found three main ways through which employees in the commercial world can gain a sense of value from their work.

First, some commercial institutions feel a deep *responsibility towards their stakeholders*. For example, in one well-known executive search company we found that the founders' values of collegiality were still strong, even after the firm had achieved global scale and worldwide success. New members were socialized into holding these values, which then determined the way business was conducted. Player Managers were to look out for each other and for new members. As one woman who had just returned from time off to look after a sick relative told us: 'I was really nervous about going away, thinking that the ground would close over after I was gone or that my work would just pile up and my clients would get dissatisfied. But it wasn't like that at all. Everyone understood my situation. We drew up a plan about who would handle my clients while I was gone. On my return I just picked up where I had left off. No one tried to move in on my patch and no one resented the extra work. I have learned something important about sharing and have a personal experience that demonstrated to me that the values we espouse are real.'

Second, a few organizations were committed to *enabling a better kind of work experience*. For example Andy Law, who founded the London advertising agency St Lukes, has been very publicly outspoken about how work at St Lukes is designed to take the advertising out of advertising. With workplace posters such as 'Profit is like health, you need it but it is not what you live for', the people at St Lukes all have an ownership stake in a venture that is meant to be creative and fun. The climate is designed to unleash creative and fresh advertising by implementing a different kind of managing, one that fits the values of the people that own the business. The result has been a climate that to date has been both high performing and psychologically rewarding.

Third we found *commitment to the idea of capitalism* itself, a belief that capitalism, while not yet a perfect system, was the least imperfect of what humankind had come up with so far. As one Player Manager told us: 'We have now merged with another firm three times, and each time this happens I feel as though I am starting all over with the task in front of me. But this is inevitable as businesses consolidate. I am confident that the people at the top know what they are doing. I'm a believer in the spread of global capitalism. I see no alternative, and I know that this spread is in the hands of people like our leaders and people in the middle like myself. We do deals and they are big ones. At times there are casualties, but I believe that the people who are running things are people like me. They are people who care.'

Although we were lifted by meeting Player Managers committed to an ideal – whether knowledge, art, quality of life, shared ownership or the values of enlightened self-interest – such people were not the norm. While one told us brightly, 'I am a capitalist and I am here to run a profitable business. I believe that the only way to work for change is from within the system,' the majority of Player Managers we spoke to sounded involved in something much less profound. They were not at work to ask questions or to make change; indeed they were naturally suspicious of anyone who was. They were there simply to get on with it.

Getting On With It

It took us a while to appreciate just how many people who were holding their own in the middle of large organizations had very little expectation of securing personal or financial enrichment from work. They were just *Getting On With It*. Probably labelled by their more ambitious and idealistic colleagues as 'life's troopers', 'business realists' or 'pragmatists', many Player Managers had been trained in an area of expertise and they came to work each day to apply it. They were doing what JFK had said was required in 1962, namely being dispassionately involved in the 'practical management of a modern economy.'[4]

For example, Rosemary started out by training to become a nurse and quickly progressed to being a ward sister in a large public hospital. A couple of years later she was taking an MA in hospital management, and after she finished that she began spending part of her time teaching other nursing students. Most of her work was now administrative or educational, although she still spent some of her time on the wards and, when short staffed, kept her hand in on patient care.

When we asked her about what motivated her to come to work she looked at us as though questions like that were an indulgent luxury. We felt humbled when she said: 'I don't have time to think about why I come to work or about what motivates me when I am here. I prepare lessons for my students that I hope will get them through their studies. I manage the bed rota and the staff rota for our ward and hopefully between the two there is enough resource to give acceptable, if not excellent, patient care. I try to keep the nurses on track with their personal lives and with the management of their finances as some of them can barely afford to live. I complete most of my paperwork for the hospital management in between all of these other activities. This is the work I know how to do, somebody has to do it and few people are better equipped than me.'

This was a pragmatic attitude to a demanding and necessary job. Maybe it was just as well Rosemary wasn't asking too many questions about the rewards.

In every organization we visited we met people like Rosemary, people seasoned in their chosen function or profession and who, as a result of their maturity and knowledge, were probably at their highest point of contribution as Player Managers. They might be flanked by commercial killers and more romantic dreamers but, as the demand grew for cheaper and better products, shorter supply times and improved services and as business processes became more streamlined and cost-effective, we were left in little doubt about who was really holding it all together.

Seizing the Day

Not everyone has a plan for living. Some people just want to see what happens, and then decide whether to go along with it or move on. We met Player Managers who, while not aroused by any great conviction or passion, were good performers and mentally healthy with it; life, for them, was simply too short to permit its total domination by work. This was the case with Cathy, a partner in a global consultancy.

'I'm surprised I am still here. I can't believe it has been more than five years. But you know, even though it is tough I must be enjoying it. Perhaps it is because we have so much change. I never have chance to get bored. I won't be here forever though. I'm just here to seize the day.'

Cathy was bright, bubbly and curious and she infected her team with the same spirit. The climate in her group was one of learning and adapting as each new change was introduced. Cathy told us that by taking the lead on how to approach each new round of change, she had demonstrated to her team that exploring new situations and unravelling complexity could be fun.

'I told them that it didn't matter if they could no longer see where they might be going long term in our business. Even in the midst of confusion, personal development can occur.'

A desire for personal development or 'what's in it for me as an experience' was something that Player Managers who wanted to 'seize the day' all had in common. This attitude arose from the fundamental changes in the climate and context of work that we discussed in Chapter One.

This is how one senior Player Manager put it: 'Knock, knock. Who's there? Not you any more. Wasn't that the Dilbert joke that summed up downsizing? Well there is another side to the coin. I meet it all the time in our first level producer managers. They are here for themselves. They want to have a blast with their teams and, yes, they want to get the work done. But commit to the company, to the long term of the institution, stay with us? I doubt it. If I asked them about it, they would say, "Why should I? You lay us off when times get tough, we move on if there's a better opportunity. That's the deal."'

We were no nearer being able to come up with a definitive response to 'Who's there?' after meeting Lou, who was just about to leave on a six-month sabbatical.

'I have done two jobs in this firm and both were great learning experiences. I was also working with a great team of people who I learned a lot from. But now I just don't know what I want. I spoke to my own manager about this and asked about some time off. I found out that this would damage my own chances of becoming a more senior manager but duh, who cares? So many people like me just don't want that path. In the end they have let me go, and they want me to return after the break. In a funny sort of way socialism is back.'

Most people now in their mid to late twenties and early thirties realized, even as students, that loyalty was dead and so was any guarantee of employment. This new generation of professional players, fed on concepts like 'portfolio careers', 'employability' and 'being your own brand manager', are now taking on Player Manager positions themselves. They are empowered in their own right and their expectations of working in large organizations, while positive, are not about 'hanging on in there' or being 'company women' or 'organization men'.

We encountered enough people like those we have just outlined, together with others whose life was more of a mixed bag but who were nevertheless on the positive side of neutral, for us to believe that under certain circumstances the empowered Player Manager was a model that could work. However, we also encountered many Player Managers who felt, as they told us, 'Under Pressure'.

Under Pressure

Top of the list of concerns for Player Managers under pressure is the constant preoccupation with production, or *Keeping Up the Numbers* as it is often described. This drive for short-term results impacts the quality of support and personal development provided and creates a second area of concern, which we discuss under *Let's Just Call It Attitude*. The third area of pressure, dealt with under *Hold That Thought*, relates to problems with work overload and confusion over reporting lines and responsibilities. Far from creating a climate of empowerment and involvement, it appears from these interviews that some organizations have created a climate of confusion and disenfranchisement. Finally, there is the problem of reconciling personal and professional integrity. Pressures here manifest themselves in such themes as work/life balance and the purpose and meaning of work. We deal with these in the section *Gone Missing*.

Keeping Up the Numbers

In contrast to an ideal scenario in which playing and managing can be balanced, in the field we discovered a marked reluctance on the part of Player Managers to give up playing as the main act. Their primary concern was often their personal contribution to results, to 'keeping up the numbers'.

In part this is due to a lack of security and a fear of the consequences of failure, which for Player Managers tends to be measured in the very short term. This insecurity was evident in the interviews that we did during the last few months of the global economic boom, but was even more pronounced after the slowdown and redundancies of 2000–1. A well-established Player Manager, whom most people would have believed to be as safely installed in her position as it is possible to be these days, told us: 'They won't sack me so long as I'm still bringing in the numbers,' by way of an explanation of her priorities. The recession had set these quite firmly as 'play first, manage later'.

A second reason that Player Managers hang on to playing is the anti-managerial culture that still surrounds some organizations, especially in the professions. This was clearly explained to us by a section leader in a financial services group: 'I'll keep respect if I play well and the team won't see that I am just not sure how to manage.'

Implicit in an anti-managerial culture is a belief that for many playing is where the heart should be, not to mention being easier and more fun than managing. One colleague of a top producer who had now taken on weighty management responsibilities as well, said to us: 'I am amazed at how well my boss has adjusted to management. His heart is in doing deals. It must be a terrible sacrifice.' Even George, a successful publisher and one of the most balanced Player Managers we met, paused in telling us about his own framework for managing to lament: 'But the playing bit is so much more exciting!'

Marjorie, who had been a Player Manager for many years and was now heading up a division of a top services firm, gave the final reason why people are reluctant to prioritize management: they don't understand the advantages of leveraging their own efforts by involving others. She told us: 'In this whole department of around fifty people I am the only one who can do a particular type of transaction that is essential for today's markets. I have been doing more and more playing because of this, even though the management demands of the role have increased dramatically as the division has grown. People wonder why I get impatient when they keep walking through my door, but I am now handling six projects directly as everyone else is so inexperienced. It is just as well I am resilient and have the determination to take this many projects on. The contribution to our numbers this year will be massive, and by bringing in these numbers I am helping us all.'

What Marjorie had never for a moment considered was the cost of her failure to manage anything more than her personal performance. It never occurred to her (nor presumably to the people who set her objectives) that through sharing her knowledge and developing others, she might by now have already replicated her expertise. Marjorie missed an opportunity to enhance the capability of the team as well as improve the numbers of the division, not to mention freeing up her time for other things.

Keeping up the numbers is important for Player Managers everywhere, and undoubtedly the pressures to deliver results in the short term are real. But keeping up with the numbers, like keeping up with the Joneses, is a game that is easy to get sucked into. Player Managers are among the first to admit that they bring this upon themselves by failing to apply any of the levers of management. This particularly applies to the areas of team development, performance management and collaborative problem solving, those 'soft' people management skills that can be developed by training programmes when the organization shows itself to be clearly committed.

Let's Just Call it Attitude

The second area of stress we identified stems from this reluctance of Player Managers to apply the levers of management. In the service sector, all the companies we investigated had expanded through a mix of organic growth and acquisition. All were operating in a more intensely competitive arena on a bigger, more sophisticated scale. Yet an unwillingness to manage remains, creating pressures for the managers and for those they manage.

The impact on those being managed is particularly severe on young professionals who, as juniors, are given workloads that border on the inhumane. Whether they are young doctors working a hundred hours a week in casualty or fresh-faced management consultants expected to 'hit the ground running', juniors are the pack horses of post-industrial society.

In medicine, legislation has curbed the worst excesses of overwork in the UK but the standards of Victorian England appear to have crossed into twenty-first century America: 'America's 400 teaching hospitals may not immediately resemble Tom Brown's Schooldays but for young resident doctors, life at a 19th century public school might seem familiar. As new boys and girls, young trainee doctors are expected to work until they drop often completing 100 hour weeks ... Around 70% of trainees reported seeing colleagues working in impaired condition, most often caused by lack of sleep.'[5]

A similar pattern prevails in professions such as Management Consultancy under the so-called 'mentorship' system of principals and partners, most of whom are Player Managers. In consultancy the practice of charging premium rates for this young, fast-learning talent supports the economics of the model and, despite growing questions about the effectiveness of such mentoring, keeps the money flowing in. Time off client projects for juniors and time away from client relationship management for partners is not encouraged, and so opportunities for team building and development or even personal communication are limited.

For people still fairly fresh out of college, the reality of their mentorship is frequently less than ideal. One person we spoke to, in a global firm of considerable cachet, described his mentorship by a Player Manager as follows: 'For the first six months my boss insisted I hung around him all day. This was to learn first hand just what he did. I would sit listening to him on client calls and meetings, and I joined all the meetings where he gave direction to everyone in his group. At the end of the day he would ask me what I had learned and then hand me a pile of work, for example a market analysis or a report to prepare that he would be using with a client later that week. He would expect progress on this in the morning, and I would often be up past midnight to get a decent piece of work done. I got tired of my colleagues asking me, "How was the sunrise?" It was too close to home, that one. Why we worked like this was never clear. I could never figure out whether it was a punishing form of initiation into the firm, or whether he was so truly disorganized and caught up in each moment that he never took time out to think about the best way to arrange his and my tasks. I never asked or complained. His sponsorship was important to me in the early years. I simply put my head down, and through sheer determination got everything I was asked to do done. As for the attitude of our partners about our wellbeing, well, let's just call it attitude.'

One reason that juniors are treated like this is that, according to our research, many of their Player Manager mentors are treated in exactly the same way by the people to whom they report. The case of Andy, who sought help when the demands of combining his producer/ manager role became overwhelming, illustrates how far some organizations are from making empowerment work.

One of the first things Andy told us about was a conversation he had with the CEO and Managing Partner of the firm. He asked this revered leader how people adjusted to the pace.

'They either get addicted or they leave,' came the reply.

Andy was smart enough to believe that neither outcome was healthy for the firm; he was also smart enough to keep this opinion to himself. But in the end the pace overwhelmed Andy, as he struggled to organize the work of a fairly junior team. He tried to make up for their lack of experience and his own lack of management expertise by taking on too many assignments himself. In the end he wore himself out, and asked to return to a less senior 'player only' role.

Andy's experience illustrates a contradiction that stems from the changes in professional services firms that we described in Chapter Two, changes which imply a requirement for more management, not less. The contradiction is that only the top players in such organizations have the kudos to manage, but they lack the time and often the right attributes to do so. The consequence of this for young talent is a growing sense of isolation as true mentors are harder to find. 'Talent is fungible despite what they say,' and 'No one, not one single person, cares about me here,' are two other examples that typify what we heard from those being 'managed'.

Some organizations have begun to notice this. We came across several efforts to move away from ad hoc approaches to managing people. The use of 360 evaluations, leadership and personal effectiveness coaching, and communication skills training is becoming more common. All are intended to provide a more systematic means of measuring and developing Player Management talent. One well-known example is Morgan Stanley's 360 evaluation system in use for upward feedback which has been the subject of a Harvard Business School case study.

At another major company we were told: 'Several of our very best producers got hit this year in both their compensation and promotions because they neglected the non-playing parts of their role. Gone are the days when it was enough to be a star producer who made life difficult for everyone else in the team. It's a hard message to swallow if clients love you and your commercial results are outstanding, but if you get bad upward reviews in our firm the consequences are now very real.'

But such enlightened attitudes are still the exception and not the norm. In many sectors the most widespread definition of management was that used by a managing director at an investment bank: 'Something to do when a problem walked through the door.'

Hold That Thought

For others we interviewed, the pressure point wasn't so much lack of support and isolation as sheer overload and confusion. Everyone we met had too much to do and faced some kind of compromise as a result. While on the surface some people shrugged their shoulders and said, 'That's life,' we discerned signs of exhaustion and burnout. We found frustration in buckets, as well as the loss of self-esteem that can develop when high achievers feel they are failing to make progress.

For some, this was compounded by confusion caused by the disappearance of any semblance of workable structure and reporting arrangements. There were many examples of the sense of frustration and cynicism that accompanies an impossible job. One technical manager from a large industrial multinational said: 'With the flattening of our hierarchical structure, we have spread job enrichment and team empowerment. Truth is, more people feel powerless and "put upon". We can change very little and are cynical that promotion prospects are now reduced.'

Our conclusion was that producer managers in all sectors had come under ever increasing workloads from the drive for 'more from less' and that the people in the middle of most corporations now had less freedom than ever. For Player Managers, command and control from above is alive and well, as the much vaunted 'empowerment' is overlaid with multiple authorities and reporting requirements. Many people reported that they felt micro-managed and second-guessed. The result was more frustration, loss of trust and a sense that there was too much risk associated with being either creative or passionate about change.

According to a Player Manager in the service function of an electronics company, 'Since we restructured we have had no end of reorganizing of roles and responsibilities. This has meant upheaval and confusion for most of us despite all the talk of the business benefits of being agile. I am here to produce revenues while managing and motivating "flat" multidisciplinary teams, but everyone knows that a matrix is just two hierarchies constantly bumping into each other at multiple points of internal competition and control. It is hard not to get defensive or impatient when it takes so long to make decisions and when you don't know who you can trust.'

Another gave us a telling account of the feeling of isolation that we heard many times: ' "Hold that thought!" has become one of my boss's favourite expressions. It's not surprising as he is just too busy to think about anything. I long ago gave up expecting quality time with him. We are lucky to snatch phone calls from airports on our respective travels, which is one cost of globalization we have both felt since our function integrated a year ago. We used to be part of regional sectors, but in a drive for one global approach to market, our function is now responsible for ensuring consistent strategy and positioning in over twenty countries. Without the support of the regional teams though, we will not be successful. Like all "global" functions we run the risk of becoming marginal and an unwelcome overhead if we lose sensitivity to the fact that what we can say in Japan, Italy and Australia will be different. To avoid this we spend a lot of time working the countries, building relationships, and being sensitive to local needs and at the same time promoting ideas and programmes that tie to the global image.

'Are we succeeding? I don't know. If I can cover off my most critical Lotus Notes without appearing too distracted from wall-to-wall conference calls, I feel that I have had a good day. My boss says, "Hang in there!" but in eighteen months we have had three significant reorganizations. Frankly I am beginning to lose the plot.'

It wasn't just this person who was losing the plot. What we learned was that Player Managers, often among the most talented and most determined to succeed in their organizations, feel that something significant has gone wrong.

Some, like this Player Manager, are phlegmatic: 'I have had seven different bosses in five years. They come in with new ideas, full of enthusiasm and the latest jargon and dump them all on us. We are like guinea pigs in laboratory experiments, just part of someone else's learning curve. After a while they move on, up, or out. I just get on with my job and take as little notice as possible. At the end of the day, I am still here, they've all gone.'

Others are more desperate: 'I spend a third of my life at work, a third at leisure and a third asleep, and guess which third I hate. My boss ignores me until she needs me, then I'm her special friend, sisterhood and all that, and the moment the crisis is solved I'm forgotten. I can't see the point. My work completely lacks any meaning. I am a hired gun.'

This last comment is telling of an environment where people feel more demands, more confusion, and have no time to think about how to develop a framework for getting on top of things. The result is often the loss of one intangible reward of work: the intrinsic pleasure of seeing a job well done and knowing it was you that made the difference. In the absence of this kind of job satisfaction, Player Managers and their teams feel a loss of emotional energy and involvement. They turn up and work long hours, but many are just going through the motions.

Gone Missing

One noticeable feature of our conversations with Player Managers was that so many of them were dreaming of getting out of whatever it was they were doing. We met wannabe fish farmers, furniture restorers, guesthouse keepers, home designers and landscape gardeners. We were asked more times than we care to remember questions like: 'Is work/ life balance really attainable, or is it just a fantasy fed by the dream of having it all?'

For most people we spoke to, work/life balance wasn't attainable. It had gone missing, and so too had they – from the lives of their families at least. What had also gone missing was any real expectation that this balance could be achieved in the near term, combined with the belief that their organization was willing to do anything to promote it beyond rhetoric.

At a very fundamental level Player Managers are struggling to handle everything their roles require them to do. Further, in many cases both business and personal partners are demanding rather than sympathetic. It can feel as though support has gone missing as well. The result is that the Player Manager ends up isolated and sandwiched in an impossible and permanently stressful situation.

On one side of this sandwich is the 'work ethic', a requirement for dedication to delivery at work. This can manifest itself as quiet coercion or by 'in your face' demands for commitment. 'When I was being interviewed for this job three years ago I asked, perhaps naively, about the prospects of work/life balance. When asked to expand on what I meant by this, I said quite straightforwardly that it was about balancing three things – work, family, and outside interests. The Managing Director who was interviewing me looked me straight in the eye and said, "People who work here find that if they work on it they can balance, say, two of those three things. If you join us, be sure to pick the two important ones." '

At least this Managing Director was honest. Another Player Manager we interviewed had been misled by a firm that had headhunted him: 'They fed me a line about the quality of life away from London, how everyone dropped their kids off at school before coming in to work, left on time in the evening and how weekends were for family, not work. That was an important factor in deciding to move up here, uprooting the family away from relatives, friends, jobs and schools.

'The reality was totally different: raised eyebrows if you were in later than 8 am or if you left before 7 pm and an impossible workload that always spilled over into evenings and weekends. At my first appraisal, the same guy that had wooed me at the interviews with all that quality of life stuff marked me down for commitment. What was I supposed to do? I had dragged my wife and young children 200 miles north on the promise that they would see more of me, and when I tried to deliver to them got C scores at work and blame at home.'

This, the situation at home, is the other side of the sandwich. Many Player Managers feel inadequate in terms of the support they provide to their families and stressed by complaints from loved ones who feel short-changed in terms of involvement and time. When, in the end, the family gives up expecting them to be around during weekdays and even weekends, more stress, not less, ensues.

'Daddy, how come you are home so early? Have you been fired?' is what the seven-year-old daughter of one Player Manager asked when he walked through the door one night before 7 pm. Being home so early in the middle of the week, so soon after he had been assigned to the image management of a firm that had undergone a high profile public offering, was indeed unusual. A few months in, Steve was feeling the pressure – and so was his family.

'I don't want a crisis management job on my hands and neither do the senior partners of my own firm. They have said in no uncertain terms that I must do what it takes to "keep this one happy". I know my family wish I hadn't taken this on and taken it so to heart, but I have to keep on top of this 24/7. It's no easy task.'

The inability to reconcile the split between professional and personal values in some of the brightest and most educated people in the workforce is raising important questions about the meaning of work. It follows that questions are also being asked about definitions of success and the hidden costs of 'having it all'. Fortunately for business, Player Managers are usually high achievers and have high levels of what psychologists refer to as the 'self-skills' of emotional intelligence.[6] They are confident and optimistic, which gives them a more than average capacity to take things in their stride and deal well with reversals in their life circumstances. Yet despite the fact that modern professionals are supposed to be life's winners, with a broader array of options than most – of which being a Player Manager in business is but one – many feel like one Player Manager we spoke to: 'I know I am on a treadmill but I have forgotten how to get off. Beneath the surface I am just not there.'

It Wasn't Supposed to be Like This

It is clear from our fieldwork that many organizations have failed to create the right climate to deliver properly on empowerment. Whether as a result of reengineering or otherwise, most people described their organizations as becoming increasingly complex in their business processes and operations. Despite this additional complexity there was lower tolerance of failure. Player Managers are more tightly squeezed from above and below than they ever were previously. Whilst some have undoubtedly come to terms with this either by throwing themselves wholeheartedly into competing or seeking refuge in their ideals or simply 'going with the flow', others have not. Many such survivors of restructuring have become narrow minded, self-absorbed and scared of taking risks. They are more shell shocked than empowered.

In reviewing our fieldwork, we detected some differences between 'professional' and 'corporate' organizations. In professional practice, where senior people's identity and continued success remains invested in being a player, the balance errs towards more playing and less managing. This tends to create climates that, to use an old but clear distinction, are more 'task' than 'people' oriented, emphasizing performance and short-term results. It seems as though keeping up the numbers is the entirety of many Player Managers' end game, setting the unspoken benchmark that others should follow suit. In such cases there is little investment in developing people beyond a coercive approach geared to short-term targets that does nothing for commitment or team spirit.

In the corporate environment, where Player Managers spend more energy formally managing – whether reporting results, negotiating resources, managing upward or building the team – the balance can go either way. If it is towards less managing, then the effects on the immediate team culture are similar to those in professional services firms. If the balance errs towards more managing and less playing, then the effects on climate can be more positive, but not necessarily so. It depends on the Player Manager's attention to, and confidence in, their dealings with the human factors.[7]

When one commentator said about reengineering that 'it wasn't supposed to be the last gasp of industrial-age management,' they could equally have been speaking about the effect of empowerment on climate.[8] What started out in the 1980s as an attempt to bring about a more empowered, more involved workforce in order to use human capital well has become a parody. Unfortunately, the joke is mainly on those supposedly empowered to deliver on empowerment: the Player Managers. Far from creating a climate where people feel motivated and able to be involved, the movement has created a group of disoriented, overworked and overstressed individuals. Why has this gap emerged between hope and reality?

We found the key to this in the many comments that we got from Player Managers about how they see their jobs. There was a fairly common acceptance that what they had to do above all else was to get short-term results. Pressure to achieve this overrode many of the other important objectives of management mentioned by a sizeable number, such as planning for growth, strategy or developing the team. Even well-intentioned and enlightened Player Managers find it hard to live up to the ideal. Despite the rhetorical emphasis on 'participatory styles of management', 'collaborative leadership' and 'empowerment', the majority of those charged with making it happen see their priorities as being rooted very firmly in the short term.

In following this line, Player Managers are responding to signals from CEOs and others at the top of their organization who have to satisfy shareholders looking for immediate results. Institutional shareholders are measured by short-term results – quarterly in many cases – and it is no surprise that they expect the managers of the companies in which they hold shares to deliver to the same schedule. This is unrealistic. As one investment banker revealed when discussing Barclays' decision to sell its investment bank, the time-frame for results given by shareholders is adrift from business reality: 'It's the difference between ownership and management. There is no one at Barclays able to take a longer-term view. The chief executive probably thinks he's only got a year or two to sort it out. The institutional shareholders are working on an even shorter time horizon. Building an investment bank is a thirty year process and Barclays are about a third of the way through it, but no one is around for that long.'[9]

In the public sector, Player Managers also faced an increasing need to meet short-term targets following the introduction of what Margaret Thatcher clinically described as 'new and more efficient working practices'.[10] Many of the characteristics we found in the private sector – anti-managerial cultures, confused reporting lines, pressure on costs to meet short-term budgets – apply equally to the public sector. The pressure in the public sector is such that it is very hard for Player Managers to win a share of budget for essential management training purposes, increasing the danger of a downward spiral in managerial standards.

There is no relief for those in the professional services sector, where many firms are in a vicious circle. The need to pay higher packages to talented staff leads to a search for compensatory cost savings elsewhere. To avoid this constraint on resources showing through in an inferior service to clients, Player Managers take on even greater loads. The most talented sense this and can threaten to move on. As a quick fix the firm pays higher packages to retain them, and so the cycle resumes. With one eye on hoped-for IPOs and the other on partners' annual profit expectations, organizations in this sector have been driven to increasingly short-term expedients as momentum in the economy has slowed.

Short-termism, we believe, is the reason why so many Player Managers have to operate in a high pressure climate. Too often they report to people who feel under pressure to deliver results that quarter or that year and who believe that they do not have time to wait for developmental work to pay off. They also face incessant pressure to keep costs down, cutting them whenever and wherever possible. The

Player Managers therefore find themselves under-resourced for anything except items which have a very direct bearing on the immediate results. It goes without saying that people development costs are not usually seen as falling into this category. Player Managers find themselves understaffed and underprepared. As for changing the climate, the pressures of the short term mean that most Player Managers have more than enough to do.

PART TWO

Player Managers at Work

4
Looking Both Ways

If the stories from the field outlined in the previous chapter are anything to go by, many Player Managers are trapped between myth and reality. From above they are accountable for business results delivered through their own production and the performance of their teams. Their organization tells them that they are 'empowered' and, in all probability, boasts of its commitment to its people in its annual report to shareholders, in its mission statement and in its advertising to the public. The people at the top believe that they are proponents of modern management theory. They have invested in various platforms for people and are handing on power to those in the senior and middle ranks 'who probably know better than we do what is best for the business these days.'

From below it can look very different. Empowered Player Managers are being overloaded with production responsibilities and managerial duties. They have received little or no training in how to manage others yet they are accountable for their results. There is no margin for error and little patience for those who do not produce in the short term. The Player Manager probably reports to someone who is experiencing exactly the same problems with those to whom they report; thus impatience and pressure become instilled as features of the organization's climate. With little knowledge of the disciplines and techniques required to get leverage from the team, the Player Managers, if many of those we met are typical, react the only way they know how – by doing more themselves, by working longer hours and by veiling their growing frustration. Unless their personal circumstances are very unusual, work pressures can produce domestic ones, as tiredness and long hours spent away from home eat into their quality of life.

Regardless of whether the view is taken from above or below, Player

Managers are carrying the load; they are at the fulcrum of a fragile uneasy balance. We discovered that Player Managers are, as usual, doing it for themselves. They are not expecting a sudden sea-change in global managerial practice or an easing of the post-1990's economic straitjacket that grips many of their organizations. Instead, in a continuing effort to do what is expected of them and at the same time to keep their heads above water, they are taking the initiative and learning to survive for themselves.

They might be interested in the story of Amanda Sage, who knows how to face the Player Manager challenge. She has the attributes of a born survivor. With very little help from the person to whom she reports, she has worked out independently the levers to pull that enable her to get the best results personally and from her team.

Just Perfect

It had been a long time since Amanda Sage had sat back and thought about her options. When we questioned her about what had first attracted her to a career in business, she seemed genuinely surprised.

Opting for a job in business

'I started in business in 1983. At that time I was considering an MA in Communication Arts. I had always imagined I would write screenplays, or do something associated with films. I felt a year on a master's programme would take me further along that road. But I quickly realized how much competition there was and how hard life would be as an MA student. Grants were scarce and getting scarcer. After thinking realistically about another year with a significant overdraft that would get sizeably bigger, I opted for a job instead.

'Most of my friends were making similar choices, and so when I accepted my position as an analyst at a mid-size computer services consultancy I was by no means alone. After all, we were Thatcher's newborns. We had heard there was no such thing as society, especially for financing dreams. I must admit that for a few years I wondered if this had been the right thing to do. But in the late 1980s I opted to take a part time MBA at business school. My company offered to fund this and to support the study programme with some time off, and frankly since then I have never looked back. I met my husband at business school and I was quickly promoted through to associate partner after completing the programme. Sure, we were classic eighties Yuppies or Dinkies or both – but we really had done it for ourselves. And boy, it was fun!

'By this time the computer sector, well the whole IT thing really, was exploding. High tech was the place to be, although the pace was accelerating and it was getting harder to keep up. I suppose I really started to pull ahead of my class at that time; I just got such a charge from the buzz in our industry. When our firm was merged with a much bigger full service consultancy a couple of years after I finished my MBA, I was given my first responsibility for Europe, which has afforded great travel opportunities and the chance to become more culturally aware.

'The only really big change for me occurred when our first child was born in 1994. I must admit I had a few guilt pangs then. Could I be a good mother and good professional without compromising both roles? Would my promotion prospects to partner start to evaporate now that I was juggling a baby and a job? And would the firm still believe I was serious about my career?

'The first year was tough but, like anything else, it's all about organization and good support. Once I had worked out what this meant in terms of practical help, things started to feel less pressured. And I must say both the partners here and my husband have been brilliant about it; everyone has offered such tremendous help. I remember that by the beginning of 1998 I even found time to join a gym and I still go out after work with the team fairly often. And here I am – back in my pre-baby body and up for partner this year. I have a very exciting business challenge in front of me and my two children, who as you can see from the pictures round the office are so cute that people want to hug them, are getting settled into school. With effort, work/life balance is achievable. Without wishing to sound smug, I believe that if you work at it systematically with dedication as well as realism and efficiency, it is possible to juggle and have it all.'

Spinning Plates

Curious to know more, we asked Amanda Sage about the challenges and pressures she faced. She replied that her role was like spinning plates, and keeping them all spinning at the same time was how she defined success.

Amanda's Day.　Spinning plates sounded to us like a rather precarious pastime and we couldn't quite associate it with the calm and confident woman seated in front of us. When we asked Amanda to describe what she meant by spinning plates she replied: 'Take this morning for example. Up at 5.30 to check messages, fortunately no major catastrophes, so onto the Stairmaster while checking "the barometer" as I call it. This is actually a quick scan of the markets to catch any overnight changes to the share prices of my clients. I have noticed in the last couple of years just how sensitive clients are to their share price, particularly at quarter end. On some of our big ticket items, the mood about quarterly earnings can mean the difference between a close and another three to six months of hanging in there for the order.

'Anyway, by 6.30 I was warmed up and fairly well organized – a schedule for the nanny, a note and money for the dog walker, a list and a cheque for the joiner who, if the nanny remembered to be back on time to let him in, should be starting cabinet refurbishing today. Then it was just a matter of a few "get your shoes on we are leaving right now" to the household at large and a quick check in with my husband about which of us was likely to be home first. We aim for the nanny to finish on schedule so that the kids can have at least one parent for hugs and early evening quality time. By 7.15 we were on our way to the school – where thankfully they have a great early start programme – and I was the first to arrive at the office, coffee in hand, for a meeting that had been set up at 8.00.'

We wondered why Amanda was describing her life and her journey to work in such detail when it was her work life and not her home life we were interested in. But then we realized that for Amanda these two had become one and the same. To meet the demands placed on her, she operated constantly as some kind of super juggling machine without any evident down time. The fact that pragmatic micro-management of all aspects of her life was something Amanda took for granted and sounded proud of, told us something about what it takes to be successful in a role made up of spinning plates. This was no ordinary personality. It included a steely focus, relentless commitment to keeping things going, the resolve to drive things through and an overarching optimism that all would come good in the end. Amanda had all these qualities in abundance, and if she ever needed to detune, take a break or felt less than optimistic, we doubted whether she would ever have the space or time to notice.

Amanda At Work. We described the Player Manager concept to Amanda and asked her how it compared to her own job.

'It sounds surprisingly similar – more juggling, more spinning plates.

'I'm responsible for a line of service across Europe. I am expected to deliver results in three areas. First is our short-term performance, the delivery of results to plan. Second is our growth, the numbers in our mid-term plan. We are targeting 20 per cent growth over the next three years, a chunk of which depends on us stealing market share from our top three competitors. Most of the action will be in Europe – it's a critical geography for us in the near- to mid-term, so the eyes are on my team and me. This brings me to the third area of results, sustainability. I am expected to deliver the plan that will keep us in the game for the long haul and the team of talent for ensuring that we get there.

'Of course my boss is much more worried about the first one than any of the others, and I know that without bringing in this year's numbers the case for putting me up as partner this year will be weakened. But I also know that the others are important, especially if I become a partner and part of the stewardship of the firm. So many small players in our industry ended up being sold off because they mortgaged their futures, and I don't want that to happen to us. We also have no plans to go public, that I know of at any rate. Our culture is such that our independence is still important to us. We will have to be commercially savvy to protect that.

'Of course I have to deliver results within various budget constraints, and that means seeing myself as part of the team. I am one of the elephant hunters shooting to kill some of the time, but I'm also the head of the tribe. For example in Italy we lost a few people last year, and the strength of our client base is much less than I supposed when

I moved into the service line. We had made a small acquisition and it was left alone for too long without being given a clear sense of what its contribution was supposed to be. People became disenchanted and left. This means I have had to take on responsibility for maintaining accounts with several clients, rebuilding relationships with them as well as trying to grow the business in the local market.

'I have personal targets to achieve and this year a big part of keeping up the numbers comes from Italy. I have been there a lot in the last six months prospecting and handling bids, not to mention dealing with aggravation in some of our service contracts there. This is all detailed and time-consuming work, and at the moment I am the only one up to handling it. Unless I make some hits, we will miss our target for the year. At the same time I don't want to be handling it forever or we will never achieve our objective for growth. Next year I will need to be much more hands on in other markets, and this will be represented in my targets. So at the same time I have had to prioritize putting in place a programme for replacing the people we lost.

'As head of the service line I interview all the candidates personally, and more than that I try to give them a compelling reason to join us. Just last week our top candidate to become head of Italian sales asked to clarify things in a follow-up interview. We haven't offered the job yet but we are likely to. To keep the candidate warm I flew out at the end of the week, after just getting back from two client pitches at the beginning of the week. Now I need to find time to put through the paperwork internally so that we can offer in an acceptable timeframe. This is as well as turning the pitches last week into concrete proposals and keeping in contact with the clients that we already have there.

'All this work in Italy means that the people here and in other parts of Europe have to wait for my attention. Understandably their needs build up and I am permanently awash in Lotus notes and voicemails. I don't like to hold up other people's progress, so I play a game with myself about emptying the voicebox and inbox daily. But I have worked out that the faster I respond, the faster the next tranche builds up, so I am getting a little more discerning about what I respond to and how fast. It's a more selective and subjective prioritization, but by putting some levers in place upfront, I have done enough to build up sufficient understanding and goodwill from the team to be able to do that without cost.'

Before we could ask Amanda more specific questions about these levers, she continued her account of her job.

'In the emerging markets we are nowhere and, to be honest, our product isn't as good as it needs to be there. Unless this changes we will miss our growth target. Nobody at the global level knows what we are trying to do here and how much effort is required. I sometimes feel as though I am completely on my own with this problem. To top it all, the head of the UK team just cannot collaborate with the head of marketing. Their inability to work together is driving all sorts of problems my way, and I am involved much more in the detail of this than I would want to be. But unless I pick up the ball and drive this one, their disconnect will damage our performance as well as morale in both the UK and the marketing team. Now I am accountable for the result and for sorting out their relationship as well.'

We acknowledged that Amanda did indeed have her hands full and that we were beginning to get the picture of what she meant when she described it all as spinning plates. It was a precarious position, with plenty of potential for things to go wrong. How did she keep her cool, we wondered, and to whom did she look to share the burden of her load? Did she, for example, get any help from her boss?

Amanda's Boss. 'It is funny you should ask that now,' Amanda replied. 'I spoke to my boss about the disconnect between marketing and the UK team last week. He took the time to listen to me and he was sympathetic enough, if not of much practical value. I am pretty much on my own with all of this. Heads of service lines like me are all thrown into the deep end with precious little guidance from above. My boss joined us from a much more established public company shortly after the merger a few years back. They hired him for his big company experience at a time when our sector began to grow and consolidate. He is supposed to be the one with the managerial experience, but I wonder sometimes if he and I are operating in parallel universes.

'Anyway, when I spoke to him about my concerns, he said: "You know, Amanda, time was when understanding how to manage was very simple. Like the earth in the days before Galileo insisted on making things more complicated, managers were the part that everything else in the universe revolved around. It was about knowing enough soon enough to be right enough to be boss. If you watched your back, shared as little as possible and had a boss that liked you, you could keep things under control. That was then though, Amanda.

' "Now nothing is that simple. Nobody knows enough. Too many things are changing faster than our ability to keep up. We all spend many more hours sharing everything we know, yet nobody knows who is right or not as there are too many uncertainties involved. So don't expect to fix everything or try to take it all on. The head of marketing and the head of the UK are never going to get along. They are both type A males for a start and one is European and the other isn't. In any case, marketing and sales were never meant to get along; it's just like cats and dogs.

' "Don't be so idealistic about all this collaboration and cross-functional stuff they are spreading down from the top. Turf is turf. It's all about looking after your own. Take my advice. Watch your back 24/7, be charming enough to keep all the guys onside, and then you might just be kept in the loop long enough not to feel totally out of control. I know that cannot sound particularly helpful, but it is good advice."

'That is honestly what he said to me. I'd like to think he genuinely believed he was helping me by sharing his philosophy on management. But to be frank, I think his real message was "Don't get too dragged into the people issues, Amanda, or you will take your eye off the ball". He has a lot riding on me really, more than he appreciates. In this place rainmaker skills are paramount, regardless of all the things we do to champion people. And my rainmaker skills in Italy this year are important to my boss. He doesn't exactly have egg on his face because we lost the Italian team and some clients, but he is accountable for making the acquisition in Italy starting to show some payback soon. The easiest way is for it to show positive numbers in the short term and that means me making rain fast.

'He isn't wrong, just a bit blinkered and biased towards the short term. If we'd had a better relationship between some of the teams we might have made a better go of the business integration in the first place, and we cannot afford to lose a second team which is why getting all this in place is important. My boss is really on the line for the headway we make in Europe, and if I only concentrated on the numbers we would be in trouble halfway through next year. We need strength on the ground in our local markets and we need to get rid of the fault line in our service contracts – otherwise the territory just won't be ours. So, as I said when we started talking, it is all so many plates up in the air.'

Amanda's Levers. 'How do you feel about all the plates waiting to come crashing down?' we asked Amanda. 'Do you really have to watch your back all the time, and if everything is on the verge of being out of control then isn't that a disheartening feeling?' It was a while before Amanda replied.

'Do I get disheartened? Not really. Before I took over this job I knew it would present a lot of challenges, but I made it my business to take command quickly. I'm a natural when it comes to prioritizing. My time management is good and people always tell me that I am pretty good at motivating and developing the team. We have held 360s here for a few years now and my upward feedback has been consistently upper quartile. It has been so good, in fact, that I keep being asked by the partners to give talks to the other principals about leadership and retention. I think it helps that in all the years that I have had responsibility for other people, I have also had to deliver personal results. The people I work with respect my point of view, not because I have been in their shoes but because I am in their shoes; we are in the game together.

'I take the team offsite a couple of times a year, as I believe away days are great for personal development and for building team bonds. They demonstrate empowerment; everyone has the chance to participate in formal decisions about business plans. Mentoring others individually is another fulfilling part of the role. I've never really understood the "time drain" my colleagues often complain of when faced with having to do these people development things.'

We asked Amanda if the things she was describing about her interaction with the team were examples of what she had meant earlier when she had mentioned 'putting in levers'.

'To a point, yes, but it is more accurate to say that they are examples of the levers being pulled after they are in place. You asked me earlier what I am expected to do as a Player Manager and I said three things. Keep up with the numbers short term, deliver growth, and deliver a sustainable future via the plan and the team. When I first took over this job, I asked myself what I would need to put in place to be able to do this job day by day while making progress on all three fronts. This is more precisely what I meant by putting in the levers.'*

We realized that we had come to the crux of what Amanda was doing to make her life as a Player Manager enjoyable and workable, despite the lack of support she got from those above her in the organization. The reason Amanda felt able to spin so many plates without feeling out of control was that the ground was fairly safe beneath her as a consequence of the foundation she had built. We asked her to outline her levers.

'I have never articulated this fully before, but I believe there are six levers for what you term "player managing". If you think about it they are obvious. Without them it is easy to get swamped, to disappear into the day to day and, even if you are delivering on your personal targets, to lose the support of the team.

The End Game.   'The first lever is direction. Some people call it the overarching goal, I call it the picture of the end game. This picture needs painting in everyone's mind as soon as possible, ideally while settling into the job or else at the first possible moment. Painting this picture not only helped me take command by clarifying what I was up to, but by defining and communicating the end game to others it gave the team something to identify with. Now they have a good idea of where they are headed – of where I am taking them and why.

'The picture does not need to be an agency-designed mission statement or anything like that. In fact what has always worked best for me is something simple and real. I said earlier that to grow by the 20 per cent expected of us we will need to take share. We need to take it from the existing top three in the European market, "so being number one or two in our line in Europe" is the end game for me and the team all know it.

'Before we leave the end game, I should add that the stating is nearly as important as the defining. It is no good having a great picture of the end result if you keep it in your head. And saying it once isn't enough. It has to become the backcloth of every conversation we are having and of every action we take.

---

* The levers outlined in this chapter are a refinement of the six factors of organization climate discussed in the notes to the previous chapter.

The Game Plan. 'Once you give people an end game it not only gives them an aiming point, it also makes it possible to come up with the second lever and that is the game plan. It's the "what and how" of playing and it needs formulating and stating regularly. Some people call it strategy; I call it the way through the game. Believe me, coming up with a game plan that has some edge is not easy.

'As you no doubt worked out from what I told you, we are spread pretty thinly across Europe and the risk for us, as we try to build share in more countries, is that we go from one patch to another without building a sustainable presence anywhere. I am still working out the game plan for this, but having a team in Italy is one obvious piece as is the relationship between the project managers, sales, marketing and service. I don't want the sales people developing clients that are too out of line with the market plan, otherwise we end up bidding too tactically – or worse – on things we cannot deliver. Sales need to be playing to the same game plan as everyone.

'One feature of our game plan, which will maybe give us some edge, is team coverage of accounts. I began introducing this after taking over the job. Instead of having just the salesperson involved upstream we are trying to get a client dialogue with the bid manager, the sector analyst and the service manager also involved. I think there would be more leverage in us working as an account team with everyone pointing in the same direction. This is the piece I just can't get the people above me to understand, and naturally there is some resistance on the ground especially from those that don't directly report to me. You can see why this is making my boss nervous, given his views on "turf" as he puts it.

'I don't think of the game plan as fixed. Circumstances change, and the game plan is something that needs thinking about and working on all the time. But if you don't do it, then the team doesn't have a common way forward even with the end game in place.

The Benchmark. 'Once a game plan has been set, it is important to give people something against which they can measure themselves. I call this "benchmarking performance". It is the third lever a Player Manager can pull, and it is still a mystery to me why so few pull it. It strikes me as vital to have some standards and to set and communicate these as your expectations of the team. In our business, where there are external market share surveys, benchmarks are easy to find and track. These are tied in to our desired end game. If we are trying to be our clients' first choice service provider as an end game, then we can measure our progress in the surveys. From the top-level benchmark the goals, the targets and the pace of play for each player and for the team as a whole fall out.

'Obviously it's unrealistic to go from fifth to, say, second in one jump, so interim targets have been defined. I set all of these, and if they are clear no one is confused about what the benchmark is, where they stand in relation to it and how well their contribution matches it.

'Of course I don't develop the benchmark unilaterally. Parts of it can be formulated as a group. But everyone expects me to be clear about this in my own mind. Some partners I have worked for have done this better than others. My current boss – well, as I think I highlighted, he is a bit jaded and cynical. He would never set a benchmark along these lines, unless watching my back is some kind of standard.'

Amanda paused, and we remarked that all of the items mentioned so far in her framework were practical and concrete. We wondered if this was enough to secure involvement and high performance?

'It's not a bad point. I said these things were obvious. But it doesn't make them less powerful or real as levers. So far I have given you half of my list of six and you are right to a point in that they are concrete. They create the map of the terrain and the approach, but how we get across it depends on the emotional energy we put in.

'The benchmark is more than a detached standard. Attached to it is my personal expectation, or faith in a person's ability to be able to meet it. I can motivate or demotivate someone by the way I communicate this. Without even opening my mouth, I can say to someone, "You are an idiot, and if we get there with you on the team it will be a miracle," or I can say, "Hey, you are great and without you we would never do it." These signals about how the players relate to the benchmark make all the difference to whether our team spirit is encouraging or critical. If I set unrealistic standards it would be demotivating, either because the benchmark is too tough or even because it is too easy. People need stretch, but they don't need to be overstretched. It is important to get rhythm and flow as well as pace into how we play.

'It is similar with the game plan and end game. These can be interpreted as management babble or as the main reason for showing up to work. If our game plan isn't taken to heart by the team, then that is a failure on my part. We all hear of organizations that think that posting the vision is enough, that information is equal to empower-ment. Nothing could be further from the truth, and that kind of thinking explains why so many people feel lost. You can only get these levers to work when you combine the message with the less obvious aspects of influencing.'

We asked Amanda to explain what she meant and she said that the fourth lever she was about to discuss was a good example.

Team Enablers.   'The fourth lever is enabling the team to play. It's a mix of how we structure work and create the freedom to get it done. I don't know whether it is process or permission that is most enabling, but I do know that my team needs the tools and the space to achieve their best.

'A key to it is resisting the urge to do it all myself. It is natural for hustlers like me to want to do everything. But I have to involve others who want the freedom to do their thing and to have an impact on what happens around here. And that's fine. Over the years I have realized that enabling the team is part attitude and part organization. The attitude part is to trust others to do it or to learn to do it. It is vital to keep listening to where the team is, to step in only when necessary and to respond flexibly to their ideas.

'Everyone wants the resources to do things for themselves and the room to do it. It is so competitive out there that winning takes the whole team. I need them and they need my trust. Enabling the team is an attitude that says "Over to you", together with an appreciation that people can't do it unless they have the skills and resources. The one without the other is not enough.

Feedback.   'If you are going to trust people and give them room to play, it is important to give them feedback, and this is the fifth factor. Everyone wants to understand their part in the game, both what they are meant to be doing and how well they are doing it. The more transparent this is for everyone and for the team as a whole, then the better off we are. Empowerment in my book doesn't just come from handing over authority. It comes from quality of information, the ability to know how well you are doing against the standard of what you have said you should be doing. Feedback out of the context of an end game, game plan and benchmark is not nearly so meaningful or powerful.

'Of course the danger is that I become the conduit for this information about performance. This isn't what I want. I want the team to be more independent than that. We as a team can set things up so this information is available directly to those who need it. We enable feedback, if you like, via the systems we set up. With real time feedback, everyone can see where they are relative to the benchmark and can adjust their game accordingly. My judgement is still important, but unless the team can see how they are doing they will be reactive.

'Feedback also ties to rewards. If my team feels that rewards and recognition are unfair relative to how well we are playing both individually and as a team, then there is something wrong. Sure, you cannot please all of the people all of the time. But you can take out much of the noise and bias when it comes to expectations and decisions about how to divvy up rewards. If in my 360 feedback people were telling me my decisions were unfair or that I preferred favourites, I know I would be storing up some long-term problems of resentment and cynicism that would impact morale and performance. Feedback means that even if people do not agree with your decisions, at least they can understand why you have come to them.

Commitment.   'This brings me to the sixth and final lever, securing the commitment of the team. My job is to spark us all into raising the bar. I want us to make a difference, to create a result that wasn't going to happen anyway. All great sports coaches and managers do that for their teams. In business, so many teams and combinations fail even when they are rich with talent and all the other resources. I can name a few in my industry alone that are like that. They have a great squad but they never pull off anything remarkable. I want my performance and the team's performance to be nothing less than remarkable. And it will be. My own sense of responsibility and commitment to our end game and to everyone else in the team will ensure that.'

We asked Amanda if there was any advice she could give people about how to make the various levers work well together.

'One thing I would add is something I learned from a good friend and mentor. A subtle, but vital ingredient of making it happen is just letting it happen. Things have a rhythm and a dynamic and a way of playing themselves out. I don't need to hold the reins too tightly or to be totally in control. With good sensors and intelligence, there is time to anticipate most problems and to bring things back on track if the game is going wrong. It also leaves space for new ways of doing things to emerge as play unfolds. This is just as well. Otherwise I wouldn't get even a few hours sleep each night.'

Looking Both Ways

We asked Amanda whether she was happy.

'This would never work for me unless I enjoyed it, but I wouldn't enjoy it unless I worked at it. It struck me a couple of years back when the pace hotted up that I was like Janus, the Roman god of gates and doors.

'Janus, as I am sure you know, had two heads, one to look forward and one to look back. He could keep his eye on both sides of the gate by constantly looking in two directions at once. In the Roman Empire, when his gates were closed it meant peace, when they were open it was war. Well, the gates here are well and truly open, and I need my one head to be in two places at once.

'On one side of my gate is playing, my personal performance, where I am pitted against every other rainmaker in our industry and where there's little margin for error. I have to keep my eye on this. On the other side of the gate is managing the performance of the team and the business, and I need to watch that too.

'The instinct just to drive forward can get in the way here because I can start seeing the team as an encumbrance, something that is slowing me down. But I was given this job to be a leader, someone who can influence other people and the things they achieve, and I have learned to resist the urge to do it all myself. In any case, unless I leverage the team I will burn out, and then I really would be unhappy.

'Janus was also the god of new beginnings, and my work offers me plenty of those. If I am not learning something new or striving for a new challenge, I am not fulfilled. It's always a sixty hour week or more and it invariably intrudes into weekends, but hey, I have to do something with my life. Right now, this is fun.'

With that Amanda smiled and signalled to her assistant. She was ready to resume her day's work. Her own personal playing was a part of this, but her main act was guarding the gate using the six levers she had just described.

Amanda firstly defined her *end game* and then secondly translated this into a *game plan*. Each of her team was aware of this. They were also aware of their part and the expected standard, because Amanda thirdly specified the *benchmark* of performance and then fourthly put in place *enablers* for this to be achieved. Next she made sure that *feedback* was available to everyone, with strong ties between feedback, performance and rewards. Her sixth lever was to engender *commitment*, by giving all those involved the chance to achieve something out of the ordinary and by setting a personal example of enthusiasm for the cause.

Amanda did all this through a level of organization and discipline at home and at work that bordered on the superhuman. When things became messy and demanding, as they had become in the relationship with her boss, she remained both optimistic and pragmatic. All in all, for Amanda Sage things sounded pretty perfect. There was only one problem. Amanda wasn't real.

In all our years of management, executive coaching and management education we have never met anyone like Amanda Sage; she is a fantasy of management theory. Amanda holds humane values, and always displays positive regard for others while never failing to deliver as she runs herself smoothly and efficiently like a machine. She is how it is meant to be when juggling with the multiple demands of Player Managing, but the fieldwork outlined in Chapter Three suggests we are not going to meet anyone like Amanda anytime soon.

We Imperfect Types

The rest of us are real and most of us have failings. We know that taking time out to look ahead and plan makes us more effective in the long run; yet few of us make the time to do it well. We are reactive and biased in favour of what we know how to do, what we prefer to do and what is right there in front of us. The only thing that real Player Managers have in common with Amanda Sage is her quantity of work.

Whatever the economic and cultural reasons for the shifting balance between managing and producing, Player Managers are back, their dual function posing more challenges than management theory and education suggest. From the safe distance of the educator, it is easy to say, 'Look two ways with one head.' But from our own less than perfect results when trying to manage and from our fieldwork, we have learned that it is easier to lose your head than to look both ways.

We have found that whether it is work/life balance, support from above, directing teams, having prospects and purpose or even finding the most basic level of meaning, something essential is lacking in the average Player Manager's work satisfaction. If this is so, then how can Player Managers who directly produce while holding responsibility for the business performance and management of functions, product lines, customers and teams, sustain their efforts? Can anyone, other than the mythical Amanda Sage, really balance it all?

The key to bridging the gap between those of us stuck in the real world outlined in Chapter Three and the mythically well-managed life of Amanda Sage lies in Amanda's analysis. Her definition of what she was expected to deliver – short-term results, growth in the mid-term plan and sustainability to keep in the game for the long haul – would be accepted as the ideal by most organizations. The problem, as we have outlined, is that there is an excessive focus on the near horizon and no real commitment to the longer term, beyond a hope that if all is well in the short term the long term will look after itself.

Amanda's six levers for getting the best from her team offer a way of connecting fantasy with reality. We went back into the field to find out more about the attributes of Player Managers in action in order to test the ideal – Amanda's storm-proof personality and her framework for leveraging the team – against the real types of Player Managers that were out there at work.

We discovered that in the real world there are Player Managers who are just about balancing it all, although they can go closer to the edge of failure than either they or their teams would like. As we got to understand their situation and explored with them the ways they are striving to improve their performance and happiness, our observations led us to believe that most Player Managers can develop through experience. There is no single pathway to success, but amongst the broad spread of 'Believers' and those 'Under Pressure' we have identified six types of Player Manager. Each type displays some common characteristics and faces a similar kind of challenge, and we have written one story, often an amalgamation of several people and situations, to illustrate each. How will they measure up to Amanda's ideal?

5

Introducing the Player Managers

Objective self-appraisal is always difficult to achieve, particularly at work. Day-to-day situations and relationships sweep us along and cloud our judgements. Opportunities to stand back and appreciate the overall situation are rare, occurring for example after a break, on taking up a new job or on changing roles.

For Player Managers, who have to keep looking both ways to survive, stepping back to see things is especially difficult. They are probably tired, stressed and lacking enough time to think, all circumstances that make it more essential than ever to stand back but which also make doing so less likely. An easy way for busy Player Managers to get perspective is to measure themselves against someone else's style, and the characters that follow are designed to serve as models for comparison.

First is *the Rookie*, a character who is new to the role but keen to succeed. The Rookie's challenge is to step up and take command without doing it all personally.

Players' Players are much admired stars. With a love of the game and a demonstrated excellence in most areas of it the Players' Player's challenge is to replicate their own success in others.

Player Coaches are personable and empathetic. Their challenge is to develop talent without losing sight of the bigger picture.

Veterans are the old hands. Their challenge is to manage the institution as well as the team whilst keeping both fresh.

Play Makers are change agents. Labelled as brilliant but difficult, because they agitate for change, they must lead the team in new directions without disappearing out of sight.

Each type has different strengths. They each generate their own kind of support as well as making different contributions to the business, to their teams and to the climate that prevails in the groups that they manage. Each type also has potential shortcomings and it is these that lead to the distinct challenges identified above. These shortcomings arise from the personal and cultural factors that influence behaviour and affect the capability of a Player Manager to adapt 'what comes naturally' into approaches that generate 'better outcomes', however these might be defined.

Some Player Managers step up to their challenges admirably. Others face a constant struggle to improve their contribution in the role. For some it is simply impossible, and for this reason we include *the Player Again*, a person who returns to pure playing, as the final type in our framework. Unsuited to or overwhelmed by the demands of managing, the challenge for the Player Again is to get out sooner rather than later regardless of perceived loss of face. Most Player Managers will find that they contain elements of some or all of the six types outlined, starting with Roger the Rookie.

The Rookie

When we met Roger he had just left the market research agency where he worked to start a career in a completely different industry. He was widely regarded as a success in a field which employed many professionals, but where star status was comparatively rare. His departure had caused a few shock waves, especially since his next job would represent quite a change of direction, and we were eager to hear his story. We were lucky that he seemed in reflective mood and we asked him about the job he had just left.

He told us in a quiet, modulated tone that it had been his first experience of managing, that it was a job we recognized as being a Player Manager role and that it had been difficult for him: 'Almost everything about it and me was wrong. I managed to scrape through only at a huge personal cost. The strain of coping with new situations and an impossible workload burned me out within a couple of years. I felt fed up and exhausted and just had to leave in order to recover. Even now, talking about it makes my stomach tighten.'

We asked him to tell us more about how 'everything about it was wrong'.

'I was to take charge of a team of four professionals who carried out direct research and also of two salespeople, whose role was to telephone clients and prospects in our sector to keep them abreast of trends and find out their views. It was a classic producer manager role: in addition to managing the team, I had work to do as a researcher. I had been a player in another sector and this was a promotion for me.

'The team had been under-achieving. It had been jointly managed by a senior researcher and a senior account director. It had not been made clear to the senior researcher that she was no longer running things. She was supposedly moved on to a new area but was allowed to believe she still had some responsibilities in the team. This gave her a position from which she could undermine me, of which she took full advantage, for she did not accept that there was a new leader.

'To top that, the senior account director had also not been told that I was to be in charge; we were just left to sort it out. He was senior to me in age, experience and status in the firm, and of course, having done the job for several years, he knew more about the sector issues and products we were researching. Although he was a decent guy and we rubbed along OK, I never addressed the lack of clarity, which confused clients, colleagues and especially us!'

Roger looked embarrassed when we asked him to recall the confusion. He told us that in retrospect they just seemed silly trivial things but they mattered to all concerned at the time.

'If we had a client event, we would be manoeuvring for position to see who would chair it; if we did a joint presentation to clients, games would be played to see who would introduce whom; all of this must have been obvious to the staff and to outsiders. Worse, I suppose, was that we would leave decisions to one another. Sometimes we cancelled each other out because we took opposite sides and no view was taken. We must have looked indecisive, and despite the fact that we got on well at the personal level there were some uncomfortable moments. I have no doubt that we wasted emotional energy on internal wrangling, energy that would have been better spent in more creative ways.'

We asked him who else was involved.

'Most of the members of the previous team had left, so we had a few very good young graduates, the former team leaders, and me. Then another problem occurred: we desperately needed new and experienced researchers and I had assumed when taking the job that I would be responsible for hiring them. But no, the Client Services Director presented me with two candidates, good people, actually, but with no experience of our field, and told me that he expected me to approve their recruitment. I should have stood up to him there and then and told him that if I was to manage the team, I would also want to pick it. Even if he insisted in being involved, I should have insisted that at that stage we needed experience above potential. Instead, I took a back seat in the selection process and did not object to the newcomers.

'So there we were: a bunch of graduates who were just learning the job, two recruits from outside who knew nothing at all about product research, a displaced team leader who probably wanted us to fail and a senior salesperson who thought he was leading the team, a role that had just been given to me, a team leader who knew nothing about the sector.'

We agreed that all of this would have been a handful even for an experienced Player Manager, let alone for a rookie. We wondered whether Roger's company had given him any training for his new responsibility and how he had prepared himself for it.

'The only training I got was to be told that the firm believed that the way to learn was to get in at the deep end and start swimming. Unfortunately I started drowning instead. I had no knowledge of the companies that we were trying to sell research to, so I had to learn the industry sector. As the new leader of this team I had to spend a lot of time getting up to speed as well as trying to take over. Even when I was up to speed, the demands of doing research, writing to a tight timetable, delivering reports back to clients, thinking coolly about product marketing decisions and managing the team required time management and prioritization skills that I had never needed before.

'Also, I had no experience of managing people or of office politics. I did not know how to do it. Things like how to train people, how to blend encouragement with correction, all this was foreign to me. I had always worked in a small, unified team before and I did not know how to cope with the undermining that went on within this new larger unit. I had no training about how to cope with difficult situations. I was in the deep end all right, and sinking like a stone.

'The only way that I could see to do things was to learn fast and lead by example. On the managerial issues, I made the best of things with my two rivals and avoided confrontation. Frankly, this gave me two years of hell. Trying to master a new sector was difficult: lots of reading in the evenings and at weekends after the family had gone to bed. This meant that I was getting up already feeling exhausted before I even started the next day's challenges. I was forever trying to prove myself as someone that the team would look up to, so I tried to be better than they were: better informed, more insightful, harder working. I thought they would only respect me if I was the best.

'The deposed team leader eventually ceased to be a problem once she established herself in her new area, although there were a number of annoying and upsetting incidents before then, which as far as outside appearances were concerned, I just ignored. Inwardly however, I was boiling. The senior account director and I just rubbed along. We liked each other, needed each other and although there were moments of mutual irritation when we were jockeying for position, we avoided serious rows.'

We were relieved to hear that no lives were lost but wanted to know Roger's perception about the whole episode. In hindsight, how did he think it had all worked out?

'The team succeeded in its business aims and most of the individuals within it got the career progression that they wanted. For me personally, it did not work. It left me exhausted and unhappy. I was so tired that I could not analyse my personal situation properly, I just knew that I was unhappy. There was no one at the office I could discuss this with because it was not done to admit to weakness. Therefore I took the first opportunity that I could find to leave the industry with my dignity, if not my nerves, intact.'

The Rookie's Challenge

The Rookie's challenge is to step up and take command without doing it all personally.

Roger is a good example of our first Player Manager type, the Rookie who, as the name suggests, is new to the job and inevitably puts a few steps wrong. Rookies are in a significant transition from specialist or technical work to a role that requires a wider and often more political outlook as well as a broader set of skills. Quite often, as Roger discovered, the situation into which they are going is less than optimal.

When a top producer is offered a management role it sounds like, and usually is, a promotion. Most people just accept, without thinking if they want it or will be any good at it. Rookie Player Managers tend to be appointed from their organization's pool of expert producers, and this determines how they respond. Experts just dive in; they don't ask for help, they are experts. One notable characteristic of experts is their self-reliance. When Spike Milligan won an award for lifetime achievement in 1995 he said in his acceptance speech: 'I'm not going to thank anyone, because I did it all myself.'

This sentiment is often felt, if not expressed, by Rookies. They display high self-esteem but low esteem for others, even if internally they are experiencing some doubt. Instead of dealing with this issue, they determinedly hold to the belief that they have to do everything. In their anxiety about getting everything done, they underestimate others. 'No one in my team is up to doing much at all,' is a common Rookie complaint.

To succeed, Rookies have to see the world through a broader lens than they used as an expert player. Transitioning from pure playing to taking on additional responsibilities is the hardest thing to address. Giving up or doing less of what made you so successful in the first place and for which you are still accountable is not easy. But the alternative is to be like Roger: burned out and alienated from your colleagues.

Over time the Rookie does one of three things – gives up, reverts to playing, or learns how to step up to take command without burning out in the process. In Chapter Six we return to Roger, offering ways to reduce the chances of this transition being painful and prolonged.

Rookie's Profile

Typical Strengths
- Never done it before
- Keen to step up
- Gets things done
- Determined to succeed
- Technically expert
- Works long hours

Possible Shortcomings
- 'Task' not 'people' oriented
- Fails to delegate
- Feels responsible for everything
- Relies on expert status
- Doesn't seek feedback
- Prone to denial

The Players' Player

We heard about Nicola from a satisfied client, someone who described her as the most charismatic relationship manager they had ever met. What really interested us was the client's view that 'Nicola's people would knock down walls for her', and we decided to find out more. Getting the meeting was the hardest bit. Nicola doesn't have an assistant, was always on the phone and, although colleagues took messages, our calls were never returned. We finally got our original contact to set up the meeting for 6 pm one Wednesday evening.

It was nearly 6.45 pm when Nicola eventually walked in. Actually she didn't walk in, she made an entrance, designer dressed from her neck down to her shoes. The door burst open and she was upon us with a profusion of apologies for being late, a warm smile and firm handshake with 'I've got all the time you need, the rest of the evening is for you.' We agreed that Nicola had great charisma and that her confidence betrayed the fact she had never had a self-doubt in her life.

We asked Nicola to explain how she managed her bond sales team.

'First of all I've got to be the biggest producer in the team. The clients have to ask for me more than anyone else, I have to win and keep the biggest clients, my revenues must be bigger, maybe twice as big as anyone else's. That's the secret. The boys and girls in the team have to look up to me, they have to say, "Nicola does it and so can I." When I close a deal, I want them all to know and to share in the excitement. I want them to draw energy from success, to feel uplifted, to get a buzz. And I want them to do it for themselves.'

We asked her if she gave them any training on how to do it.

'Not in the formal sense. I don't believe in wasting time away from the business going on courses or stuff like that. HR try to get in the way with a load of forms to fill out with nonsense about development and objectives and so on, but I pay scant attention to them and, to be honest, I've never read a book about selling in my life. But I do try to give them on-the-job training by setting a good example. I let them know that knowledge of the product and the client are absolute "must haves". If you are not up to date with the latest developments you do not deserve to work here and, quite frankly, unless you are, you won't last for very long. Same with the clients. I always take one of the team along to meetings with me, they can see for themselves how much I know about every client's needs. I know the names of their partners and spouses, I know where they live, how they get to work, where they go on holiday, which sport they like, what team they support and what they like to do in the evening.

'The team knows I am available and I spend a lot of time getting to know what they are good at. I like to think I know as much about the expertise of my boys and girls as I do about the clients and the product. Thursday night is team night. After work we all go across the road and have some drinks. Everyone has to come to that bit. A few of the older ones leave then, most of the rest of us go on to a restaurant, nothing fancy, maybe some good Thai food, something like that. I make a point of talking to everyone and of grabbing a serious chat with anyone who needs it. If it is someone who has done really well, I let them know that I am pleased and I let everyone else see that I am pleased. If it is someone who is having a problem, if I think they are trying, I let them know, subtly, that I understand that it's tough at the moment, to keep trying and so on. If it's someone who is not trying or who is bullshitting me, I ignore them, give them very little attention, so they can sense my displeasure. That way there's no embarrassment when we cut them.

'I've no time for people that don't put the effort in. We can't have passengers; it would eat into morale – not to mention rewards.

'I don't really believe in strategy planning or that kind of management nonsense, but once in a while I will give everything a real shake-up. I might change the seating plan, reallocate clients, alter the pairings so that people are not always out on the road with the same partner, or change our research so we are selling slightly different opinions. Before I do anything like that, I talk to a few of them to sound out my ideas and they usually agree with what I propose. I let them know that they are contributing to my thinking and that although I might be the best salesperson twice over, I never give up learning. In the end though, it's my gut feel that tells me whether to go with a new idea. I then tell everyone what has been decided and waste no time in getting it implemented.'

We were a bit stunned by this. We had rarely seen such a combination of ego, compassion and enthusiasm all wrapped up in manipulation, which was either cynically calculated or alarmingly naive.

We started to challenge some of her assumptions and were promptly 'Nicked': 'Look, I respect you both for what you have achieved. I bought both of your previous books and if I read them, I am sure I could learn from them. Tim told me he had learned a lot from working with you and that he respects you, that's why we are here. But don't tell me about how to do my job. It works for me, my people love me, my clients are amongst my best friends and I just don't need help. And by the way, if you don't believe me, talk to the team!'

Nicola grinned, gave us the latest sales brochure with everyone's phone number in it, told us to call who we wanted and made an exit as pronounced as her entrance.

The following day we each took two numbers at random from Nicola's list and called them. We were impressed that Nicola had already voicemailed them with a message that we might call and all four agreed to meet us. Three of them could not speak highly enough of Nicola; for example, one of them said, 'I would do anything for her and I believe she would do anything for me. She's such a great person. You have to admire her energy and the commitment. She lets me know what she expects from me. It's always a tough target, but she has such an engaging way of letting you know how pleased she is when we succeed. It sounds corny, but I find her inspiring. I do things to win her approval and respect. I want to please her.'

Only one of the four gave us a different perspective: 'Sure Nicola's great and if you are too, then that's great, you are in the club. Once you are in the club, and I am not, so this might be jealousy, she is very loyal to you and it is difficult to get thrown out. The trouble is, she just rushes off yelling for the rest of us to follow and if we can't, then it's tough luck and then "goodbye". There is never any instruction, we are just meant to watch her and pick it up, I don't know, by osmosis or something like that.

'Actually it can be very disheartening seeing her and her acolytes land plum orders, "high fives" all round, and the rest of us just plug away and try to look pleased. I have never found any of her favourites willing to help me. I get to go on their client meetings, say my prepared piece, watch how it's done, but no one helps me put it into practice in my own life.

'The worst thing is when we have a bad run. Boy, does she let her disappointment show. When she is frustrated she projects onto us, shouts a lot, steps up the pace and completely loses perspective and all sense of humour. All the jokes stop and she becomes intimidating, almost bullying in style.

'Nicola is all about the moment. She once said to me that the firm did not need a strategy, it just needed momentum. But what happens when the momentum stops? I worry about my own future, and this is not the environment for an open discussion, but I also worry about the firm's future. We are heading off at 250 miles an hour, 300 miles an hour, 400 miles an hour, and who knows if there is a roadblock ahead? I don't plan to be around to find out.'

We asked Danny if he minded us using his real name in this chapter.

'Sure, someone might take some notice of me if you do.'

The Players' Player's Challenge

The challenge for the Players' Player is to replicate their own success in others.

The Players' Player has moved on from the Rookie, yet still retains an emphasis on the game and how it is played. Through high personal standards and achievements and an orientation towards excellence, the Players' Player sets an astonishing pace. This can lift the contribution of the whole team by inspiring others to raise their game several gears.

When standards are met, the Players' Player gets excited and very engaged. This inspires others, and people respect them for the quality of results. With the Players' Player though, it's all about achievement and performance, and if standards are not met disappointment is made known. Talent is valued but expected to hit the ground running. The Players' Player doesn't invest in providing much coaching and managing. And if anyone on the team has a personal problem and is in need of some support, the chances are that the Players' Player hasn't noticed. Their attention is all on the momentum of the game.

Problems can arise when, as is inevitable in business, the momentum stops. To begin with, Players' Players tend to redouble their efforts and if the business responds, then all is well. But if problems are more serious and persist in spite of the leader's efforts, the atmosphere can turn very quickly. Players' Players do not cope well with failure and find it hard to inspire others when they personally feel deflated. Their followers can be very fickle under such circumstances and do not stay loyal to their wounded leader, preferring to move on to the next momentum wave.

Players' Players who are new Player Managers are not that different to the old hands. Both tend to dismiss the management and people development shortfalls that show up in their reviews by saying, 'But my team think I'm great. They would follow me anywhere.' With a tendency to equate 'managing' with well-meaning but nevertheless misguided types from HR, Finance and Planning, they often find ways to delegate administrative work to others in the team.

Over time, Players' Players tend to do one of two things. They either stay where they are, building maximum momentum in their units, or they address the challenge of developing others so that their own talents can be replicated. If they stay where they are, some Players' Players end up frustrated and feeling they never really progressed as far as they would have hoped. Because they lead through their own energy and charisma, they are not aware of others around them and do not learn the statesmanship required in larger more senior roles. As one person we interviewed put it: 'Our most clever people are stuck in the morass of eating what they kill. They are swamped in deals. There is no time to think about navigation and stewardship of the business. It is very frustrating.'

We will address these and other issues when we revisit Nicola in Chapter Seven.

Players' Player Profile

Typical Strengths

- Sets the pace
- Creates a climate of 'excellence'
- Inspirational
- Serves as role model
- Mentors star players
- Earns respect and admiration

Possible Shortcomings

- Can overextend and divide the team
- Secrets of greatness often tacit
- Intolerant
- Less of a mentor to the average player
- Vulnerable to loss of momentum

The Player Coach

Our Alex experience was definitely 'high touch'. From the moment we arrived until the end of our meeting, when Alex accompanied us to the lobby, we felt as though we were with somebody warm and attentive. As he greeted us with a firm handshake he looked us fully in the eye, clear signals that he wanted to get to know us. He listened to our questions, sought our opinions, made helpful suggestions about our project and, when we left, said we must get back together sometime for a drink.

Alex is a Marketing Programme Director in the drinks business, with a reputation for being a developer of people as well as brands: 'I handle the performance of several core brands. I run marketing through a matrix of category teams, specialist teams such as market research and customer service, and regional sector teams. In the last few years we have moved towards global branding of all our core brands, but this by no means indicates that regional differences have disappeared. In fact I am convinced that face-to-face visits to get insight into local distinctions are more important than ever. We interface heavily with product development, planning, distribution and sales. All of us are delivering on programmes and accounts that spread across all three regional time zones, although our team mostly operates out of Chicago, Paris and Singapore. There are about sixty of us in total, with fifteen reporting directly to me. We are charged with building market share across all products, while enhancing the target position of each brand.

'I have been here just over fifteen years. I was recruited as a graduate trainee into a well-structured marketing programme, where I was rotated across several brands and specialisms before settling down as a sector head in this line a few years ago. I was made associate director and then director in very quick order after my predecessor was lured to a competitor. In this industry, even in marketing, no one appreciates the "high-concept" types. There is nothing very complicated about our customers or our products. The culture here rewards hands-on doers, especially those associated with high impact marketing pro-grammes. We want people who can deliver and people who can deliver. Those that can't deliver depart. That's it.

'When I first took over as Director, I tried to keep up everything I had been doing as well as taking on all sorts of new responsibilities, but it was impossible. I am single again with no family commitments and my work is my life, but even so there were not enough hours in the day. I found that my conversations with colleagues were rushed, often mobile-to-mobile, and that my grasp of key programmes wasn't as good as it had been. I made a couple of bad calls which the overall head of marketing and the CEO pulled me up on, something that had never happened to me before.

'Then the wrong kind of person left. We have a practice of working second and third year graduates pretty hard; some decide it's not for them, others thrive. Richard, one of our brightest young prospects and one we had earmarked for early promotion, left to join my prede-cessor at his new company; his exit interview did not make good reading for me. He felt that he had been handled badly by his immediate management, no attention was being paid to his personal develop-ment and he was being treated, he said, like a cross between a mush-room and a donkey. Since I was meant to be his mentor and manager, the loss of Richard was down to me. It sent a terrible signal to the team.

'It was coming up to Christmas and I had a few days to take a step back. For the first time for ages, I had time to think. I was looking for a better way and I thought seriously about stepping down to a sales-only role, something I knew that I could do. However I am bloody-minded and do not like to fail, so I resolved to find a way of sorting things out.

'I found the key in a most unlikely place. Believe it or not, it was in an interview with Shelly Lazarus, known as the queen of Madison Avenue, in *Advertising Age*, a magazine I was reading at the gym. In 1998, two years after she became CEO of Ogilvy & Mather and after twenty-seven years in advertising, she told the magazine: "This is a rather simple statement, but this business is all about people. We're only as good as the people we have. The agency with the best people wins. You have to be able to motivate and direct people and create an environment where people can do great work. That's the hardest part of this job actually."[1]

'Now, while not generally modelling myself on the queens of Madison Avenue – especially as agency types don't go down too well in our industry – I began to wonder whether I could apply these principles to my team. Carrying on the way that I was would lead, probably, to more of the team leaving, to more bad calls and to me burning myself out without any progress to show for it. The best way was to hand over some of my key programmes for others to champion while spending more of my energy bringing on the team. For that to happen, I would need to reprogramme myself into believing that managing people was at least as important as managing products. Since carrying on the way that I was seemed to be damaging my own image all round, it seemed like a low risk leap of faith.'

We asked Alex how he had gone about reprogramming himself.

'I really approached it as I would a problem with underperforming brands. I cleared some space in my schedule by handing the management of a couple of the most difficult projects over to my two best people and began to map everyone's attributes. I sat down with everyone on the team, explained how I planned to take a more active role in their development, asked them to tell me about themselves and promised to take them out for a beer afterwards. We don't have a history of great mentoring here, but the fact that my people all respect me for my own know-how helped open the conversations up. I wrote everything down, made sure that each meeting was relaxed, not rushed, and did only one a day. I remember my first boss used to do six annual appraisals a day. He thought he was efficient. We all felt it was like a production line. Sounds corny, but before long I really got to know each player's hopes and fears and began to form a view of their distinctive strengths and weaknesses, especially those areas where they needed developing or pairing with a complementary person.

'I'm not sure I want you to write this down but I sat down with a Human Resources advisor who put forward some frameworks and ideas for personal development work. I did not want to send people off on training courses; I wanted to do the development work myself and to get the team to learn from each other. We had a marketing group dinner of all the associate directors and senior category and geography managers. I explained Richard's leaving was down to me, that we all needed to get better at developing and retaining talent, and asked each of them to regard mentoring the graduates as a part of their role. They all seemed up for it, although in the end only a couple of them had enough conviction to follow through. I guess it's a matter of temperament and personal interest.

'I focused on my weaker players. I asked them to tell me what their goals were and where they thought they could contribute to the business. I was surprised how candid people were. Afterwards I felt much closer to who was in my team and how the dynamic worked between them. I think they felt much closer to me too.

'I soon realized that each person has to work to their own way of learning, so very often I did no more than listen and probe into what they were thinking. Fairly superficial issues of presentation were holding some people back. For others, issues were more substantive. Other times it was more personal. I had to ask Rupert to buy a second suit because his habit of wearing the same one every day was causing comment in the office, and I suggested that Jo's prankish and giggly manner was not helping her to be treated as a professional. I spent hours discussing and going over everyone's work and helping them bring it to a conclusion. I kept up with the progress on the projects I had handed over just to make sure there would be no surprises, but for a while my involvement in them really was a lower priority.

'After about a year I re-evaluated all our positions. Out of my team of fifteen, two were not going to make it. Despite masses of my time and the support of colleagues, they were no closer to delivering. Both of them knew it anyway, so we sat down to work out the best way for them to move on.

'The others broke down into three equal categories. A third had always played to high standards and continued to do so. I felt the two people who had taken over my project work had stepped up well, and another two had added a new dimension by acting as good mentors to the others. Another third had really raised their game and would soon present us with the nicest kind of management problem: could they all be promoted at once?

'As for the rest, the jury was still out. One old stager had made some improvement, but not enough, and for him the next year would be crucial. Some of our newest graduates were moving fast through the learning curve and time would tell how far they could go. One thing pleasing to me though is that no one had resigned, and quite a few people had approached me to see if we had any openings in our group. I felt I had learned a lot from Richard's departure.'

Alex had spoken non-stop about his team; we wanted to know how he felt about himself.

'I made a leap of faith and it proved itself well founded. I am here to get results for this business, and for me that now incorporates working with the team. We need each other to succeed.'

He glanced up at the clock; it was time to move to other things: 'We can walk through the office on the way out and you can see the people I have been telling you about.'

The Player Coach's Challenge

The challenge for the Player Coach is to develop talent without losing sight of the bigger picture.

Alex is a good example of our third Player Manager type, the Player Coach. The Player Coach, as this title borrowed from sport suggests, places an emphasis not only on the game but also on the people playing it. The Player Coach understands that not everyone plays the game as well as he or she does. The Player Coach focuses therefore on their potential to develop. Good Player Coaches look at people's attributes and see not just how they are now, but also how they could be. From this understanding, they can help them realize their potential in ways that otherwise would not have happened.

Being a good Player Coach requires a lot of interpersonal commitment, and to develop the team they first need to spend time understanding the makeup as well as the talents of the people within it. Player Coaches are not afraid to use emotions as a way of bringing about understanding and change. This can generate a very dedicated following.

The approach of the Player Coach tends to foster climates where the pace is demanding but not draining. Creating a climate where people feel valued is something that some organizations aspire to once they understand the impact on people of colder and harsher cultures. One small example of this came from an unlikely source, a Player Manager who runs a large trading floor in the macho culture of Wall Street: 'See the floor out there? See how many people on it? See the man in the yellow shirt? How do we make him feel special, helping him to stand out and feel that he counts?'

The Player Coach does have some downsides. In the early days of Alex's attempts to be more developmental, his nickname amongst the most hard-nosed in his team was 'Mother Hen'. Player Coaches also tread a delicate line between being one of the guys and the boss, as recalled by the head coach of one American football team soon after he had made the transition from player: 'If we're on the road, I may be with players for a team lunch, but I'm not going to go over to a player's house and play cards. More than in the past, I have to separate myself.' Some Player Coaches fail to create enough distance for themselves, bringing a dependency effect as well as a demanding workload. Others can become so absorbed in one-to-one development that they lose sight of the end game.

To remain in command of the game, strong Player Coaches must step back and assess the whole team's capabilities against the challenges faced. They must also communicate clearly to each team member the part they are playing for the whole. In large measure, Alex had taken on the Player Coach's challenge. 'Playing' and 'coaching', however, were still distinct categories in his own mind, and this separation was to cause problems as we shall see when we revisit Alex in Chapter Eight.

Player Coach Profile

Typical Strengths

- Knows the players and how they play
- Develops and motivates others
- Generates team spirit
- Secures trust and commitment
- Improves everyone's game

Possible Shortcomings

- Gets distracted from player role
- Loses sight of the end game
- Gets stuck in one-on-one meetings
- Doesn't build infrastructure
- Overprotective

The Veteran

'Managing partner's office' announced a calm, clear voice when we phoned to arrange a meeting with George Dunlop Jones, head of a well respected firm of solicitors. We had visions of Miss Moneypenny, coffee in china cups, chocolate biscuits, leather sofas, antique objects and an all-round ambience of good order. Some three weeks later, we were not disappointed when we met the great man ('Just call me Dun, everyone else does') and his secretary Marilyn. His desk was as neat and tidy as the man himself, an elegant figure with exactly the right amount of cuff showing from the sleeve of his pinstriped suit.

'I joined Read and Williams straight from Oxford in 1965, did my articles here, became a specialist in corporate law and was invited to join the partnership towards the end of the seventies. The next ten years were my best years. There was a mergers and acquisitions boom and I was lucky enough to get my name attached to some interesting deals. At this time corporate law overtook some of our more traditional activities as the biggest fee earner, and people seemed to look to me as the leader of the area. I did not really pay much attention to how the partnership was being run. I went to partners' weekends, that sort of thing, was happy to take my draw and share of the profits, but mainly I just enjoyed getting stuck into my cases.

'I first became aware that some of the partners were getting disgruntled at the partners' weekend in 1995. In the bar on the Saturday night there was a lot of talk about the firm expanding everywhere except on the bottom line, and someone said, half jokingly I thought, that it was time JHB stood down to let a younger man take over. "Maybe you should do it, Dun," I remember one of them saying. The following morning we had the closing session, and I noticed how tired JHB looked and how the reaction to his closing remarks was polite, but no more than that. A few weeks later he had his stroke, and although I am delighted to say it was only a slight one, he never came back to work. We still see him on social occasions; there was a terrific retirement dinner for him and Jane, but we were suddenly all aware that we had a hole at the top.

'Anyway, to cut a long story short, they asked me to take over, and after a lot of soul searching I accepted and started at the Easter of 1996. The only two conditions I set were that I would have a free hand to make whatever changes I thought necessary, and that I could keep some of my clients. The second of those was especially important; I did not want to become one of those chaps that are supposed to run businesses but have lost all touch with reality.'

We asked Dun how he had got to grips with the job and how he managed to balance playing with managing.

'To start with, it was pretty hellish. I was quite shocked by what I found. We had expanded like crazy in the 1970s and 1980s. Aside from corporate work we were doing a lot of private work. This involved masses of resources but it was work with quite low margins. I found that the total staff numbered 400, with more in an associate firm of ours. The focus had been on high professional standards, doing the best thing for the client all the time, but the costs regime had been deteriorating. When I actually looked at the profit numbers, my little corporate law team was bringing in nearly all the profits if you accounted for overhead properly.

'I could see that I had to do two things: keep up the profitability of my own unit, because if that went we as a partnership were in serious financial trouble, and restructure the rest of the business. The first year was difficult. As often happens, it is not so easy to cast off from old relationships, and one of my biggest clients became involved in corporate action that required a lot of input from me. Simultaneously, the partners were waiting expectantly for me to do something with the business.

'I called in consultants to prepare a report and make some recommendations. This gave me some breathing space, and by the time they reported I had a little bit more time to deal with the management issues. In a nutshell, we had too many partners and senior executives sitting on their own cottage industries and not enough juniors to liberate senior people for winning new business.

'I then followed a strategy to put some structure into my own team and professionalize the management of the firm. My own team was fairly easy. There were three senior partners who had been with me a long time and they were well able to look after the execution of client business. I redefined my role so that the clients saw me at critical moments but I did less of the donkeywork. Because the team was regarded as something of a market leader in our particular niche, we had always found it easy to attract bright young lawyers and they were able to step up.

'That freed me up to work with the rest of the firm. An outfit of our size needed an infrastructure and we appointed a chief operating officer and heads of Finance, IT, HR and Training. The partners' assistant who had historically done most of this herself was a bit upset about it, and there was some muttering from the partners about 'more bloody overhead at a time like this,' but it was what the consultants suggested and it made sense to me. This took a lot of the detail out of my in-tray and I turned my attention to how the business was actually done.

'Without boring you with the detail, lots of people were reinventing the wheel every day. We introduced templates and business processes for areas that had lots in common and sharpened up on client delivery. That involved giving the clients less of some things and more of others, and meant that we came across as a taut, more professional organization.

'We had not been good at playing as a team, so we were not getting full leverage from our staff. We introduced year-end appraisals that emphasized cross-divisional co-operation and created benchmarks for rewarding people that were a lot fairer than the old lockstep, length of service basis. We also worked hard at team-building exercises, not corny stuff like going off to Dartmoor together, but offsite conferences built around solving real issues.

'It is very important that I set the right example. I spend about a day a week on client business, although the staff probably think that I do more because the things I do are high profile. I work through my functional heads and we have a management committee meeting every week. The business is now divided into service lines with someone in charge of each. I try to empower them as much as possible, as well as providing intelligent support and setting stretching targets. There is no point in my trying to micro-manage; I just set a framework that will hopefully catch problems before they get serious and stimulate new ideas.

'I get round the staff as often as I can. I go to every office every year and shake as many hands as I can. I hold an annual town hall meeting about a week after we have announced the profit share. Everyone is invited to head office for it but if they can't come, or don't want to, there are video and telephone links.

'None of this is very original. I got some of the ideas from the consultants we use and others from the chief executive of a media company I am close to. All in all, however, I think it has worked. I am happy keeping my hand in and running the shop, the partners are earning more and the staff tell me that they think I've got vision.

'All of this wouldn't have been achieved without the groundwork laid by JHB. It is a pity that he wasn't able to stay around long enough to reap the benefits. I am just lucky to have been in the right place at the right time.'

Marilyn opened the door and packed the coffee cups back onto the silver tray. We deduced it was time to leave, thanked Dun for the meeting and Marilyn showed us out. We had just met our fourth Player Manager type, the Veteran.

The Veteran's Challenge

The Veteran's challenge is to manage the institution as well as the team whilst keeping both fresh.

To some, the term 'manager' implies the dullness of administration rather than the thrill of the chase. For the Veteran, however, it offers the opportunity of making a significant difference to the organization.

Veterans understand that by implementing business process, procedure and organization, they can create more bang per buck. They prefer things to be systematic rather than ad hoc and often implement methods for measuring and evaluating the performance of individuals, teams and the unit as a whole. Good at prioritizing and getting things done, the Veteran has a detached perspective. They have grown to be a commander of the enterprise, an agent for the institution as well as the team.

Achieving this isn't always easy. As Tom Tierney of Bain has said, 'You can't just walk into your office on a Monday morning and say, OK, today I am going to generate a sort of gravity to keep the business centered and exude energy to motivate stars.'[2] In any case, talented producers often resent any attempt to ring-fence and harness their performance: 'I don't need managing' is a common defence against what they perceive as interference. They often resist anything that will reduce the autonomy that is so important to their sense of wellbeing and their discretionary freedom 'to make decisions that benefit my clients.'

Veterans need to tackle this opposition. Inevitably they will face the prevailing anti-managerial culture and will have to run the risk of becoming less popular than either the much admired Players' Player or the much loved Player Coach. As one member of the Bain partnership committee said: 'One of the criticisms of Tom is that he is not close enough to clients any more. There is always a tendency for global client heads to feel superior to Tom, because they have led client engagements whereas he has simply managed and led the firm.'

However, growth and complexity trigger the need for protocols, and although the climate that ensues will feel more regulated, in the long run successful Veterans win recognition. Having succeeded, their next challenge is to keep the organization fresh.

Veteran Profile

Typical Strengths

- Builds systems and protocols
- Hones execution
- Identifies goals
- Creates acceptable boundaries
- Instils effectiveness
- Playing skills critical at times

Possible Shortcomings

- Wedded to the status quo
- Overly detached
- Not always charismatic
- Demotivates free spirits
- Protocols applied too rigidly
- Overmanages and underleads

The Play Maker

'A Play Maker?' mused Vikram, touching the New Age jewellery on his thumb and round the neck of his black t-shirt. 'Well, it depends what you mean. Let me tell you what I do round here, and you can tell me whether or not I am your Play Maker.

'There are various parts to my role. I double up as overseer of operations across our entire portfolio and as hands-on troubleshooter for what we call our "Big Bets". These are special projects where either the design is taking us into new territory or the customer relationship is high profile, or we have messed up and need to get things back on track. When we code something a Big Bet I become its project director, and the project sits in operations and not the regions for its design and delivery phases. This protects the regions from losing focus on their overall portfolio when we bring in difficult work. It suits me fine, because I like orchestrating complex projects.

'On top of these two things I sit on the executive that runs the global business. It is a fairly open system, everyone that works here is entitled to say what they think, and even if they weren't they are wilful enough to say it anyway. There is very little hierarchy by necessity and design. The eight core members of the executive sit with four open slots that we fill from our pool of senior designers and programme managers according to specific business needs. The four original founders do tend to shape the strategy and drive the business forward, but at the same time we try to give everyone a voice. The executive is a delicate balance, but it generates a healthy amount of flux.'

Vikram was definitely a Player Manager, but we needed to know a bit more about how he operated to know if he was our Play Maker. We asked him about the firm's history as a way of breaking into the subject.

Vikram settled back onto his sofa and said reflectively: 'That really means going back to "the Schism of 1994". I was handling the portfolio in the Americas as well as two turnkey projects in Europe. We were organized into designers and programme managers, although some people like myself straddled both roles. Programme managers tended to be producers who had excelled at project management before moving into the programme office and away from client sites. Designers were either early twentysomethings who loved code and had bright design ideas, or thirtysomethings who had enough presence to handle clients and keep the younger producers grounded. We were fairly chaotic in approach, yet became leading edge in open systems.

'In the eighties we won a reputation for being the place to call. We worked hard, played hard and never drew lines between the two. We shared the gains through a fairly simple profit share amongst the executive founders. Top designers and the members of the best programme teams were rewarded with bonuses, "technology leader awards" we called them.

'By 1994 there were grumblings from the programme managers. They were working all hours to meet milestones and change requests, but received no share of the profits and had little say in the way we were run. They even pointed out that they were much less likely to receive bonuses than the designers they were managing. Our 1993 Christmas party was a bad moment. A few of our big name clients sent polite apologies, others sent quite junior representatives. The buzz, to the extent that there was one, came from guests not invited by the executive. We all felt like outsiders and our trade rag picked up that our party, "the thrash of the year" as they had called it, had not quite rocked.

'Anyway, early into the New Year, a handful of the programme managers told us that they were leaving to start up a new firm and that they were taking the best of the design staff with them. They had even told some important clients and they had promised to go with them. This seemed to come out of the blue. I had been very focused on a health management system in the US. I missed all the vital signs of wider dissent. We tried to turn it round but it was all too late, despite the non-compete clauses in their contracts. Our talent had rebelled, they were leaving home and there was zip we could do to stop them. We did what damage limitation we could, but there was no doubt we were in big trouble.

'The Saturday after they left, the other founders met at my house to decide what to do. We had to face the world on Monday and we needed either a survival plan or an exit strategy. Everyone was down in the dumps but I felt strangely excited, hurt yet curious to discover why our own team had deserted us. I even felt a fleeting urge to go with them but then thought, "No, we can come back from this". The atmosphere was terrible, flat, defeatist. As I was least flattened, I took the lead.

'I asked if we could bounce back by next year. No one met me in the eye or even spoke. How about in two years? Again, silence. I pushed the horizon out to five years. The meeting stirred a bit. Someone said that over five years we could recruit new designers, train up a strong team of programme managers and win back some clients from today's low base. I asked them what we could do to our platform to make us attractive to join in the short term. Flatten the structure, said someone; give everyone a say in how the business is run, be open and widen the distribution of profit-based rewards, said others.

'The mood was lifting by the second. All of us could see that on a five-year view we could create something that was different and better. Once the mood was up, I proposed that we called two of the people we had lost and ask them to listen to our plans and reconsider. It also gave us deeper insight into where we were going wrong. People felt that the technology founders who had started the business operated too exclusively and that our design teams were compartmentalized and partisan. Apparently designers pandered to particular programme managers who sponsored their allocation onto hot projects. What I thought was still a fairly loose collaborative outfit had developed big company politics. We were the opposite of the systems that we were advocating to our clients.

'All through this process my role had been only to ask the questions. None of what emerged to transform our business had been my own. But I became the spokesperson for New AlphaSolva, using the same principles to run the business that we used for design, removing every-thing that got in the way of a spirit of enquiry and excitement.'

We told Vikram that what he had just described fitted very closely the role model for our Play Maker. We wanted to know about the second part of his job, troubleshooting on Big Bets. Was he a Play Maker in that role too?

'I take a number of different positions in these. It is part client management, part persuasion that the impossible is in fact possible, and part project management. Take the Monday meeting. For each Big Bet we review work in progress. I act as an agent provocateur rather than identifying or solving the project issues, and I challenge and stretch what others put forward. Quite often they look alarmed. If we are having a bad run or client confidence about our ability to service the contract is suffering, they can be pretty dismissive of me as an outsider who doesn't know the nuts and bolts of the contract. But to jolt complacency, I persist. I do not get discouraged and I do not compromise my suggestions. I never insist, these are just suggestions, but I have noticed that a few of my ideas reappear later on in a slightly different form. When that happens I know that I have done my job.

'Other times the programme managers say, "Vikram, put your software hat on," and then I am off into a world of my own. People complain that I go into a void at these times, but they trust me to come up with the goods. Then we all quietly appreciate the result. You would have to be a designer to know what I mean. Of course it doesn't always work out. Then people grumble about me being off the wall.

'In our culture nothing is sacrosanct other than the principles of design. Recently we even scrapped the regular Monday meeting. It was becoming part of the furniture, so I suggested no fixed meetings until someone had a problem that needed extra brains. It created a bit of confusion at first. But it is easier to run a meeting around an issue than run issues around a tired meeting!'

By now we were confident that Vikram was indeed our fifth Player Manager type. He was a Play Maker, the master of the unexpected.

The Play Maker's Challenge

The Play Maker's challenge is to lead the team in new directions without disappearing out of sight.

Play Makers seize the moment. They can create advantages from performing the unexpected, even changing the rules of the game. Visionary when originating new options and known for their innovative enthusiasm for change, Play Makers stimulate the team to think and act differently. Sometimes they are accused of going too far out on a limb and losing a sense of what will work under today's constraints. Their focus is usually so much on the future that like Vikram before the Schism of 1994, they can miss current problems.

One example of both the upside and downside of Play Makers is Bill Gross, the founder of Idealab. Profiled by Joseph Nocera of *Fortune* as a leading entrepreneur, he was also described as 'a stupendously poor manager and a tragic figure of the Internet bust.'[3] Up there with the best of the Internet thinkers, Gross created an incubator model that gave birth to such stars as eToys, which was worth $7.8 billion when it went public in 1999. Idealab then consumed $800m in eight months. No wonder a colleague of Gross said, 'Sometimes with Bill you would say wow and sometimes yikes.'

It's the imagination and instinct for new moves that distinguishes Play Makers from other Player Manager types. They tend to come into their own in times of turnaround and industry turbulence, when rules are being redefined. But they sometimes leave what the rest of us would call 'our better judgement' behind and risk losing organizational support for their ideas. Unlike the Veteran, they can lose sight of the needs and the boundaries of the institution. A sense of timing and an understanding of how to overcome resistance are important skills for Play Makers to develop if they are to meet their challenge. Being a few steps ahead of everybody else is both their greatest strength and their greatest weakness.

Play Makers need the mental strength to be a lone voice. Like Machiavelli's Prince, Play Makers need to be mindful that most people would rather get on and play instead of fighting to change the game. 'There is nothing more difficult to plan, more doubtful of success, nor more dangerous to manage than the creation of a new system. For the initiator has the enmity of all who would profit by the preservation of the old institutions and merely lukewarm defenders in those who should gain by the new ones.'[4]

Play Maker Profile

Typical Strengths

- Thinks on the edge
- Unafraid to challenge authority
- Catalyst
- Undeterred by adversity
- Transforms the game

Possible Shortcomings

- Disruptive
- Not always responsible or credible
- Expensive user of resources
- Disconnected from others
- Chaotic

Player Again

It took us quite a while to track down Maggi. She had slipped out of her company and not kept in touch with her old colleagues, and when we finally made contact she was unsure about meeting us. After some gentle persuasion and the promise of anonymity, we met for lunch at a place on the outskirts of the town where she lived. She made it plain at the beginning that this was going to be a short meeting, that she did not relish going over matters she still found painful, and that her only reason for seeing us was to help others avoid her fate.

'I became the director of client services in the call centre because I was the best producer. Soon after that a new person took over at the top who was all for automated marketing. Profiles were to be drawn up, calls were to be targeted more scientifically, reps were to be given less discretion and tighter supervision. I had to implement this, but there was not enough time to set everything up so we were always doing things on the run.

'In the meantime the culture of the team was that if your ratings slipped you lost respect, so I was striving very hard to keep up my numbers, motivate the team and introduce this automated sales system. I was the first in, the last to leave, and became exhausted. My ratings began to fall; the harder I tried, the worse it got. I became irritable with the people that I was managing. As I got exasperated, no doubt I became a rather unattractive person to be with. Then came the tap on the shoulder. "You've done a great job for us, but it is time we looked to the future. We'd like Mark to step into your role and hope you will stay on as a programme rep and support him," was how the speech went.

'In some ways it was a relief when they took the job away, because some balance returned to my life and I was able to concentrate on what I do best, which is selling. However I have never come to terms with failing at that job. I could not forgive my colleagues who I suspected had been behind my demotion, and I found it difficult to respect Mark who quite quickly ran into the same problems that I had.

'After the pain of working twelve hours a day stopped and with the satisfaction of building up my client ratings again, I became much more balanced. But I was uneasy. I just couldn't look my former team in the eye and I always suspected Mark would rather I was gone. I was very pleased when we found an old house to renovate. It gave me a perfect reason to stop working at a place where the memories were painful and where I felt I had failed.'

Maggi would not be drawn on whether she should have taken the job in the first place, or on what kind of support she had got from her senior management as she made her transition into and back out of Player Managing. She told us that she had to get back to meet a designer who was due to show her some plans for a refit in her basement, thanked us for lunch and jumped into her 4×4 with some alacrity.

We stayed on after Maggi left and wondered whether there were better ways out of an unsatisfactory Player Manager situation than being tapped on the shoulder like Maggi. Joy remembered the Deputy Head at her son's school. A great success in that role, he was widely tipped to be the next Head. Yet he surprised everyone by returning to his former position as a full time maths teacher. We wanted to find out whether, unlike Maggi, he had come to terms with being a Player Again.

Martin invited us round to his house for tea to discuss the matter: 'Make it after next week, can you? We'll be in the summer holidays then and I will have more time to talk.'

Joy had some trouble disentangling this pleasant middle-aged man, whose twinkling eyes seemed to hold people's gaze, from the tyrant described by her son, but as Martin said, teaching is at least 25 per cent playacting. We asked him why he had gone back to the classroom instead of taking the widely predicted step up.

'I had been Deputy Head for six years, teaching a reduced timetable, supporting the Head in administrative work and representing her at meetings in the rest of the week. I much preferred the classroom work, and although the money was useful it was not enough to compensate me for doing something I did not really enjoy. It was suggested that I might like to take over from the Head when she retired. After discussing it at home for a few weeks, we concluded that just because you have the ability to do something does not necessarily mean you have to do it. I was happier teaching than managing the school and I wanted to get back to it. I did not want to put the school in the difficult position of having to find a new Head and Deputy at the same time, so I went back to the Governors and asked to step down.'

We wondered whether Martin had found it difficult taking a less senior role, perhaps involving reporting to someone he had once been in charge of.

'I think had I been asked to move aside that might have occurred, but in my heart I knew that teaching was something I cared about passionately. I made a decision to come into it despite the unattractive rewards and limited career path. So in making the decision not to be Head, I was being true to myself. I had no doubt it was the right thing to do. I love the classroom and I enjoy doing what I do best. I miss the money but I get home at a predictable time, I have energy left over for my family and I know that I did a good job while I was there. Besides, do you know how many children seek top-up tutoring in maths?'

The Player Again Challenge

The challenge for the Player Again is to get out sooner rather than later, regardless of perceived loss of face.

Boat owners often say there are really only two memorable days when owning a boat. The first is the day you buy it and the second is the day you sell it. In Player Managing – where some people despite training, coaching and the application of will are not suited to managing at all – high spots can be akin to boat owning, coming only on the day you accept the job and the day you give it up. As such, giving it up sooner rather than later can sometimes be best.

Martin and Maggi offer contrasting experiences of what it is like to become a Player Again, our sixth Player Manager type. The trick is to remain clear that being a Player Manager is an option and not the only choice. This is easy to forget when seeking to establish a career and when progression is so often seen in terms of getting a management position, despite the much-proclaimed 'end of hierarchy'.

To maintain balance, all Player Managers need to assess continually how things are going and whether they are still making the right choices for themselves. Those who are confident, and at the same time open and honest, know they have a choice. It is not the end of the world to get out. The alternative, as Maggi's experience shows, is to hang around too long and have someone else make the choice for you with all the injured pride that implies. Achievers do not like to fail, and if success has been externally defined by certain roles in the organization then it is these roles that high-achieving players tend to pursue. Peer and downward pressure only adds to their sense that 'managing' is something they need to accomplish.

Player Again

Typical Strengths
- Returns as a better player
- Strengthens the team
- Lesson to others – the only way isn't up
- Advocates value of pure playing
- Less stressed individual

Possible Shortcomings
- Leaves it too late
- Re-entry can be difficult
- Loss of face
- Reward issues
- Who does the managing?

Survivors in Our Midst

Our perfect Player Manager, Amanda Sage, and our six types are not role models to follow slavishly. Their value is that they offer a benchmark for comparison. The perspective this brings opens up ways of bridging the gap between myth and reality, between the myth of the perfect climate in an empowered organization and the reality of life as a Player Manager under pressure.

The stories of our six types show that none of them is perfect and, as we later discovered, many faced problems around their challenge. Like the Believers in our field work, some were happy at being fully stretched, others by contrast became very stressed at being kept 'Under Pressure'. In every case we offered our help in the hope of improving their mastery of the role. Amanda's six levers, as we explain in Chapter Twelve, often provided the means of bridging the gap.

6

The Rookie

Recap. *When we first met Roger, the Rookie Player Manager, he had just left the market research agency where he had worked to start a career in a completely different industry. As a widely regarded success his departure had caused a few shock waves. But we discovered that Roger's first experience of managing had been difficult – 'almost everything about it and me was wrong' – and that the strain and an impossible workload had burned him out. We said that Roger was a good example of the Rookie Player Manager, someone who, as the name suggests, is new to the job and inevitably puts a few steps wrong. We concluded that the Rookie's principal challenge is 'to step up and take command without doing it all personally', and listed the Rookie attributes as follows:*

Typical Strengths
- *Never done it before*
- *Keen to step up*
- *Gets things done*
- *Determined to succeed*
- *Technically expert*
- *Works long hours*

Possible Shortcomings
- *'Task' not 'people' oriented*
- *Fails to delegate*
- *Feels responsible for everything*
- *Relies on expert status*
- *Doesn't seek feedback*
- *Prone to denial*

In this chapter we meet Roger again and we also talk to his former colleagues. We try to get to the bottom of the circumstances that drove Roger to quit, circumstances that despite his hard work and best efforts he never previously understood or mastered. We follow him into his new job and fear that history is about to repeat itself. Can Roger get it right this time round?

Roger's Story

Shortly after first meeting Roger we received an unexpected call from him. He sounded a bit terse but said he wanted to show us something. He asked us to call round to his house early on Friday evening.

When we arrived, however, Roger wasn't there. His wife, Sarah, who had just restarted work after a few years as a full time mother, let us in saying that Roger had probably got tied up finishing something in the office and would no doubt be back before long. She told us that she was glad to be back at work herself, even though she had fond memories of her baby years at home. We asked her about those years, including what she thought of Roger's change of career.

'I am pleased he left at the top. I expect he has some happy memories,' she replied. Somewhat taken aback by Sarah's lack of awareness of the stresses Roger had been under, we gently probed some more.

'I don't remember Roger having problems at work. The time you are asking about was when the children were babies really, and we were both stretched just keeping up with day-to-day things. Roger was good about getting home to help with bath time as often as he could, although of course there were times when he was away on trips. I used to crash out at about nine o'clock most evenings and I seem to remember that Roger did stay up quite late working. One day he told me it was time to move on and I just accepted that he knew himself best.'

Before we had chance to dig deeper, Roger arrived. Sarah seemed relieved to be able to get on with her evening, and we hoped we hadn't started a chain of thinking that would lead her to doubt Roger's apparent success and happiness.

Roger's Year-end Appraisal

Roger invited us into his study, and without making eye contact, any preliminary small talk or even thanking us for coming he handed over a copy of a report: 'My boss gave me this last week and told me to fix it fast.'

We realized that it was a 360 document on Roger compiled as part of his year-end appraisal. The people working for him had been asked to give their views on his leadership.

'What do you think?' he asked before we had even glanced through it. He did not wait for us to reply and continued abruptly: 'Well, let me tell you my view. I think it's bloody unfair.'

We flipped through the ten or so pages of the report noting comments such as:

'Roger is now our team leader anointed for being a good producer. He is inaccessible, and neither inspiring nor enjoyable to work with. We have too many people like that. They kid themselves. They are blind to their personal weaknesses.'

'Roger is so hardworking and conscientious it is hard to fault his performance – unless of course he is supposed to be helping me develop mine. On that we haven't got off the starting block.'

'Although Roger is involved in the detail of everything I am doing and although he clearly knows what we need to do to succeed, I can't say his leadership leaves me turned on and inspired. Sometimes it is just the opposite.'

'Roger is so desperate to prove himself against I don't know who or what that he butts in at client meetings. Clients can clearly see, and one actually told me afterwards, that we are not pulling together as a team.'

Most of the other comments were similar. They too contrasted Roger's hard work and commitment with a poor management style and bore a striking resemblance to what we had surmised about Roger's performance in his previous job. We thought that it was probably the fear of history repeating itself that had prompted his request to see us. However, we had barely started to comment when

Roger interjected: 'But this isn't about me, it's about them, that's what makes it so unfair.'

Roger was clearly very agitated and unwilling to say directly either that he needed help or that he wanted us to do anything about it. We offered to help in any way that we could, including talking to some of those involved.

'No, that won't be necessary,' Roger replied curtly. 'It's the last thing I need letting anyone know that I am actually bothered by this. Someone obviously has something against me. But I can stick this out. I have faced this before. And I know I am good at my job and working hard. My boss will see that in the end.'

Not wanting Roger to close things down completely, we suggested that instead of talking to anyone in Roger's current organization we could track down some of his former colleagues and interview them. Roger wasn't too keen on us raking over his past at first, but reluctantly agreed that he might think about the whole experience differently as a result. 'Just tell them you are doing more research for your book,' he said, 'I don't want them to think there is anything wrong.'

At this point Sarah walked into the study to remind Roger they had promised to take the children out to a movie and they needed to get ready. 'Everything is all right isn't it, Roger?' she asked brightly.

'Of course it is, darling,' he replied as he accompanied us to the front door. 'Everything is absolutely fine.'

Going Back Over Old Ground

Roger's Old Boss. Our first discussion was with the Client Services Director who had given Roger his Player Manager job, Dr B, as he liked to be called. Having heard Roger's side of the story, we expected that Dr B might not relish the idea of taking the lid off an unhappy episode but we were wrong.

'Roger? Of course I remember Roger, we think very highly of him here. It was a gamble appointing him to that job but one we had to take. The previous set-up was falling apart, we had tried recruiting from the outside and there were no takers. I was under a lot of pressure from my MD to sort things out, and it became obvious that it would have to be an internal solution.'

We asked Dr B whether there were any other internal candidates besides Roger.

'Well, strictly speaking there were, but the appeal of Roger was that he knew the business and – unlike some of the other possibilities – he could be spared from his existing role. Taking him out of his previous team left a gap, but one that I felt we could fill fairly easily. Weighing it up, Roger was not the first choice – getting a ready-made recruit would have been preferable – but he was an acceptable second choice and it got senior management off my back.'

We had long ago ceased being surprised when collecting 360 degree feedback, so it was no great shock to learn that poor old Roger was Dr B's 'quick fix'. We suggested to Dr B that his expectations must have been low given Roger's position in the pecking order.

'I wasn't sure how it would work out but I was pleasantly surprised,' he said. 'Once he had the job Roger took to it like a duck to water. I hardly ever had to get involved, I just left him to sort it out. It was a relief to me, I was able to move on to other problem areas and just left them to get on with it. I kept my lines of communication open with the co-head of the team just so that I would hear if anything went wrong, and I made sure that Roger's predecessor, Suzy, stayed partly involved just to keep my options open and of course to keep Roger on his toes.

'If I was surprised by Roger's success, I had an even bigger surprise when he left. There had been no sign of it coming, the team was pulling in the business and we were going to promote Roger. But you know him, once he's made his mind up there's no going back. The fact that he left the industry was a consolation; at least he wasn't going to join a competitor. I suppose it was just a lifestyle thing. Never did really get to the bottom of it.'

We thanked Dr B for his time, thanked our lucky stars that we did not work for him and moved on to talk to Roger's co-head, the account director with whom Roger had spent three years jockeying for position.

Roger's Rivals.   When we met Robert, we couldn't tell if he was in his mid thirties and not wearing too well or in his early forties and looking better than might be expected. He had the firm yet winning voice of someone practised at telephone sales. We started off by asking him how he came to be working with Roger.

'I was account director in the firm and I had been selling our technology product for about ten years, pretty much ever since it had become recognized as an important area in the economy. Because it was a hot area, we always had endless problems retaining staff, they were always getting headhunted by rival firms, so that by the time Roger came along there were only the two of us left, Suzy the senior researcher, and me. Our Head of Client Services, who likes to be known as Dr B, asked my opinion. We agreed to phase out Suzy who was always a pain and getting stale, bring in and refocus Roger, and adopt a policy of recruiting bright youngsters.

'Roger did a good job. I was able to help him along with my industry and client knowledge, and his understanding of the process meant that he was a quick learner.'

Robert had the knack of making us feel as though we had known him for years, and we had no hesitation in asking a direct question about his personal relationship with Roger.

He smiled: 'Ah, you want to discuss the great undiscussable! When we appointed Roger, Dr B told me that we would have to call him co-head of the team, although it was obvious that in practice I would be *primus inter pares* given my greater experience and status as director. I am not sure if Roger ever accepted that I was the real leader and I sometimes got the idea that he wanted to upstage me with clients. But we never once discussed it. For the most part, we got on with things and with each other. Overall it was OK.'

Robert was much less buttoned and intense than Roger and we could see how they would have formed a complementary team. Robert confirmed that the business was going well until, quite unexpectedly, Roger had phoned him one night to say that he was moving on.

'I was shocked when he left,' Robert told us, 'but what can you do if someone wants a change?'

If Roger had faced some difficulties with Robert, they were nothing compared to the run-in with Suzy, the senior market researcher who, according to Roger, had tried to undermine him. By the time we tracked Suzy down, she was well established as a director at another firm but was happy enough to spare us the time to discuss events at her previous employer.

'I could never understand why they appointed Roger. He knew

nothing about the sector, it was like getting a plumber in to do the decorating. I was not surprised he walked out. He just wasn't hacking it, was he? They had a bit of success, but it was all about to blow up in his face and he ran away before the problems emerged. In a way it wasn't his fault, but he was pigheaded. He never once asked me what I thought about the situation and would have rather died than ask me for advice.'

Suzy was getting quite worked up by this stage, so to calm her down we spent the rest of our time chatting about industry-related issues about which she had some forthright views herself but not much time for anyone else's. Overall, we had growing sympathy for Roger who, ill prepared and largely ignored, had been dropped into a difficult situation by Dr B. But it was already clear that Roger had done very little to help himself.

Roger's Team.   Our next step was to question the associates in the team, by this time becoming experienced and successful in their own right. The first had joined just before Roger took over and originally worked for Suzy.

'Working for Roger was a bit like being back at school,' he re-marked. 'Regular lessons, detailed instructions and constant "grading" of my work. It was, frankly, patronizing. Our opinion was equally valid to his. After all, he had only been in the sector for a short while – less than we had in fact. Why was his opinion any better than mine? If only he could have chilled out from time to time, but he really did not know when to let go or when to shut up. When we were under pressure Roger gave off the air of a burning martyr, when what we all could have done with was a few words of encouragement and a beer. Roger was just too heavy, the sort of person who leaves his sense of humour at home.'

This feedback struck a chord. Given the comments we had read in Roger's 360 report and the tight-lipped manner in which Roger had given it to us, we couldn't put it entirely down to either the certainty of youth or to the speaker's close links with Suzy. The low regard in which Roger was generally held by those people who reported to him was shared by a former supporter, a young man who had been recruited by Roger: 'Roger? Don't even speak to me about Roger. He really let us down sloping off like that when the team was at a critical stage of its development. He did not give a damn about the rest of us so long as his future was sorted out. That was one of the most selfish acts I have ever seen.'

Only one young researcher, a quietly impressive young woman, had much that was positive to say: 'I owe Roger a lot. He was involved in my recruitment and taught me everything I know. I don't come from this kind of background and I felt very uncomfortable to begin with. I was scared of giving my opinion because of the gaps in my knowledge and I felt vulnerable. Roger taught me how to fill the gaps quickly and to compensate for any remaining weaknesses. With his help I gained in confidence and learned when to speak up. Without him I would have been two years longer learning the business. The thing that most people never realized with Roger was just how tough things were for him.'

By this time we had done enough listening. We were tempted to go off and analyse all that we had heard to uncover the real Roger: a burnt out shell, an anxious but potentially good role model for new Player Managers and working fathers or a disloyal, over-promoted self-seeker?

Instead of giving in to our temptation to dissect poor Roger there and then, we called him instead. Sarah answered and we asked her when it would be convenient to come back over to see Roger.

'Nothing to worry about,' we reassured her, 'just an update on our research.'

The Story Unfolds

Still In Denial

'The truth is,' said Philip on the way over to Roger's house, 'that I think the man is all and none of the things people say about him. He was – and to my mind still is – simply a Rookie, a new Player Manager doing his best in a tricky and unfamiliar situation. Roger's response was to try to do it all himself, which is what most new Player Managers do.'

We agreed that people under pressure often lean on the things they know how to do, even though those things are usually what has caused the pressure in the first place. Roger's fallback position was an approach that said 'leave it all to me'. The rest of the team felt uninvolved, put upon, and uninspired with the result that they did not perform. Roger's response was to do yet more himself and this alienated the team still further.

When leading producers first move into the different role of managing, they go from all-star player to all-new Player Manager overnight and often nothing else changes, not least their view of themselves as an expert who can solve every problem on their own. Yet the skills and assumptions that go to make a successful player are not always appropriate to managing.

Philip reflected that 'although Roger was in a difficult situation, his response made things worse. He did not discuss his problems with any of the people that were involved or could have helped, not Dr B, Robert, or even Sarah.'

'And that,' added Joy, 'is what experts are trained to do. If you appoint a Player Manager out of your pool of experts, you should not be surprised if they conform to type. It's right there in his most current feedback. "Roger was anointed to team leader because he was a good producer." It's the classic appointment of a Player Manager from the organization's leading producers, and his response was a typical expert's solution. Experts don't ask for help, they just dive in and do it themselves. They say, "This is all my problem and I must reveal no weaknesses to anyone as I try to sort it out."

'This is Roger all over. He hasn't levelled with anyone, even himself, about the problems. No wonder his stomach tightens talking about the whole episode; the man hasn't stopped to ask what happened or what else he might have done.'

We had arrived at Roger's house and he opened the front door to us. 'Roger, how are you?' we said a little too brightly, embarrassed that we had just been talking about him intently. 'It is so good to see you again.'

'Is it?' replied Roger, as he welcomed us once more into his study.

'Roger,' Joy started off very quickly, 'we want you to know that the feedback from the people you used to work with is in some ways very consistent with that of the people you are working with now. But some is very different as well.'

'So it was bloody unfair then,' Roger cut in before she had finished.

'Yes Roger, it was bloody unfair,' said Joy steadily and much to Philip's surprise. Roger looked relieved, but not for long as Joy continued: 'But what if I were to suggest that the person who has been most unfair is you, and that the person you have been most unfair to is yourself?'

Noticing Roger's stunned expression, Philip felt he needed to bring the point home to Roger more gently by relating it to a story of his own.

'Roger, your situation reminds me of my own first Player Manager job. I felt that I needed to handle everything people threw at me. There was a lot to learn, but I was determined to succeed and worked all the hours necessary to get things done. In the end though, I felt put upon as well as unrecognized. I was often irritable and tempted to blame those around me, including my family and friends. I felt everyone was being insensitive to me and to what was really going on. But looking back, I realize that I never told a soul how I felt either at work or at home.

'I was reminded of this when we went into your old firm and learned that neither Dr B nor Robert had any idea about your true feelings. They had no inkling that you were unhappy and were both sorry and surprised when you left.'

We sensed that it was time for Roger to react, and so the study fell uncomfortably silent. Roger said nothing at first. He seemed lost in thoughts of his own until he declared to no one in particular: 'No one was more committed to the success of that group than me and no one could have worked harder to get up to speed in an area they knew nothing about. OK, I never had frank discussions with anyone about turf issues but I was on top of every practical problem in the team. I had pretty much sorted everything out before it got too much for me. Now you seem to be saying I should have stuck it out and admitted to everyone that I was unhappy.'

'Not necessarily,' said Joy, 'but before you decided to leave, did you ever stop to think about alternatives to doing it all yourself? To be blunt, a critic could say that you overestimated your own capacity and gave a false impression about how well you were coping to those who could have helped you. As a result, you missed out on getting help, help that might have enabled you to leverage the talents of your team and reduce the burden on you.'

'Don't worry,' Philip told Roger, 'Joy is always this sweet with people! Seriously though, there is nothing unusual about any of this. Like most new Player Managers, you responded to the best of your ability in a way that had served you well in the past. If you had been aware of alternative approaches, you might well have adopted one of them with better results.'

'Will one of you enlighten me,' asked Roger stonily, 'as to how I could have dealt with the situation differently given the people I had to work with and, more to the point, what shall I do about my situation now?'

Before we could answer however, Sarah was at the door to the study. 'Roger, would your colleagues like to join us for supper?' she asked.

'Although it was kind of you to think of them, Sarah, that won't be necessary. They were just leaving.'

And before we had had chance to think much about it, we were doing just that.

Admitting There's a Problem

We regretted that we had been shown the door before telling Roger about the researcher, who had said that without him she would not have developed nearly so fast. Neither had we had a chance to discuss with Roger alternative approaches to 'doing it yourself', so we decided to drop him an email to include the positive feedback and a coaching exercise, *What Do I Want?*, which we hoped would encourage him to broaden his perspective. We received a response within a couple of hours.

To: Philip and Joy
From: Roger
Sent: 18 November 2001 21:36
Subject: WHAT I WANT

Thanks. I will give it a go. By the way I asked Sarah what she thought was my biggest strength and my biggest weakness after you had left. She said my biggest strength was self-evident; it was my sense of duty and determination to succeed. My biggest weakness apparently is that I am contemptuous of others' advice and so self-reliant that others can feel I don't need them. She added that I seemed to have descended from a long line of clams to which I replied that actually I talked a lot, I just didn't use as many words as she did.

By the way let's not meet at my house in future.
Roger

After reading Roger's response we concluded that he might at last be coming out of denial. The exercise we had sent Roger was in two parts and was designed to get him to focus on what he really wanted from work. We hoped that by getting him to stop and reflect on that, he would be able to break the habit of seeing work as an endless stream of tasks to be sorted out, and were mildly encouraged when we received his longer reply three days later.

To: Philip and Joy
From: Roger
Sent: 21 November 2001 23:48
Subject: WHAT DO I WANT

I have answered the questions you posed as honestly as I can, as you can see from my italics underneath your original. I know I am supposed to feel all changed and empowered after an exercise like this but the truth is something is 'stopping' me.

I still feel very resentful about what has happened. I can't say I know what I want apart from it's something that I don't have now. I feel there is something repeatedly being asked of me that I just don't get and unless I get it before long I might blow another job.

Part One: Problem Focus
    What is your problem?
    I feel overloaded and under appreciated
    How long have you had it?
    Ever since I took on my last job
    Whose fault is it?
    That's a good question. Maybe my own. But certainly the company as well. No one told me just what it would be like.

Who is to blame?

Dr B and my new boss and probably my mother. They all want something extra from me but they never say what.

What is your worst experience with this problem?

In a word Suzy. And a last client meeting with Robert

Why haven't you solved it yet?

I have. I moved on. OK that's a cop out

What will you do about it?

Look cheerful. Try harder still. Tell my new team that if they want something more from me they only have to ask. And tell my new boss I'm fixing things just like he said to.

Part Two: Outcome Focus

What do you want?

Who knows what I want. To get better feedback I suppose. Boy what a measly goal.

How will you know when you have got it?

My stomach won't tighten and people will be off my back. I will smile more at the kids, maybe even Sarah as well.

What else in your life will improve when you get it?

People will respect me more. Our results will be better. I won't feel so exhausted.

What resources do you already have to help you achieve this outcome?

My determination and my team

What is something similar where you have already had success?

I can't think of anything similar, except that when I work at something I usually succeed

What is the next step?

Face the feedback

What could stop you?

Not knowing how to face it

How will you stop it stopping you?

Right now I don't know

After reading Roger's long reply a couple of times over, we could tell that he was moving on and sent another email to arrange the next meeting in a couple of weeks.

To: Roger
From: Philip and Joy
Sent: 7 December 2001 10:14
Subject: FACING THE FEEDBACK

Roger, so far so good. You have acknowledged that you feel over-loaded and under-appreciated. You have identified that what you really want is to achieve better results and earn the respect of your colleagues. You understand that the benefits of that are that you will feel better and less tired. The main thing stopping you from achieving all this is that you don't know how to face the feedback.

Isn't it now time to face the feedback? And are you sure there weren't any alternatives to doing it all yourself?

Philip and Joy

We felt our growing faith in Roger was validated by his reply about a week later.

To: Philip and Joy
From: Roger
Sent: 16 December 2001 20:38
Subject: DEALING WITH THE BOSS

Call me stupid or something but I have only just realized that my determination to deal with everything myself caused a lot of the problems. It was most damaging with Dr B, the B*S%#*D Head of Client Services. By failing to address the biggies with him, I consigned myself to torture via permanent lack of clarity of position and I waived my rights to any kind of preparation for the role I was about to take up. The communication from me was so poor that you said he was surprised when I resigned. I should have simply gone in and demanded that he sorted his team structure and let me sort mine, clarified my role relative to Suzy and Robert and recognized some need for training and mentoring on how to manage a team.

Why I didn't ask for Sick Suzy to be removed from the team in order to give me a clean start I don't know. I just didn't assert myself in the situation at all. By keeping quiet and seething inwardly I contributed hugely to the tiredness that precipitated my departure. If I had got the issue out into the open early on the period of stress would have been shorter, perhaps more painful in the short term (I hate confrontation) but less debilitating by virtue of its brevity. Dr B contributed to this situation by trying to hedge his bets but I let him get away with it. I see now what Joy meant when she said the unfairness was an own goal.

I can also see that I should have tackled the Robert issue too. Every time that we went off to a meeting, I was planning how to avoid coming out second best. In addition to the stress and anxiety of having to meet and impress clients, I sucked us both into mind games that must have been as tiresome for Robert as they were for me. If I had been less of a rookie I would have got the issue on the table with the head of client services, forcing Dr B to deal with the consequences of his own actions. Likewise I should not have gone along with proposals to bring in two raw recruits that I was not happy with, especially as I lived with the problems day by day. No doubt I would have irritated Dr B in the short term but it would have avoided midterm problems.

The pattern is now all too familiar. I was blind to it then though. No wonder Dr B was sorry to see me go. I was his obedient puppy.

This time we replied back immediately.

To: Roger
From: Philip and Joy
Sent: 16 December 2001 21:59
Subject: RE DEALING WITH THE BOSS

We support everything you say. One course of action would have been to raise the issues directly with Robert and Suzy and try to work through the awkwardness of your respective positions. After that a frank discussion of the team leadership would probably have been more possible with Dr B.

Philip and Joy

To: Philip and Joy
From: Roger
Sent: 16 December 2001 22:33
Subject: RE RE DEALING WITH PEERS

Robert yes. But Suzy – really? Think I am missing something on this one. A discussion with Robert might have worked, no one in their right mind would have advised me to tackle Suzy 'the most senior' researcher. There wasn't a single drop of rapport between us. Indeed only antipathy and irritation. She would have tipped if I had brought matters to a head. This was really one for more of a man than me to sort out. R

To: Roger
From: Philip and Joy
Sent: 16 December 2001 23:02
Subject: DEALING WITH SUZY

So what if she had tipped? Then what?

Philip and Joy

He's a People's Person

We received a voicemail from Roger the next afternoon thanking us for our additional insights, telling us that he was still thinking about Suzy and asking us what we thought about management training. This was a good question, as many people we met in the field asked us if their early performance as a Player Manager might have been different had they received training before taking up the role.

We replied to the voicemail, saying that if he had asked for a short management induction course or some personal coaching, the chances are that many of the mistakes he had made would have been avoided. We added that he was unfortunate in reporting to someone who believed in the 'deep end' method of learning, but that for Player Managers this was still the norm. Most organizations still underestimate the importance and difficulties of the Rookie's transition, especially in the professions. To conclude, we suggested that he should

follow up with his new boss the management training option to acceler-
ate the 'fixing' he still needed to do.

A few weeks later another email landed in the inbox.

To: Philip and Joy
From: Roger
Sent: 9 January 2002 16:49
Subject: I'M A PEOPLE PERSON

My new executive coach and I have surfaced how much it stung me when
the associates wrote that I was 'inaccessible' and 'uninspiring'. It felt like
the management equivalent of being told that I was a bad lover. You know
it makes you feel inadequate deep down. But after Sarah came up with her
clam quip I did kind of wonder what it must be like to hang out with me all
day at work. I concluded that my tendency to be preoccupied with
everything that was going on probably created inaccessibility that stopped
people from testing me out.

With my coach I worked out that I was so hung up about proving myself as
the top player in my last job that I just didn't deal with the people. I saw
the job as a continuous stream of tasks, to be completed. I would often
stay in my office for hours to clear all the stuff from my inbox. If I had
thought about the job in a different way I would have seen that locking
myself away like that made me appear unfriendly. I always used to
squirm when people like Robert set up team lunches and dinners and
other social events, but I guess as a Player Manager I have to accept
they oil the wheels. I am reprogramming myself to believe that chats
around the coffee machine are not a waste of time. I have set up a few
things myself in the last few days so that this team can form stronger
ties with each other and gain a more mutual picture of what is going
on.

Roger

We were glad things were still moving forward for Roger and sent
back an encouraging response.

To: Roger
From: Philip and Joy
Sent: 10 January 2002 18:15
Subject: RE I'M A PEOPLE PERSON

We are not prepared to make any disclosure at this point about what makes either of us feel inadequate deep down. Yet we agree that good management involves both dealing with tasks and broader emotional aspects. If you simply do the job in hand and forget to consider how people feel, you will inevitably be considered uninspiring!

Philip and Joy

One Hundred Days On

As we were to do with all of our Player Managers, we called again on Roger one hundred days after our 'closing' session. He was keen to meet, because although the coaching had helped him rebuild relations with his current colleagues, there was something else on his mind. An opportunity had arisen to go back to his old firm and replace Dr B who was considering early retirement. It seemed that our discussion with Dr B had reminded him of Roger's strengths, and some preliminary meetings had been held. We asked Roger whether he had thought about being 'once bitten, twice shy'.

'I have to say that I am looking much more carefully about what is on offer this time! I have already had one of Dr B's "once in a lifetime opportunities", so I am asking more questions about reporting lines and responsibilities. Robert has been made Business Development Director and I would be his counterpart in Client Services. I need to check out that relationship very carefully.

'Suzy, I have discovered, is no longer there. She is a director in a different company, and before either of you say anything I called her last week to see if she is free for lunch sometime. Needless to say, I haven't heard back from her yet.'

Taking Command

We suggested to Roger that if he was thinking seriously about returning to his old firm, he should work out how he would establish credibility as a leader, especially as the people who had once worked for him were now much less junior. We could see him looking uncomfortable and felt we had come to the heart of what Roger had found most difficult in his transition.

Joy broke the silence: 'Expert players can experience a difficult transition to a Player Manager role because they do not realize that people are now listening to them in a different way and for different things. The Rookie Player Manager assumes that the audience is looking for informed answers; the Veteran Player Manager has learned that above all the audience is looking for someone they can relate to and trust.'

We showed Roger a table outlining how the expertise-centred Rookie and the Veteran think differently about establishing credibility with their teams. While the Rookie tries to impress through superior knowledge, the Veteran does not try to impress at all, instead seeking to build rapport by giving the team something they can fasten on to.

We told Roger about the case of Maria. When Joy began coaching her on team leadership skills, she noticed that Maria came across much better when 'off script', talking naturally and looking at her team directly. All too often, however, she spent more time interacting with the equipment around her and the content of her material than she did with the people in the room.

Regardless of her obvious mastery of the business and all the prep-

Table 1: Taking Command

A Rookie asks:	A Veteran asks:
What do they need to know?	What do they need to understand?
What is the evidence?	What will get attention?
Have I got all the facts?	Have I got memorable headlines?
Does the case speak for itself?	What will people object to?
Is it coherent?	Is it compelling?
Am I ready to tell them?	Are people receptive to me?
Did I win the argument?	What message did they take out?

aration effort that went into Maria's presentations, her feedback at review time was that she was 'aloof, analytical and dry' rather than 'accessible, powerful and inspiring'. No one ever doubted her professional competence. Her style of communicating reinforced that she knew everything there was to know. But in reinforcing her expertise she inadvertently undermined her credibility as a leader. Like many other Rookie Player Managers she made no connection to her team and signalled, inadvertently, that she was detached, commercially focused and not interested in them as people.

People told Joy that Maria would be much better if she could be more like Tyrone. Apparently he was always interested in what the team saw as key issues, and in a funny, relaxed way gave lots of great advice. Tyrone gave the impression that he was a born communicator, and a lot of people wondered why he wasn't leader of Maria's team as well as his own. It seemed that all he had to do to win people's hearts and minds was to show up on time.

Joy asked Tyrone to talk to Maria about the secrets of his success. Maria's eyes widened when Tyrone said the key was preparation; after all, everything he did seemed so off the cuff.

Tyrone outlined how he thought through the process of reaching the team at the outset of each meeting so that they would connect and stay with him throughout: 'Once the story comes, then I write it down, and then say it out loud a few times. I rehearse several times exactly what I want to say. Once I am sure of that, I can relax and just enjoy being in front of the crowd.'

Roger picked up that the message for him and Maria was to connect with the team. Impressing them with technical expertise was less important than he had believed. More important was to convey a vision for the business and a passion for people. Roger saw that to take over successfully from Dr B meant making up ground with his former team members; we advised him to study the right hand side of Table 1.

Doing It Through Others

Although he agreed that establishing rapport with people was a top priority, Roger sounded less convinced that delegation could replace his personal involvement as a means of production: 'Looking back, I can see that it would have been better for me to have stopped trying to impress the team with my knowledge and to have concentrated on winning their support by showing that I cared about them as people and by passing on my technique. But even now, I am not sure how I would have done this or how well it would have worked in such a junior team. They just could not have done it without constant input from me.'

We asked him to profile his old team for us.

'To do a good job, each person in the team had to be able to write cogently and handle data; they also needed technical knowledge about the industry we were covering, presentational skills, and predictive powers. That's five broad areas of ability. Now we had people who could write but knew nothing about the industry, people who knew lots about the industry but nothing about forecasting, and others who were great with numbers but unable to construct an argument on paper. Another could construct a beautiful picture about what had just happened but was nearly always wrong about the future; someone else had great intuition but could not write clearly. All of them wanted to be involved in the "front end" business of presentation, but not all had the presence to carry it off.'

Philip sketched something on to a piece of paper, which he handed to Roger.

'One solution,' said Philip, 'would have been to draw up a matrix comprising each team member and their skills and then to compare this to the skills required for each project. You could then have put together mini-teams on a flexible basis, around key research projects. Each team could have contained a blend of the five critical skills, your role could have then changed to one of integrating, guiding and developing others rather than jumping in to fill all the individual gaps.'

Roger looked unimpressed by Philip's tables and charts until Joy asked him to 'imagine a soccer player manager trying to play in goal, in defence, in midfield, in attack all at the same time in a single match. It just wouldn't happen. But in a sense, that is what you tried to do. Player Managers in soccer pick specialists for each position and blend them into a team in which they themselves also play. Might that have worked for you?'

Roger looked at her with renewed respect. Whether it was Joy's unexpected knowledge of soccer or the power of her argument that had made the connection did not much matter; he was now fully engaged and that, as we had just been saying, was all that mattered.

Table 2: Skills Matrix

Team Member	Skills Needed	Actual Skills
Stephen	Writing Data handling Technical Presentational Predictive	Writing Data handling Presentational
Andrea	Writing Data handling Technical Presentational Predictive	Data handling Technical Predictive
Jan	Writing Data handling Technical Presentational Predictive	Writing Technical Presentational

Did Roger Meet the Rookie's Challenge?

The Rookie's challenge is to step up and take command without doing it all personally.

We gleaned that Roger had taken up Dr B's new offer when we took delivery of a case of champagne and a card marked 'Your headhunting

Table 3: Skills and Resource Matrix

Client Project	Skills Needed	Skills Supplied By
'Windsor'	Writing	Stephen, Jan
	Data handling	Stephen, Andrea
	Technical	Jan, Andrea
	Presentational	Stephen, Jan
	Predictive	Andrea

fee, with gratitude from Tony B'. We called Roger to congratulate him and, to our surprise, he invited us back to his house to celebrate. We accepted on the understanding that he would allow us to provide the champagne.

Sarah briefly joined us to toast Roger's success and she thanked us for, as she put it, 'opening Roger's eyes and mine to what had happened', and then disappeared upstairs to put the children to bed. Roger told us that he was on 'garden leave' at present and that he would appreciate our spending a few minutes with him to run through the key messages of the past few months before he started back at work on Monday.

We started off by talking about the importance of *admitting that there was a problem,* not only to oneself but also to colleagues and other confidantes, including those close to home. Roger nodded and smiled ruefully.

His problem last time was his *belief that the team would only respect him if he was an expert* in all areas. We told him that our research showed this to be a recurring theme amongst Player Managers, particularly in the professions.

Roger did not seem surprised: 'This belief that credibility with the team can only be established by being the top producer or player is real, born partly out of insecurity and partly out of our culture. I come across it often.'

We asked him what he intended to do about it now that he was

Client Services Director. He agreed that in his new role he would be in a position to change the culture, but believed that this would take some time.

First he intended to mobilize the Player Managers beneath him: 'They will need *a framework for involving all people in their teams*, possibly something similar to your skills and resources matrix. With that in place they can *set the team's expectations about how roles are changing* and how they plan to handle management responsibilities.'

We agreed with this as a priority and added: 'Complaints about the leader's lack of production are usually a symptom, not a cause, of managerial problems. Your Player Managers will need to learn that *involving others is a much better strategy than trying to do it all themselves*. It builds team spirit, gets leverage from the other team members and keeps the workload down to achievable proportions.'

Roger needed to develop *a different approach to influencing the team* if he was to step up and take command effectively. We suggested that he reveal his passion for the job and his interest in his team as individuals, as a way of engaging them.

Roger had not met the Rookie's challenge first time round. However, he now understood the circumstances that had caused him to burn out and leave. With his alternative strategies in hand, we felt confident he would take over successfully from Dr B. Roger, we believed, was no longer a Rookie.

7
The Players' Player

Recap. *In this chapter we return to meet Nicola, the Players' Player, who led a bond sales team in an investment bank by charisma and example. Nicola believed that the secret of her success was to be the top producer in the team. 'I have to win and keep the biggest clients, my revenues must be bigger, maybe twice as big as anyone else's,' was how she put it. Nicola clearly loved the thrill of playing and generated a buzz that made her an exciting person to work with. This was confirmed by several of her team, but it wasn't a universal view and we detected rumblings of discontent from those excluded from the in-crowd. When we last met Nicola, we concluded that the challenge for Players' Players like her is to replicate their own success in others, and we described the Players' Player Profile as follows:*

Typical Strengths
- *Sets the pace*
- *Creates a climate of 'excellence'*
- *Inspirational*
- *Serves as role model*
- *Mentors star players*
- *Earns respect and admiration*

Possible Shortcomings
- *Can overextend and divide the team*
- *Secrets of greatness often tacit*
- *Intolerant*
- *Less of a mentor to the average player*
- *Vulnerable to loss of momentum*

In this chapter, to our surprise and Nicola's, we uncover mounting discontent from her team. We hear both from her dedicated and her disaffected followers, including Danny, the lost soul who wanted his name in the book so someone would take notice of him. Can Nicola pull it all together?

Nicola's Story

Nicola from All Angles

We were somewhat taken aback when, following our initial meeting with Nicola and subsequent telephone contact with four of the people whose names she had given us, we started to receive calls from other people in her team. We were not sure whether this was being triggered through word of mouth about our initial calls or was being propagated by Nicola, but either way the calls kept coming. It was clear that Nicola's character was not one that could be ignored. Now that there was an opportunity to comment on her style, people seemed very keen to take it.

The In-crowd

As we talked to Nicola's team, we realized that she had an in-crowd of people around her. Tak Lee was one of these and was the first to call after hearing that we were doing research on Player Managers.

He introduced himself as one of the biggest producers in the team after Nicola and as someone who had earned Nicola's total trust: 'Nicola and I met at the firm's recruitment stand at university. We got to know each other a bit during those last months at uni, went through graduate training together here, and I'd say since then we have matched each other stride for stride.

'It helps that I am not interested in a leadership role or anything like that, so we have never been rivals after the same job, we just push each other on to do better and better. It's competitive but not bitchy; in the end there are some months she does better than me and others when I win. That's how we decide who's going to buy the beers!

'What I like about working for Nicola is that she has a way of making me want to please her. It's to do with the right amount of praise, not lightly given but not so sparing that you think it's never going to come. I want her praise because I respect her as a producer. I think to myself, "Well, if she thinks that's a blast, it must have been good", and I feel proud of myself and I want to do it again for her. I notice that others feel the same, and wanting to get a nod from Nicola is almost as important to many of us as getting a bonus. I did say almost!'

Tak was not alone in his view. David is two years younger than Tak and has been with the firm for three years: 'It's fair to say I joined because of Nicola. We met at a charity party organized by a mutual client and they suggested we get together. We had a drink the next night and she sold me the story really.

'Basically I just like working with her, she is intensely focused on bringing in business, she works very hard and somehow I get the feeling she cares fiercely about us all. It's us against the rest; we are doing it all together, for each other, the best united against the rest. I do it for the good days. When we are on a roll the atmosphere is electric, there is no place on earth I'd rather be on days like that.'

The Outsiders

We knew that not everyone felt this way, 'us against the rest' as David described it. When we had first talked to Danny he had made it clear he was one of Nicola's outsiders. Was he unusual in feeling unloved and unwanted?

'It's a good question. If you came in here and watched us all day you'd think to yourself, what a happy, committed, bunch of people. Same if you came on one of her nights out, fun and games all round the table.

'But see what happens on those nights out after she and her poodles have gone on to a club. There's a few of us left, maybe a self-selecting group, and we all feel the same; this place is great if you are winning but it's no town for losers.'

Danny had mentioned Emma, Nicola's exact contemporary, who was now struggling after a flying start to her career. He had told us that Emma dressed and sounded like Nicola, which is perhaps why when she called us we felt as though we were actually talking to Nicola.

But behind the positive pattern was a sadder tone: 'Danny suggested I call you with some input about Nicola's style. I'll start at the beginning. To begin with there were three of us, girls in a man's world and the best of buddies. We enjoyed knocking down the walls together. In those early days I could handle being out four nights a week with clients and got to work in the morning still feeling good. I had the hunger to be interested in the clients as people and, to be truthful, I got the business by being their friend.

'But after a few years the novelty wore off. The doormen at the night clubs got to know me and I realized that other people's pleasure was just a job for me and that it could not go on. Nikki and I talked about this, she felt the same, but she was able to add an edge to her game that I have not been able to match. She was able to throttle back on the socializing and raise her game in working hours. For some reason I can only get them to give me business if I become part of their lives; Nikki has that knack of staying friendly with them without getting too close. She gets business in a way that I don't understand.

'Anyway, as my numbers slipped and Nicola's stayed high, she got on really well. I was pleased about that, there were a few of us who got right behind her, pushed her forward and probably helped her get the head of sales job. To start with it was fine, we were still all in it together and Nicola gave me every reason to believe that there was something special between us.

'But then I noticed a subtle change; the messages got less friendly, I was not included in on everything. Business decisions were being made without my input. It began to affect our personal relationship, and now I'd say we have neither a business nor a personal relationship. It's incredible when you think how close we have been. Why didn't she help me see the things I couldn't understand? What kind of leader is that?'

We asked Emma what had happened to the third of the original three friends.

'Good question. She left a year or two ago to join AMSS. Her name is Katie. I'll get her to give you a call, she'd have an interesting story to tell.' We were feeling more and more uncomfortable about receiving these calls and told Emma that although we appreciated hearing her story, she really didn't need to go to the trouble of contacting Katie.

Nevertheless, the very next day Katie called. We learned that AMSS was a rapidly emerging competitor to Nicola's firm and that Katie had settled in well there. She was keen to tell us how good AMSS was and how well she was doing: 'I came here because this is the place to be nowadays. We have state-of-the-art technology, a building that looks like a home not a factory, a buzz in the office that Nicola lost years ago and a vision for the future that Nicola will never get in a month of Sundays.'

It was clear that Katie and Nicola had fallen out and we asked when this had happened.

'Two years ago the numbers over there stopped growing at quite the same rate. The harder we tried, the more Nikki leaped up and down, the more frustrated we all became when things just plodded on. It wasn't going wrong, you understand, but it wasn't going right either. Nikki did not react well. She changed everything round, drove herself harder and harder, seemed to trust others less, just wanted to do it all herself. The atmosphere turned flat, the team nights became an embarrassment, and it was clear there was another game in town. Nikki was not a nice person to be with at this time, but I would have stayed with her if she or those goons she reports to had shown any vision. But they could see no alternative to doing more of the same and I had to go.'

We listened to Katie with a mixture of sympathy, discomfort and growing concern. Beneath the glowing surface of Nicola's performance and the results of her team were clearly some more fundamental and less glowing issues. We were beginning to feel implicated as 'keepers' of those issues and were unsure about how to handle them. How could we let Nicola know something of what we had heard without betraying the confidence of the people who had called us? We decided that Nicola needed to know and that we would fix a meeting, say that we had talked to some people as she suggested and that whilst the team perception of her style was broadly consistent with her own, there were some areas of mismatch that she might want to know about.

It took several attempts to set up a meeting, but when we arrived we discovered Nicola wasn't there. 'Oh, she had to fly to France at short notice,' we learned from a helpful associate. 'Don't worry, you probably wouldn't have got to see her anyway as there was an internal cross-divisional sales meeting scheduled for that time as well. Why don't you hang on a minute while I try to track her down? She might want to talk to you by phone.'

While we waited to discover whether or not we were going to speak to, if not meet, Nicola, Danny spotted us from across the desks. 'So you two are back,' he said. 'I'm not surprised. Have you met Steve? He is one of Nik's bosses, although I sometimes wonder who is bossing who. I have just come out of a meeting with him. Let's see if he has time to say hello.'

The Co-heads

Steve was co-head of Europe and operated from a glass walled area raised a few feet above the trading desks where Nicola's and the other teams worked. He greeted us with 'Welcome to the fish tank, can I get you a coffee?'

As Steve disappeared to the machine to get the drinks, we looked out over the trading area. It was crowded, energized, but unmistakeably dingy and very untidy, with discarded food wrappers, old newspapers and reports overflowing the bins.

Steve came back with a couple of plastic cups and saw us looking out: 'We call it "The Pits". I have been trying for two years to get the senior producers to approve new plans but they won't spare me the time to think seriously about it, fobbing me off with the old argument about not wanting to add overhead.'

'Even Nicola?' we asked innocently.

'She's about the worst. A couple of years ago I could have got through to her, but ever since she "hit the wall" she's been impossible to live with. Jean Marie – he's my co-head – and I have been trying to get the department heads to do some "blue sky" thinking about this place for years, but Nicola will only focus on the present.

'In a way I see her point of view; her numbers are still fantastic, and even if they are not growing like they used to, the return on sales is still up there with the best. She says any time not spent with her team or clients is time wasted, but we are a big business now and we have to plan. She won't come to offsites, will only come to meetings after 6 pm and is usually late or fails to show at the last minute [we glanced at each other, 'we know, Steve, we know'] and when she does turn up, she shouts down the other department heads and the support people. But she's so important to us, she's impossible to fire.'

At that point the door opened and a man carrying a Euroshuttle bag walked in: 'It has to be Nicola you are talking about,' said Jean Marie. 'I am not so sure we shouldn't fire her. Talk to anyone in Paris or any other European office and you will not hear very nice things.

She is not a team player, she will not play the matrix, and despite great personal performance she is holding the business back. We should let her go.'

Jean Marie slung his suitcase into the corner, cursed the traffic for making him late and went to his desk.

'Excuse my colleague,' said Steve, 'we have our own cross-Channel divide on this one. He gets a little impetuous in matters concerning Nicola.'

Jean Marie would have none of it: 'It's not about London versus Paris, Steve, it's about client service. The client decides how we service them, not Nicola, and unless you recognize that soon we are going to blow apart.'

Not wishing to intrude on a family argument, we thanked Steve for the coffee, commiserated with Jean Marie about the London traffic and made our way to the floor below to find out if there was any progress on setting up a call with Nicola.

'Look, why don't we just come back another day?' we suggested to the associate who had not yet been able to reach Nicola because 'it's a bit hectic round here' and 'other things keep cropping up.'

'Another day isn't likely to be any better,' he replied. 'Just give me a minute and I will try to reach her now.'

The associate came back looking apologetic: 'Nik says sorry to you both for not being here, but she doesn't think you will have had a wasted journey. She said it was a great opportunity for me to show you around and that you should treat the place as an open research site. She especially asked me to introduce you to "The Elders". If you hang on a minute, I'll try to track them down. Nik plans to be back tomorrow afternoon and will call you as soon as she can.'

We knew we should leave, but didn't wish to appear ungracious in the face of a generous invitation to stay from the woman who had just stood us up. We felt that if Nicola knew what we knew and why we had come to see her, the charming offer to wander freely around would be abruptly withdrawn. We decided to stay.

The Elders

During our contact with Nicola's team we had come across frequent references to the Elders, a pair of veteran salesmen who had a place in the firm's folklore. John and James had each run the desk in their time.

Now they worked as a big producing duo – only the production wasn't quite so big any more according to what we had heard from the team.

After being introduced to them by Nicola's enthusiastic associate, we agreed to meet them later in a well-known local bar. When we arrived James gave the barman a twenty-pound tip with the first round 'so you don't forget us.' To judge by the pace of the drinking there was little chance of that. They were briefly interested in what we were doing but very soon got on to war stories: deals they had closed, places they had been and nights they had had. John standing Rambo-like on the top of a grand piano while James played *Blue Suede Shoes* on the keyboard was one of the few printable tales. It was impossible to get them focused on the business, so after Joy left early Philip had to do the drinking for two.

Late into the evening John went on to other things, and Philip was able to talk to James who had slipped into a wistful mood.

'Don't let all this fool you,' James confided. 'Five years ago, no, two years ago, you wouldn't have got near us for clients and colleagues on a night like this. But the game moves on. We have team night on Thursdays, a few nights like tonight but the rest of the time they don't want to know us.

'I'm a fool really, I had it all but fell out with Steve because I was too busy to listen. When I was head of the desk my power was greater than his. If I had played politics I could have taken his job, no trouble. But instead of doing things their way, I just stamped my foot whenever I wanted something and Steve dared not say no. But then my numbers slipped and he was able to ease me out, leaving me as a relationship manager. But how long will that last? The way business is going, about two months I reckon. And then what? A smaller firm, a worse firm or the golf club? I should have paid more attention to developing the people and the business, but at that stage I had no time for all that management stuff. No one does, really. Certainly not Nicola.'

Philip asked James how he got on with Nicola.

'Personally I think she is a real class act. She hides a killer instinct and an ability to focus right in on her target under a fur coat of charm. Clients find her irresistible. The trouble is the business needs more than Nicola alone. I have tried talking to her about it, warned her to learn from my mistakes, but I can tell when she has stopped processing. She says, "I'm hearing everything you say Jamie," gives me one of her winning smiles and always finds a way to move the conversation her way.'

Philip left James later than he would have liked, but couldn't help reflecting on the new things he had heard. Nicola was personally brilliant and energizing to know; she came over as a naturally charismatic leader, but her blind spots had near fatal effects. He imagined that it would be difficult not to like and admire Nicola. If he was in her team he would want to keep up with her dazzling pace. But he also imagined that Nicola's style took its toll. She operated with herself as the centre of the universe. This blinkered her perspective and closed down her listening to the detriment of others and the health of the business long term. The downsides of her style were becoming manifest – at least to everyone else.

The Story Unfolds

Nicola's Angry

It was easy to get the next meeting with Nicola. She phoned Joy at 11 pm one evening later that week, clearly furious.

'Do you know what you two have done?' she almost shouted. 'I've just got back from the team night and they are all talking about us losing momentum. At the end of the night one of my very best people tells me they are off to AMSS, and do you know why? You two, asking lots of nosey questions and getting everyone thinking negative thoughts. Just keep well away from this place in future, will you? And if I appear in your book, I'll sue!'

Joy knew enough about handling difficult situations to stay on the front foot and invited Nicola round to talk things over there and then.

'I think you should make the effort to see me here,' said Nicola. 'I didn't make this mess. You did!'

Joy made the short cab ride to Nicola's home which turned out to be a smart mews house that was so immaculate it appeared not to have been lived in. Once Joy was inside and seated, Nicola vented. It was an impressive performance and at the end of it Nicola seemed more excited than enraged.

Joy asked if she would be interested in hearing the full story of the meetings and without giving Nicola time to say no, turned to her notes and began reading. At first Nicola interrupted, disagreeing with what was being said. But gradually she became less vehement, and for the first time since we had met her she seemed to be listening intently.

After Joy had finished, there was a long silence. Finally Nicola spoke. 'How about if we meet after work tomorrow night?'

'We could do that, but why not take a day off and we can meet in the morning?' countered Joy.

'I don't do days off, but let's meet Saturday.' Joy settled for that, feeling that this was finally the chance to handle things properly.

Nicola's Listening

For the session on Saturday we booked a meeting room in a good hotel in London, a decision we initially regretted as we worked our way through guests arriving for a wedding breakfast and others leaving for sightseeing trips. Once the room was set up though, the elegant atmosphere was exactly right for Nicola who, only three minutes late, quietly slipped in.

She looked composed, more fragile than usual, and had a strain about her face that told of a bad night's sleep. She began by telling us that she had learned yesterday the detail of David's planned departure to AMSS. It was not good news for her since her leadership was a reason for his decision, a fact of which he had made no secret. Jean Marie, who was still in the UK, had cracked a joke in front of everyone about offering to move the entire sales force to Paris if that would help keep the team in place.

'I cracked back,' said Nicola, 'that anyone leaving the team was leaving a good thing while it was still going, and that we had to doubt their judgement and not ours. I added that a move to Paris would be romantic and that being closer to Jean Marie all the time would be equally so.

'Inside however, I felt uneasy and not much like joking. I wanted to know what they all really thought of me, how many of them secretly shared David's view, and who else was planning to quit. So why don't we run through the feedback one more time?'

Nicola's Handheld

Acknowledging Nicola's talent for moving conversations and the people in them to where she wanted them to be, we went over the feedback. Then we suggested to Nicola that she draw up separate lists of the positive and negative things that were said. Nicola took her handheld from her bag, worked away for several minutes and then showed us her list of positives.

➤ Top producer
➤ Leads by example
➤ Mentors other good producers
➤ Inspiration to others
➤ Commands allegiance & respect
➤ Creates energy & buzz
➤ The return on sales from the team is excellent
➤ Clients can't get enough

Nicola looked more cheerful after she had drawn up this list: 'Maybe I'm not so bad after all,' she remarked.

We told her that thinking of herself as good or bad probably wasn't that helpful: being a Player Manager was invariably tough and it was impossible to get everything right.

'But there are real consequences of doing too many things wrong,' said Nicola. 'I remember James saying to me once that he regretted his lack of attention to management. He believes now that he had unintentionally hurt others and himself and caused undue stress for the team. So for all the positives, my main concern right now is to understand why others think I have weaknesses.'

We were beginning to realize just how smart Nicola was and how carefully she was thinking about the elements in her game. She seemed tense, as though permanently poised to pounce. It gave her an edginess that was simultaneously attractive and nerve-racking. We doubted that Nicola suffered fools gladly or tempered her style much for those who couldn't bring themselves to operate so close to the edge. We asked her whether she agreed with James that management was an important part of the job.

The Maths of Leverage

Nicola's response was almost inevitable: 'Yes it is, but it is not as important as producing. Producing is everyone's top personal priority, even mine.' She paused for a while. 'But we wouldn't be here if it was as simple as that, so let me change my answer. Let me say that for salespeople, producing is their number one aim but that the head of the desk must think about other things too. But I know in my heart that as leader producing is still what counts, both materially and for the spirit in the team. A desk head that can't pull off big transactions is a soft target for those who can. Right now I deliver 20 per cent of the team's total revenue and that's a big number. In fact it is the swing factor in our profitability. Without my 20 per cent we would be in loss.'

Philip acknowledged both the psychological and commercial importance of the business Nicola brought in, but then asked her to focus on the 80 per cent of revenue contributed by the others: 'If by concentrating on managing the team's performance you could improve their results by a quarter, that would effectively double what you bring in personally. With even my level of basic maths, that means that the firm's profits would double. It's what we mean by leverage.'

Nicola looked bemused. She conceded that the arithmetic was right, then added: 'But I do manage the team's performance. By my own example I set the standard for everyone else. Everyone knows that we cannot be less than excellent and I can feel others working to match me. You should talk to Tak Lee if you haven't already. He gets a kick out of playing alongside me. We push each other on. If I wasn't here the team's performance would drop – and probably by more than a tenth.'

Nicola was staring at Philip, as though he really wasn't grasping her ability to motivate people by her very presence in a team. She didn't say anything more, but she had clearly talked herself back up and her confidence at this point seemed impenetrable.

Joy asked her to look over the list of positives again and consider whether everything stemmed from her status as top producer, or whether it would be possible to redefine her role so that it wasn't based entirely on leading through producing. Could she add other strings to her bow? Would that cause her to lose status with the other sales people?

Nicola thought for a while and then responded that she could probably still lead the team from the front, provided that she spent more than half of her time selling and that the other team members knew what the new ground rules were and why. 'And that,' said Nicola, 'is what neither of you have sold me on so far. What would I have to gain from selling less?'

We were beginning to understand why Jean Marie, and probably Steve as well, found Nicola so hard to deal with and why, despite her results, they might fantasize about letting her go. Nevertheless she had made a smart point and it warranted a response.

Nicola's expression remained absorbed and concentrated, but before we could reply she answered her own question: 'Well, the need for new ground rules is obvious, I suppose. I would have time to attend to the causes of the negatives from the feedback. So let's make another list.'

In some ways Nicola was a delight to work with. Her mind was quick and she moved forward almost entirely on her own energy. It was refreshing to be with such a quick learner and one who seemed very capable of handling the process herself. Joy went back to her notes, going over the areas in Nicola's performance where she had been criticized. As she listened to Joy, who had decided to be fairly candid with the feedback, Nicola looked unexpectedly deflated and forlorn.

The Handheld Again

For someone who worked so hard to be excellent and who felt they were always an inspiration to the team, these comments must have been hurtful to hear. However it was anger rather than pain that came out in Nicola's voice when she said sharply: 'Sounds like Emma and Danny have had a good old bitch, but you know neither of them could do my job. Well, if that's all the appreciation I get, I had better set some new ground rules fast before every last one of them heads off for AMSS.'

With that, she drew up her second list.

➤ Ignores weak players like Danny
➤ Has favourites like Tak
➤ Disloyal to old friends like Emma
➤ Vulnerable to lost momentum – as bad as the elders
➤ Impedes investment in the business – unlike Steve
➤ Unwilling to look beyond self and team – unlike JM
➤ No strategy or vision
➤ At risk – people and growth, especially to AMSS

Nicola was certainly pulling no punches with her interpretation of her weaknesses. We weren't sure if this list was defensively exaggerated or as harsh a look at her own performance as she would have given when appraising one of her 'underachievers'. We divided the list into three areas: people management, business building and strategy. We then proceeded to tackle them in turn.

First we discussed why those people Nicola believed to be not performing well felt that she had no interest in them.

'It's not right to say that I have no interest in them,' she declared, 'but as I told you when we first met, there is a type of underachiever that I have no time for. If I think that someone is being lazy or not trying hard enough, I give them the cold shoulder in order to send a message to them and anyone else who is watching that this kind of thing will not win my approval. But if someone is trying but having a bad run, then I try to be encouraging and to give them a hand up if they are down. Then there is a third group; they are trying but they are never going to make it, I am cool with them too.'

Joy wanted to get things straight: 'So you have three groups of underachievers and you deal with them in different ways according to how you classify them. You don't explain that to them or the rest of the team, so do you think they can work it out for themselves?'

Nicola looked embarrassed and defensive. She agreed that if she was to carry on with this approach, she needed to be more open in communicating her judgements.

Philip suggested that Nicola could hand over some of her own clients to people who were ready to take on more, and use the space as management time to sit down with the others who were less strong: 'Ask them to talk about themselves and the difficulties they are facing. Do what we were doing with you: find some positive building blocks and pick off the weaknesses.'

'At least this way,' Joy argued, 'everyone would know where they stood and the atmosphere amongst the sales team would become less exclusive.'

'And old friends would know where the boundaries lay between friendship and professional relationships,' said Nicola, recalling per-haps her recent dealings, or rather lack of them, with Emma.

'Does this mean that I have to break up the club of top producers?' Nicola asked. 'Celebrating our successes is so much a way of doing things at our firm that it has become part of the culture.'

We quickly reassured Nicola that valued top players would always club together around an even better player like herself. That, as the label suggested, was the leadership pull of a Players' Player. Furthermore, we suggested to Nicola some considerations she should be aware of if the club was to continue, especially the risk that people might feel that membership was a matter of her personal sponsorship or bias.

Joy contrasted this with a more positive alternative: 'It would be more motivating for everyone to feel that membership was a matter of merit; getting there would then be seen as something to which all the team could reasonably aspire, especially if they could believe that your support was behind them.

'Achieving this shift need not involve much more than a slight but subtle change in how you communicate who you think the winners are. Encouraging everyone and bringing the whole team into celebrations, problems and plans fosters a team performance climate and not an individual one.'

We scarcely needed to point out to a person so in tune as Nicola that the loss to AMSS of one of her best people, David, and not one of her weaker ones spoke volumes about the limits of her clubby approach to fellow stars.

Building the Whole Business

Thinking about the team rather than a cluster of individual stars was something we brought up again when we turned to the second category on the list, business building. We identified three areas where Nicola was being blinkered in her approach: the matrix with the two co-heads, Steve and Jean Marie; investment in systems and facilities; and broader management issues. Our optimism about how the meeting had gone so far was punctured by Nicola's opening remarks on these issues. She launched into a set speech about Steve ('an out-of-touch pen pusher'), Jean Marie ('a typical French politician') and how meetings with either of them were a complete waste of time. We asked her how she would resolve firm-wide issues given the incompetence of her fellow managers and the unsuitability of meetings as places to deal with them.

And then a strange thing happened: she laughed. We agreed later that this was the first time either of us had seen her really laugh. It was fresh and engaging and we were encouraged that she was laughing at herself and not at other people. 'I guess it must be me then,' she acknowledged, and it was agreed that giving her co-managers the time of day would be a good use of part of the time saved from clients, which from now on could be devoted to management. And might she, with a slightly more open mind, even find a way to respect Steve and Jean Marie, or at least respect the problems they faced?

The One That's Hard to Take

We still had one area to cover: strategy, specifically related to Nicola's alleged lack of vision. 'You know, I find this one really hard to take,' she said. 'I do have a vision for the team and that is for us to be the best sales team in the industry. It's not my fault if we are already there and the job is just to stay there. That's reality. It's not a question of lacking vision. We are already the best.'

We were always troubled by such certain confidence and felt that complacency was its biggest risk. Spurred on by those people in Nicola's team who thought things were stale, we could immediately think of ways for Nicola to go forward by taking the lead. 'So how often do you tell the team that your aim is to remain number one?' we asked.

'Tell them, what do you mean tell them?' Nicola flashed back angrily. 'I should have thought it was obvious, why else would anyone be here? I've never actually spelled it out, it should be second nature to every salesperson to be top dog.'

'But is that enough?' asked Joy. 'Most of the most successful business builders believe that you need to tell them repeatedly. You really cannot repeat yourself often enough. There is no known limit to people's appetite for hearing the vision, provided of course that it's credible.'

Nicola's anger had subsided: 'Credibility is the key and it sounds as though remaining number one probably isn't enough on its own. We need to be attractive for other reasons too. AMSS aren't number one and they have certainly got some allure. I will have to be a bit creative about this. I'll sit down with Tak next week – all right, with some of the others too. Actually I might ask James and Steve to join in. We could do with brainstorming some of this stuff. Now when am I going to do this? I have so many client meetings already set up for next week. I wonder who could go instead.'

Does Nicola Do Lunch?

Nicola reached again for her handheld, looked at her calendar and started to write some notes to herself. She remained quietly immersed for a while evidently concentrating, if not reflecting, on what we had discussed and getting ready for action.

'Right what's next?' she said suddenly, taking us both by surprise.

Philip thought that lunch would be a good idea, but he had the feeling that Nicola didn't do lunch just as she didn't do days off. He didn't want to be the one to suggest it first, thereby breaking the flow or slowing down the pace. So, thinking back to his own experience of business building, he suggested: 'What about an insurance policy for the times when you are not number one?'

Nicola looked at him blankly, but he continued: 'I always found it helpful to have a range of targets. It means that you are not putting everything on black, you are not setting up an impossible goal of constantly rising momentum and you are less vulnerable to the day the momentum stops. Setting different targets hedges your bets for the periods that are bound to occur when things are off course in one area. You can relieve the pressure by pointing to broader successes. It also makes good business sense by helping to form the cross-business connections that we spoke about earlier.'

Joy could see that Nicola was struck by this. Philip was now privately thinking that he had been too quick to judge Nicola as difficult and he was warming up to the idea of her as a good Players' Player. She was surprisingly receptive – to anything that made clear sense. She just needed nudging to take a broader view of the game she was playing and the rest very quickly followed. She was even charismatic in her listening.

Feeling bolder, Philip said: 'Why don't we give you some space. We'll order some sandwiches for you and excuse ourselves for a quick lunch.'

Nicola nodded and told us she would draw up a new game plan while we were gone. 'Thank you both,' she said as we left the room. 'This morning has been helpful and constructive.'

This unexpected remark of gratitude left us with a strong desire to help her as much as we could. 'Are you sure you don't need anything more, Nicola?' asked Philip, whose regard for the woman was growing by the minute.

'No, I'll just stay here and draw everything together if you will excuse me.'

So with that we left for a quick walk and a sandwich. We returned in an hour to find Nicola working hard and a plate of untouched sandwiches still on the table.

Nicola's List

Nicola clearly had a keen mind; she assimilated quickly and prepared to move faster than many we had worked with. By the time we got back from lunch she had already completed a headline action plan and was working on how to execute it. Here is the list she had keyed into her handheld:

➤ Free up 20% of time: hand over 2 accounts to Tak (Share with Danny?) and two to David (once we persuade him to stay: share with Emma?)
➤ Brief team: I am doing this to work more on managing/business building
➤ Delegate to senior people responsibility for leading the charge when I'm busy (consider promoting Tak to Co-Head of Sales at next review)
➤ Work with Danny: giving specific advice and feedback, not just cold shoulder
➤ Make it clear to the team, starting with Emma, where they stand with me
➤ Treat fellow managers with the same respect that I give to clients
➤ Create infrastructure/facilities plan and discuss with Steve
➤ Invite Jean Marie to a 'blue sky' dinner on our future
➤ Talk to James and John about mentoring juniors
➤ Attend at least some meetings – as participant not heckler
➤ Visit Paris and other European offices, seeing is believing
➤ Revamp vision – keep on telling it

We were impressed. Nicola had more than picked up the key messages from the feedback and from our discussion, she had made them her own. There had been little attempt to deflect the feedback onto others or to argue why it was not possible to act on it at this time – both very common responses we had witnessed from others under similar circumstances.

She looked up at us and said, 'Not quite finished, if you don't mind . . .' She continued keying things into her handheld and said nothing, apart from asking us if we thought that strategy should be formulated by the team leader or by the team.

We responded that both approaches could work, but our general principle was that the more people who were included at the outset in the formulation of things that were going to affect them, the more robust the end result.

'With them then, I take it,' concluded Nicola.

We tried to engage her in further discussion but she was really too busy concentrating. She thanked us for our time, especially on a Saturday, asked for some more time to herself and for our phone numbers. She was keying away again by the time we had collected our things.

One Hundred Days On

Over the next three months we stayed in regular contact with Nicola and her colleagues. Nicola took to calling Philip quite often for advice and some of the team kept us in touch with what was happening. Steve and Jean Marie became clients of Joy's and she was asked to facilitate the European senior management conference in Paris. And yes, Nicola was there.

The Fish Tank Gets a Make Over

It seemed that Nicola had genuinely embarked on reinventing herself and the sales team, opening the way for a resurgence of the whole division. In the week after our Saturday session, Nicola went to see Steve and Jean Marie and explained that she was losing the support of her team and had begun to wonder whether she was causing the whole division a problem by being isolationist. She said that she was not prepared to offer to stand down as head of sales because she loved her job, but she was prepared to do things differently. Steve had asked her to explain what she meant by 'differently', and Nicola defined this as trying to take a broader perspective on the running of the business and in doing slightly less producing herself in order to leverage the whole sales team.

Steve and Jean Marie were sceptical at first: 'We went along with it, but quite frankly I felt she was a difficult case,' Jean Marie told Joy at the offsite. 'I did not expect her to change. I was proved wrong. Actually she can be very sweet and charming.'

Nicola began attending their Monday morning communications meetings more often than not and usually managed to avoid being too disruptive. People were surprised at first when she invited others to put their view, and when she did make a contribution of her own she offered it from a broader business perspective. She spent a whole week with the Paris team and put a programme together to visit every other European office during the next twelve months. The feedback to Steve and Jean Marie from her first few trips to the European offices showed that her visits were appreciated. Nicola displayed an understanding that good client service required co-ordination as well as single-minded determination.

Steve was especially impressed by things closer to home. Nicola brought her team in one Sunday afternoon to clean up the office and arrived with bright new bins that looked good, joking that they would hold even all of this sales team's rubbish. The rest of the division followed suit, and Steve managed to get the department heads to sign up to refit The Pits.

'Even the fish tank got a make over,' he told us with a grin.

Nicola rebuilt her relationships with everyone, it seemed. She told us: 'Once I cleared space in my calendar, I felt under less time pressure, I restored basic courtesy to my dealings with people. Once I realized that management mattered, politeness at work has become as routine as saying "thank you" to the guy that sells me my morning paper.'

Widening the Club

As Nicola gained support from Steve and Jean Marie for her adjusted role she briefed her top producers, 'The Club' as she called them, on what she planned to do. Tak Lee was asked to step up to take on more accounts and to adopt more of a 'cheerleading' role in order to provide the buzz and electricity that Nicola had previously given. David was asked to do the same after Nicola had persuaded him to stay for at least another six months 'by which time we will be better and if not, well there will still be AMSS.'

David found that this role did not work for him; it affected his production and he did not enjoy it. Tak, on the other hand, found that it added a new dimension to his work: 'It has stopped me from getting stale and if anything has made me a better salesperson. Because I have other things to think about, not just my own clients, I find that when I do come to deal with them I have that added freshness that I had probably begun to lose. I hadn't thought that I would ever say this, but I am beginning to think I wouldn't mind the role myself one day.

'There has been a small problem with David. He wants to report straight to Nicola not through me, but that's fine by me and he is still doing a great job. In fact, just between you and me, Katie has got word of the new mood around here. She is thinking of coming back on board. Next week I will position it with Nik. She and David would form a formidable pair.'

Danny was also very happy with the new Nicola: 'In the first month she called a team meeting, the first one ever that took place in a meeting room not a bar. She spoke very openly about the state of the business, how we were treading water, and how it was up to all of us to get things moving forward again. She told us that she was going to become more involved in running the business and that we should think of her as a Player Manager in future. I like that term; I am a Chelsea fan and it reminds me of the great days we had under Vialli.

'Anyway she told us that in future we were all going to be measured by how we did with our problem areas. She told us all that we were as strong as our weakest link both individually and as a team; everyone's priority was to deal with performance issues. If we had potential but were not delivering on it, this was a criminal waste. She announced with a kind of steely look that there were people in the division who were not quite getting there at the moment and that her objective would be to work with those people to improve things. She looked me straight in the eye, I thought, although two or three others also claimed the same thing when we compared notes afterwards. Anyway, the meeting broke up on a real high.

'Later we sat down together and she asked me to talk about myself. Basic stuff like where I grew up, where I went to school, what I did at university, who I was friends with in the firm. She asked me about my strongest client relationships and the ones I was struggling with.

'She set me three-monthly targets. My first task was to get "Dodgy Dave", our roughest and toughest customer, to come to the firm's suite at an industry function. Nothing more or less than that; I didn't have to get a sale, just get him to come along. I thought about it long and hard, and finally opened to him why I needed him to show up. He saw the challenge, appreciated the funny side of my being so open and agreed to be there for me. This has now developed into a good working relationship. Previously he would deal only with Nicola and then not much; now he gives me quite a bit of business. At the event, mind you, I saw him wink at Nicola, so I don't know what all that was about.

'I know that with Nicola the targets will get harder. But now I feel confident they will be achievable, and I will develop quite a revenue stream. Nicola is watching me all right, but supportively and not getting in the way. The other day I came back with a real big one and earned myself some high fives with David and Tak Lee. It felt really good, I just love my work right now. I don't know what you did with the lady, but thanks.'

We couldn't help feeling that we had done very little with the lady. Most of it she had done by herself.

It's Different

We asked Nicola directly how she was enjoying it.

'It's different. It is not better than pure selling; it is just different. I still get my ups and downs. I have not been able to rebuild things with Emma. I tried to get her to understand that we could be close personally even if I had to be hard with her at times in the business, but she wouldn't hear it. She is apparently talking about a move to AMSS. It sounds as though she will thrive there. It would be good for her to have her star back in the ascendant, though I wish she wasn't going to leave us. I guess I could have handled that better.

'One of the Elders has gone too. I lost patience after Steve finally got my attention on their expenses. It seems they have been financing a nice lifestyle at our expense for a few years now ever since their clients stopped going out with them. "D. Duck" and "M. Mouse" are not client names I recognize, and no client should be entertained quite as much as these two were getting from James and John.

'James I have kept on. His knowledge is too valuable to the juniors. He was contrite and wanted to make amends. I have doubled his target for the year and have upped by 10% the budget of every person he is mentoring. This might sound tough, but James was thrilled. It's game on.

'Looking over it all, the successes outweigh the failures. I still blow up from time to time and I get disappointed if things are not working out, but I have learned to use those emotions positively. I am not perfect, I never will be, but at least I can now see a progression in this business and that helps a lot. If I ever feel down, I think of John the Elder who has gone and how it might have been for me.'

Did Nicola Meet the Players' Player's Challenge?

The challenge for the Players' Player is to replicate their own success in others.

When we first got to know Nicola, we realized that she had 'hit the wall' and we worked with her to help her get over it. She was a quick learner and became reinvigorated as a Players' Player. She still fits into this category because her principal appeal to the team remains as a producer leading from the front, and her strongest franchise is with her team and her clients rather than with the rest of her organization.

But by learning how to leverage her team and the business, Nicola became a much more effective, much stronger Player Manager. Her team like and respect her more, her bosses have fewer doubts about her and she has taken more of a back seat in selling without losing any clients.

Six months after we had worked with Nicola, we discovered that she had been invited by the firm to present to a group of high-potential people. The old Nicola would have sneered at such a request. While the new Nicola wasn't exactly over the moon about it, she felt that her experience had been important enough to pass on. This is what she was planning to say:

Strong people like to be inspired.   The top few people in my team need leadership not management, and provided that I am growing enough to get out of the way of their growth, they do not much care what I do with the rest of my time.

Develop the whole team not just the stars.   No Player Manager can expect to have a team of all stars and no Player Manager can ignore the need to develop the weaker players. Bringing on homegrown talent is important to the team's overall blend.

Bad situations can be rescued.   A turnaround reflects well on everyone and – to judge from the high fives when Danny finally closed a big deal – is very good for morale. The occasional failures, such as I had with Emma and John, are not great but just represent reality: Player Managers cannot win them all.

Momentum is no substitute for vision.   I discovered that sales results are only one indicator of progress. Having a clear sense of direction and targets and measures for other areas of growth are important too. I and the other momentum junkies in the team now get more than one type of fix.

Set a plan and state it.   Running forward on adrenalin alone without knowing why and where you are running soon ceases to be fun. My team had never been given a reason to justify their continued commitment to the firm. Once our rate of growth started to slow, some of my people wondered why they should stay and what I stood for. I had forgotten to state the obvious: we were number one and we wanted to stay there.

Power brings responsibility.   I was always proud of running a team of stars until I realized that we exerted an unhealthy hold over the entire division. My reluctance to co-operate with other parts of Europe caused cross-divisional opportunities to be missed. Not surprisingly, resentment was building and we were vulnerable when things slowed. No one wanted us to come through, and unless I had changed that I doubt that I would have been given much of a second chance.

Regard for everyone is a quick win.   Talking down to junior staff sours morale. It is an immature abuse of position and is never worth it. Respect for all makes the atmosphere better. The same is true of the working environment. Most people spend a third of their life at work and there is no reason why standards of comfort should be low. Even a team tidy-up can have an uplifting effect.

Body language is not feedback.   People in my team always knew where they stood with me, but now I know that a lot of them didn't like the way that they found out. I now see that if someone is struggling, it is my problem as well as their problem and so we sit down to work it out together. It is equally important to give direct praise: not fawning or over-effusive, but generous on the occasions that it is deserved.

Leverage team productivity.   Raising everyone's game by 25% can be better maths than doubling one's own personal contribution. Delegation to trusted colleagues, new role definition and an explicit statement of any new rules of play help the objective of leverage to be understood.

It was an impressive list and one that few other people could have achieved in just six months. We congratulated Nicola on meeting the Players' Player's challenge of replicating their own success in others. We added that we had bumped into Katie, by now back from AMSS, and she had told us: 'This time it feels different, we have roots.'

'Coming from a momentum junkie like Kate that was praise indeed,' said Nicola, 'but also I'll let you into a secret. I am off to Paris next week to meet Jean Marie and some other senior colleagues. I have been asked to lead an acquisition taskforce, Project Mass. I'll leave you to work that one out for yourselves.'

8

The Player Coach

Recap.   *In this chapter we renew our acquaintance with Alex, the Player Coach who, when we first met him, had seemed completely on top of his game. Alex is with an alcoholic beverages group where he is responsible for marketing a portfolio of core brands. After an early scare in his managerial career, he had invested considerable time and energy into coaching and guiding his people with, he had told us, good results. Recognizing that 'managing people was at least as important as managing products', and having developed a much stronger and more stable team, Alex was now looking to direct his own and the team's attention to becoming yet more competitive and to winning an even greater market share. The success of this would determine whether Alex met both aspects of the Player Coach's challenge, which we defined as 'developing talent without losing sight of the bigger picture'. We described the profile of the Player Coach as:*

Typical Strengths
- *Knows the players and how they play*
- *Develops and motivates others*
- *Generates team spirit*
- *Secures trust and commitment*
- *Improves everyone's game*

Possible Shortcomings
- *Gets distracted from player role*
- *Loses sight of the end game*
- *Gets stuck in one-on-one meetings*
- *Doesn't build infrastructure*
- *Overprotective*

We met Alex again sooner than we had expected. He was encountering some unwelcome obstacles as he sought to make the transition from developing people into managing growth. Could Alex stay on top?

Alex's Story

We received a letter from Alex, only a few weeks after we had last seen him, asking for a meeting to talk about 'getting back into the game' as he termed it. We were surprised at this request, believing that Alex had always excelled at shuttling back and forth between playing and managing, and so it was with some curiosity that we renewed acquaintance with our Player Coach.

The Ghost of Richard

We agreed to meet Alex in the bar of a hotel on the edge of Covent Garden in London. Feeling dull in comparison to the media and marketing types who were busily watching themselves being watched by each other, we sat down to order a drink. We were only halfway through studying our choices from the three pages of Martinis on offer from the cocktail menu, thinking that it was to the credit of marketing people like Alex that something as standard as a Martini could have spawned so many fantastically named derivatives, when he arrived.

'Glad you could make it,' said Alex. 'What can I get you to drink?'

'Surprise us,' said Philip, who believed that all Martinis were equal and in any case would rather have been ordering a beer. Once our order was taken, Alex gave us an account of what had happened since we last met.

Alex Can't Find Time

'Do you remember me telling you about a problem I had a long time ago with someone called Richard? He left because I wasn't paying enough attention to his personal development and this caused me to rethink my role as a Player Manager. I took myself out of full time producing, delegated some programme management to two of our best marketing executives, Rocky and Marcella, and devoted more of my own time to bringing on the team.

'Gradually others in the team took on my own direct client and brand programme responsibilities. This left me with time to concentrate on getting leverage for the firm by making certain individuals, and eventually the team itself, more effective. I also became involved in getting the different parts of our business to work better together, which has involved an extensive travel schedule.

'The results for the group, let me tell you, have been stellar. Several people who were close to being shown the door have turned right round, and the portfolio goes from strength to strength. People have personally thanked me for bringing them on in a way that they didn't believe was possible and, without wanting to sound too soft, there is a great feeling of warmth and bonding within the team.'

We assured Alex that we remembered all of this. Despite our surprise at being asked to meet him again so soon, he was eager to fill us in. 'Well, as I said last time, we need to get more aggressive about market share. Our industry sector is maturing very fast. Volume growth is critical to our profitability and, with the category going ex-growth, we will only get that and meet shareholder expectations if we take share from our top two competitors.

'Doing that is not just a matter of getting the salespeople to make more calls or pressurizing the distributors; it needs a strategic plan for a firm-wide initiative in which all parts of the operation would have to do some things slightly differently. You know how edgy people get when it comes to change and I can see that many turf issues lie ahead. Rocky and Marcella do a great job on the sales programmes. But they don't think too much about where things are leading or the internal political issues, so that's something I have to sort out at my level.

'The problem is finding the time to do it. We are a global business and it is a huge job to ensure that the functions and the geographies work well together. I travel a lot, visiting our various locations, selling our ideas and programmes internally if you like, smoothing things down where there is a problem and generally getting across the European point of view. I spend a lot of time away from the London office, and inevitably when I am here I'm in meetings. Then when I get home I'm on voicemail to all the people in my team so that they think I'm still involved in everything that is going on.

'The team appreciate my support but tease me a bit, saying that even if I had a wife and family I wouldn't notice. It is fulfilling but exhausting, and when I do eventually get to bed it's lights out. I just don't have anything left in me to stay awake and think.

'All of this is by way of background, because last week my boss asked that we do some top-level account analysis leading to a three year growth plan. I know these plans are important and I should have taken the initiative myself ages ago, but I could never find the time to sit down to talk about them with Rocky and Marcella.'

The warm and attentive Alex we had first met, the Alex who had made everything appear to be running so smoothly, now seemed more than a little agitated. He was speaking very quickly, appeared to be overloaded and he clearly needed to take a step back and think. We felt that we should not say too much at this point and therefore encouraged him to tell the rest of his story.

Stuck in the Weeds

Alex didn't need much encouragement and continued rather hurriedly: 'I decided I had to make the time for planning. Rather than doing this behind closed doors, I went round and did some listening. Prior to opening things up with Rocky and Marcella, I chatted informally to some of the key opinion-formers in the team about where they thought we were heading and what was the best way to get there. You could have knocked me sidewise when, just as I was about to call a meeting with them, Rocky and Marcella came to see me looking very unhappy.

'Marcella told me that she and Rocky had become disillusioned. Can you believe it! They said they were now doing all of the work without me, yet I was getting all of the credit. Marcella was really quite vicious. She pulled no punches, telling me that in the old days we were all in it together, my producing was as good as anyone's, and that even though I was clearly the leader in command, we were all just one happy family. We used to go to movies, hold barbecues in the summer and have drinks after work, but now they felt there was a gulf between us.

' "You are always in meetings or travelling or working with one of the team down in the weeds," Marcella told me. "That would be fine if you contributed anything strategic. But you don't. What's the point in flying round the world gathering competitor intelligence on comparable brands when we don't have a framework for how we are going to compete with them? As for the team, they need direction not devotion. You are far too soft on half of them, and the other half think you are more of a mother than a manager."

'I was stunned. It was as though the ghost of Richard was right in front of me. I was messing it up with people all over again. I asked Marcella what she meant about me being too soft on people.

'"Look," she said, "if someone's got a problem they deserve help in sorting it out. But that shouldn't mean they come running to you every time there is a slight bump in the road. At some stage the buck stops with them. We all have to be accountable, and in any case we won't have anything to be accountable for unless we get more of a framework around what we are doing. We need a plan! There are seven or eight of us carrying the rest and we have just about had enough of running around like headless chickens."

'Marcella was being poisonous. She ranted on unendingly, with Rocky just nodding in agreement. "The bottom line is," Marcella concluded, "that you have to get out of the weeds or we won't be able to support you. We are not here to carry the can for management when the numbers start slipping."'

Putting a Flag in the Ground

Alex stopped and looked at us, his face clearly dejected. It had been a lengthy outpouring and we noticed that he had not touched his drink. Despite the fact that our glasses were empty, we felt it would be insensitive to lose the moment by ordering another even for the sake of restoring category volume growth.

Out of Touch

We reflected on all that he had said until Joy broke the silence with an anecdote about Bill Parcells, who had been the New York Jets Head Coach. She told Alex about his first press conference when he had described his role: '"I see that my job as coach is to have a system in which I believe, to put the right people into that system, and then get the players to play to their potential within that system."

'Could it be,' she asked Alex, 'that you have got the right people, you've got them playing to their potential, but the system needs an overhaul?'

Distrusting Joy's ability to sustain detailed sporting analogies, Philip pressed on: 'Alex, I think she's right, and the process of fixing the system will pick up a lot of those other problems that Marcella spoke about.'

Alex was listening intently and asked us to elaborate.

'Marcella was really saying two things,' explained Joy. 'You have lost touch with some of your key individuals and the whole team needs direction. You've spent a lot of time travelling and a lot of time developing some of your people. That's meant that you have neglected the rest of the group and the strategic direction of the business. Rocky and Marcella think you've gone soft on the team and that they are carrying the load without a sense of where they are going. They can't feel you with them.'

'Apart from that I'm doing fine?' asked Alex ironically, and as brightly as he could muster.

'Actually you probably are,' we said reassuringly. 'There are really only a couple of things you need to do to get things back on track. One is to take time out from the incessant meetings and get back in touch with the whole team, not just part of it. Explain to everyone what your priorities are. They need to know that you are very much focused on running the business as well as developing them individually. You do not need to seek their input on everything; lead from the front on this and show them that you are in command.

'Also, give them a strong sense of direction by outlining the need for a new business plan and the process you will be using to develop and execute it, and explain the benchmarks against which people will be assessed. You need to put a flag in the ground fairly fast or risk losing respect and commitment.'

Back in the Flow

We saw a flash of alarm on Alex's face at the idea of losing the team support that he had worked so hard to build, but he quickly recovered and sought clarification: 'Will letting them know that I am aware of the problem and working on it be enough to buy me some time?'

'That depends how early we've caught this,' replied Joy. 'I think you need to proceed with your planned change of role at once. If you thought that it would be a good idea to get back into the flow of production before all this blew up, the chances are that it is an even better idea now. Only my advice would be to re-establish yourself with a high profile move. If the team think you are getting too soft, then a quick way to renew command and respect is to show them what made you their leader in the first place.'

Philip added, with the conviction of someone speaking from experience: 'Don't be put off by this setback, Alex. Things have obviously gone slightly wrong but you are not the first Player Coach to have been blown off course by the demands of your team.

'Re-establish your position by giving a strong lead. At the same time though, think about what Marcella said. Is it possible that there is more truth to it than you cared to admit at first? Could it be true that you are overprotective towards some of the team? Do you spend too much time locked in meetings? Are all of those overseas trips really necessary? Have you really worked out how to integrate all aspects of playing and managing?'

Alex had a lot to absorb, and it was hard for us to read how he was feeling. When he did speak, like a true Player Coach he was trying to keep spirits up and said as buoyantly as possible: 'What you're telling me is that if Richard's departure was a "heads up" that I was too far north, Marcella is saying that I have let the needle swing too far the other way, with too much people managing and travelling and not enough playing or planning. I'm too far south and need to point more north again.'

We resisted the temptation to make comments about needing a map as well as a compass, but reminded him of the need for all managers as well as travellers to keep checking their position.

We couldn't tell how Alex really felt about the prospect of doing yet more management and yet more producing at the same time as developing a business plan. We concluded that as a Player Coach, Alex would regard it as a developmental challenge to extend what he had been already doing. We suggested that we meet up again in a couple of weeks and, as Alex was leaving to get back to 'today's stream of voicemails,' encouraged him to give us a call if he needed advice in the meantime.

The Story Unfolds

Dear Juniper . . .

Advice was something we seemed to be giving more and more of these days, and one matter in particular was demanding our immediate attention. We were due to submit replies to Juniper@Brandage.com, a weekly online advice column of a marketing magazine. As 'Juniper' we received dozens of emails a week and gave formal responses to five or six of these.

As we browsed through our inbox, we were struck by an email that bore an uncanny resemblance to Alex's story. Dismissing Joy's 'strange feeling about this one' as a case of 'Player Managers on the brain', we set to work answering the mail from someone who sounded just like Alex.

Dear Juniper,
I am a Marketing Programme Director responsible for a portfolio of brands. I have a team of over a dozen people reporting directly to me as part of the global marketing matrix. I hand reared this team myself and have spent a lot of time bringing them on. Quite a few of them actually said they would be nowhere without me and that at one level it is all down to me that the organization is such a great place to work.

Over the years I have built up some good contacts in the executive search industry. While lunching recently with Michael, one of my oldest contacts, he hinted that all might not be well with my position. He wouldn't specify exactly what – he claimed that professional ethics prevented him from saying more – but he said 'the headhunters are talking to your people. You should find out why.'

We have been doing really well so it would be easy to dismiss what Michael says but I have to admit to a nagging doubt that says I should take his words seriously. I have noticed a few occasions recently that my colleagues, the ones who all report to the same person as me, have stopped talking when I enter the room, as though there is something that people don't want me to hear. Also I have stopped being invited to their nights out. I thought this was just because I never had the time to mix socially anymore but after what Michael said I'm wondering if there is something more to it. I asked a couple of people in my own team about this and they seemed a bit evasive. I don't want to open to my boss or burden my close friends. So I thought I would try you! What should I do?

Anon

Dear Anon,
The first thing to do is to check out your source. Go back to your headhunting contact and get him to confirm the rumour. By the way it was news to me that there are professional ethics in that industry but maybe times are changing. At least get Michael to give you a bit more information about the origin of the story: did he hear it from one person, is it all over the grapevine or is it something concrete? Don't put him under so much pressure that he betrays a confidence, but as you seem to be taking his words very seriously, you need a few more clues.

Until you hear back from him do nothing. It is all too easy to react to the rumour mill. I remember the story of Coffee with Ivy. The team leader became a laughing stock because he reacted to whatever he had heard that morning from Ivy at the coffee station: 'I have decided to promote Kathleen because I hear on the grapevine that she has a tremendous following with the creatives.' Quite soon people started planting mischievous stories with Ivy and had endless fun watching the leader respond. It's a lesson that those in power have come to terms with: people play games with each other and they will try it with you.

Find out if games are being played with you here and be sure of your facts before doing anything, especially if you and the team are as close as you say, in which case they will be very sensitive to any changes in your behaviour.

Best,
Juniper@Brandage.com

Alex's New Profile

'Mixed news,' said Alex, as he greeted us two weeks to the day after our first meeting. 'The announcement that I was getting more involved with production has gone down surprisingly well. A couple of my more junior players are a bit worried that I won't have enough time for them and it took me a couple of afternoons to counsel them round, but most of the team seem pleased to see me leading more directly from the front.'

We asked Alex to tell us more about his new profile.

'I ran a successful team briefing on brand repositioning,' he answered. 'It is the first time that I have stood in front of the whole team like that for some time and I have to say I found my stride very quickly. In fact I rather enjoyed it.

'The seven or eight top people in London have started to look at me differently now. Paris, I gather, is happy not to see me so often, Chicago doesn't seem interested either way, but Singapore sent me an email saying that they hoped this would not mean a return to turf wars as they had valued my diplomatic skills. All in all, it's a load off my mind and I feel surprisingly revitalized.

'Marcella seems just fine; she has put away the acerbic tongue and has her tail up about everything. I think you were wrong about her needing my support; she just needed a demonstration that I am still in control. Her voicemails have dropped off considerably and given the smile on her face I would be surprised if she quits.

'But I am having trouble getting through to Rocky. He is very quiet, doing his job, getting his head down but avoiding me. I just don't know what to think. He doesn't seem as open with me as he was. I dread Rocky being the new Richard.' He looked at us, seeking reassurance.

Getting Out of Their Midst

We made encouraging noises, but reminded him not to leave the more dependent players to fend solely for themselves and to give them some reference points by setting benchmarks: 'Intentionally or otherwise, you have become the lynchpin of this group. The trick now is to rebuild things with those you have neglected without the others feeling dropped. It's another level of team development, and you will need to take yourself out of their midst and become the enabler not the doer. By giving them reference points to measure themselves against, you will be encouraging the team to relate more to each other and manage their own work. You can then move out of day-to-day involvement, replacing it with regular feedback on how they are doing.

'This way won't damage the positive climate you have developed within that group, but it will free up your energy for business building, for managing your strategy and for reconnecting with the stronger players.'

Next we checked whether he had done anything about our advice to give the team a better sense of direction. Alex looked pleased we had asked the question.

'In addition to the presentation on brand positioning,' he said, 'I have asked Marcella and one other person in the team to monitor resource usage on projects. I have also set up a new monthly team meeting to look at the rate of programme take-up in the geographies. Each programme team can then see their performance relative to each other much more clearly than before.'

This was all such good news that we forgot for a moment that this was only half of what Alex had to report.

Trouble With Tex

Alex remained as upbeat as he could when he continued with the bad part of his news: 'The real issue right now is with one of the people that I report to. It's the Head of Business Development who splits his time between London and Chicago. I've been "dotted line" into him ever since it became apparent that my portfolio offered our best prospects for growth. Obviously I didn't let on that anything has been amiss and I kept quiet about the Rocky and Marcella outburst, although I did clear my change of role with him. He just grunted, said "We all have to do what we all have to do," but didn't seem overly interested.

'He is a problem for me. He came to us from the food industry, which is much less glamorous than drinks. He's ... well he's ... American. He likes everyone to call him Tex. He was brought in a couple of years ago because of his acquisition experience and his record of building the value of staple brands. Beyond the fact that there is no difference in the way we spell the word "marketing", his culture and mine are worlds apart. He is all action and results. "Today is a day too late," he's always reminding us as he hands us more of what he calls "stretch" targets.'

As we tried to picture the larger-than-life character being described to us, Alex continued filling us in. 'According to Tex, who likes to think he is a champion of the culture in our company, the key to success is delivery not deliverance. He has made it very plain that he has little time for HR or people development. People are the world's most abundant commodity in his eyes and are as disposable as a used Kleenex.

'An HR person came to see him once about his attitude to diversity and he handed her business card back at the end of the meeting. It's a story he seems quite proud of. For him the key to being a good people manager is not to have sex with anyone in the direct team.

'I know he thinks I'm a bit of a wimp and he keeps asking me when I am going to get married. Not only did he disapprove of my coaching and mentoring programme, he finds opportunities to make me look soft. Just to give you an example, at the London office Christmas party last year he cut my tie off just below the knot and left me looking like a clown all evening. After a few bourbons he started flapping his arms and making clucking noises and asked me when we should introduce paternity leave for new fathers. It was after that party that the "Mother Hen" label started to stick. I'm concerned that if I told him about the meeting with Rocky and Marcella, he would make life even more difficult for me.'

This second half of the mixed news delivered by Alex left us feeling that more than his tie was at risk. We felt that as he reasserted his leadership authority with Rocky and Marcella, it was equally important that he build a relationship with Tex. We advised Alex that the only way he could do that was to win his respect by delivering a compelling formula for the future. The programme for structured business development therefore became even more important.

After Alex finished speaking we thought that many problems still lay ahead of him, but we kept some of this to ourselves. Alex seemed to be in a vulnerable position on four counts: the support of his key people had wavered and was only partially regained; he had the tricky job of redefining his relationship with those in the team who had got used to depending on him; he had a culture clash with his boss and, to top it all, his portfolio was under scrutiny as the company's best prospect in an industry going ex-growth. The tough market conditions would create, no doubt, an environment where the company would look hard at performance and costs. We had heard good news and bad news, but despite Alex's almost impervious optimism and good cheer, overall we were left with an uneasy feeling for his immediate future.

Fifteen Minutes of Fame

As Alex left he passed us an invitation, explaining that: 'By the way I have agreed to speak at a press conference given by our trade association. The subject is "alcopops", or our company's attitude towards teenage drinking to be precise. I was going to send Rocky, but now that I've got to get out in front I will do it myself. Fortunately we have a clear positioning statement on this and it will do the team good to see us take a high profile. You said have an impact, and this should do it.'

While not one hundred per cent sure that seeing Alex in lights trying to handle one of his industry's most sensitive and political issues was quite the impact we had had in mind, we were pleased to see Alex being so bullish despite the mixed news. He made us feel as though our presence mattered to him, so despite an impossible diary and a feeling that Alex might be in for fifteen minutes of the wrong kind of fame, we agreed to attend.

By the time we reached the hotel on Park Lane for the Alcoholic Beverages Association press briefing on teenage drinking, the formal proceedings were over and the journalists were doing some drinking of their own.

Marcella greeted us, glowing from being part of it all: 'You should have seen Alex delivering our statement. He was fantastic. When he is on his game Alex is just great, an example to us all! He said he would be a while getting to you. Somebody from a teenage journal has pulled him to one side. She cornered him about doing a piece on alcopops in a story they are doing on some girl who went a bit over the top. It's dodgy for us to be part of real life stories so I doubt he will do it. He just didn't want to be rude to her. Anyway, the bar is over that way. Make yourselves at home.'

Before we ordered our 'Martinis of choice', we looked around at the crowd and decided to head back outside. Although the pile of unanswered letters at our office seemed daunting, tackling them seemed more worthwhile than talking about the dangers of young people drinking alcohol with a group of drink marketing pundits in a free bar.

We heard no more about Alex's big night until a few days later when a copy of *W-kid*, '*the* magazine for young adults' as the cover modestly proclaimed, arrived through the mail with one of Alex's compliments slips attached. He had written the words 'Bloody hell! She said it was off the record' on it, and we opened the magazine with trepidation.

If Alex had been on his game while speaking at the press conference, the journalist had subsequently knocked him off it. Alex had been well and truly set up. She had evidently interviewed him at the Park Lane hotel about the company line on responsible teenage drinking and then gone on clubbing with him afterwards. She had kept a careful record of Alex's personal consumption, noted the size of the bills which Alex said he would put down to expenses, and taken a few choice quotes about how the company was relying on alcopops to restore its volume growth. The story was run under the headline 'Drinking from both sides of the glass', and the magazine suggested that its young readers boycott alcopops in general and those marketed by Alex's company in particular.

'Oh Alex,' sighed Joy as she tossed the magazine aside.

Much Less Than One Hundred Days On

We had planned to contact Alex to discuss the article but he made the first move. Joy was away for a few days, but when she returned Philip recounted how Alex's assistant had phoned to say that he was already on the way over.

Alex is Out

Alex had rushed in, and before he had even sat down said dejectedly: 'I just can't believe this, I just can't believe what is happening to me. Tex called me yesterday and told me "The hen party is over." Rocky is going to take charge of the portfolio; apparently it was all decided weeks ago. I was too stunned to take it in but I got the gist all right – Tex talking about a clash of cultures between my management style and that of the rest of the firm.'

Philip was taken aback by Tex's apparent fait accompli. Although sensing that Alex was at risk, neither of us had picked up the signs that things were terminal. In fact aside from the unfortunate incident with *W-kid*, Alex had given the impression that his situation was being brought back under control. The magazine article cannot have helped, but it appeared that Alex's fate had been planned for some time.

Alex seemed bemused: 'I have given everything to this place. There are people here who would have been dead ducks long ago without me to look after them. Half the people in London, Paris and Singapore have never set eyes on Tex and when they do, guess who will be eating who for breakfast. As for Rocky, no wonder he has been so sheepish of late. Who exactly is going to look after everybody now?

'It is so unfair. Just as I'd got everything sorted, the team was really up for it and the new work structure was bedding in so smoothly. Now I am worried about the organization even more than before. Tex offered to hold a leaving party for me, and when he did I swear his gaze moved to my tie. Anyway, I don't think I can look any of them in the face again.'

Joy was unusually quiet as Philip recounted this. She was experiencing the uneasiest of feelings, as though she knew all of this already. She decided to say nothing but to do a bit more digging and thinking on her own. We put Alex aside to prepare another column for *Brandage*, but after reading about thirty emails Joy's uneasy feeling got stronger. She was looking at another letter from 'Anon':

Dear Juniper,

I'm out of luck and out of the economy. Michael called me today offering me his services. Seemed to hear in the same breath as I did that I was out of a job. My boss was his client and I shouldn't be surprised if Michael had known about all this from the word go. It was good of him to drop me a hint, although I suppose mobility in the job market is no bad thing for his business. CC was right. There was an internal candidate for the job. All this time I thought it would be her (for obvious reasons) or me (for the right reasons). But no they've picked a real Brutus instead. Juniper, my faith in human nature is all gone.

Anon

'Dear Alex', wrote Joy with certainty now that a blinding flash of the obvious had replaced her uneasy feeling. Anon had been a regular correspondent and we had featured him several times in our columns since the first email about Michael the head hunter. We pulled up a sequence of mail from the file that showed our exchanges:

Dear Juniper,
Well I've done what you said. Michael was pretty cagey about giving too much away but it turns out that they have an assignment from us for someone who can beef up the global marketing push. Word is that they think our people numbers will treble in the next two years and they are looking for someone to spearhead the growth. Michael didn't exactly say it and I didn't exactly ask it but I think the assignment is for my job.

Juniper, I'm feeling very uneasy. What next?

Anon

Dear Anon,
The good news is your business is growing. The bad news is you may not be growing with it. You need to find out why. Forget lunch with Michael. Time to do lunch with your boss.

Bon Appetit
Juniper@Brandage.com

Dear Juniper,
I've tried getting into the boss's calendar for lunch. He is over here twice a month. So far there have been several last minute cancellations. Do you think I'm getting the cold shoulder or are we both busy? I'm feeling pretty unnerved by this. How can I find out?

Anon

Dear Anon,
Who does your boss usually talk to? It must be somebody if it isn't you. Try having lunch with one of them instead. Otherwise try to bring the conversation round to the future next time you see your boss.

Good luck.
Juniper@Brandage.com

Dear Juniper,
Thanks for the tip. Success at last. Yesterday I had lunch with CC, who is very close to my boss. I found out that I have nothing to worry about. Apparently they are just using the headhunters to benchmark the job. No one external is likely to be appointed. CC said we had a great internal candidate for the job. Phew!!

Anon
PS thanks Juniper for the great advice

After talking about the strange coincidence and checking our contract to confirm that we were not allowed to disclose our true identity, we replied to Anon:

Dear Anon,
Most careers end in failure but is yours really over yet? If it is then swallow your pride. Insist on a farewell party if it is at all possible. Invite all the team and the former whispering colleagues for a fond farewell. Your team will be feeling very vulnerable at the moment; they have trusted and depended on you. You can't just disappear from their lives without giving

them some reassurance. Your colleagues, especially Brutus, will be feeling guilty. Deep in their hearts they will know they owe you something. Give them the opportunity. But the main reason for partying is your own self-esteem. After a setback we all need to recover. A good leaving party is a turning point, allowing people to pay their respects and get ready to move on.

By the way before talking to Michael about your next move you might want to talk to HR. Ask them about the policy on unfair dismissal for one.

Juniper@Brandage.com

Tex is Toast

When we called Alex after lunch the next day, he was just off to a meeting. Briefly, we reinforced the advice we had given Anon: he didn't have to take this lying down, he should find someone to give him professional advice and if he wanted to stay, he should work on the decision being reversed.

'That's just what I am about to do,' said Alex. 'I have a meeting with the lady in HR. Remember the one Tex dismissed as irrelevant. I'll get back to you later on if there is anything new to report.'

Alex did call us back and told us that the lady in HR had been very interested to hear his story. It turned out that she had not entirely got over having her card returned by Tex and she had been noting a number of incidents where he had ridden roughshod over company protocols. She had a record of cases where, for example, Tex had brought in unapproved headhunters and others where he had run up entertaining expenses that blew the company guidelines to bits. Apparently, a sharp-eyed person in Finance had noticed that one of these had been with the journalist from *W-kid* just the week before Alex's speech and had reported this 'coincidence' back to Alex's friend in HR. Now Alex was handing her a gift – payback time.

He added that she had been 'pretty awesome, describing leaders who thought exclusively of commercial success as being history, and producer managers who could generate results while attracting and retaining diverse groups of talent as being the future. "Trust me, Alex," she said. "Tex is toast."'

Alex had also learned that HR produced two indexes from the annual employee survey to tell them how the organization's senior managers were doing. For both the 'Committed People' index and 'Manager Satisfaction' index, Alex was in the upper quartile while Tex was barely at midpoint. To make Tex's position worse, lots of people in his group had skipped questions, saying that Tex had not given them enough information to answer the items listed.

The lady in HR wasn't going to let matters rest. She had already asked to see the overall head of marketing and was ready to take Tex's unjust treatment of Alex, not to mention her other complaints and suspicions, to the board if necessary.

'The best thing,' Alex said finally, 'was that Marcella had already called HR to say this was a terrible injustice, that I had the support of the team and that, if anything, I should be getting promoted rather than fired.'

As we parted from Alex we told him we were really pleased that his situation was not as black as it had appeared two days ago. A week later we found out what had happened via Juniper:

Dear Juniper,
I'm back. Brutus is being transferred to Chicago and my boss is toast. CC and I are to be Co-Heads of a new function – Programme Marketing Business Development. My team all clapped when I walked in the office today. I couldn't have done it without your excellent advice and a certain woman in HR.

Anon

When we read what we supposed would be Anon's final email to Juniper, we breathed a sigh of relief for our Player Coach. He may have struggled, but now he seemed to be coming out where he deserved – on top of the game and still supporting, and supported by, the team. We began to compose Juniper's response:

Dear Anon,
I know that the postman is always supposed to ring twice, but in this case I was getting worried that there was something about you and the way you managed that was bringing him back again so soon and carrying the same

letter. Glad the worry was unfounded. Now you are back, be magnanimous. Throw the party anyway.

By the way Michael might appreciate an intro to the lady in HR.

Juniper@Brandage.com

Did Alex Meet the Player Coach's Challenge?

The challenge for the Player Coach is to develop talent without losing sight of the bigger picture.

Soon after Juniper's final letter, we met to discuss Alex and Philip remarked: 'There is an Alex in every organization who has lost sight of the business goal. They spend all their time down in the weeds micro-managing and not enough time at the top getting a perspective.'

We agreed that this was the main reason why Alex had nearly failed the Player Coach's challenge. He had lost sight of the bigger picture, becoming out of touch and vulnerable.

Philip had come across many Player Managers like Alex in his time and believed that Alex had become too accommodating of some people at the expense of his own game and that of the team as a whole: 'People who try to accommodate everyone and everything cannot be effective managers. Good Player Managers take a view, at times providing decisive leadership. Knowing when to stop listening and start directing is a key judgement.'

Joy agreed: 'Lots of things were going on with Alex, but the crux of it was that for all of his many positive attributes and the good work that he did with the team, he forgot about what came next. People don't sit still on the shelf like bottles of booze. They have motives of their own and emotions that change all the time. They need constant reassurance, remotivation and reappraisal, and a strong Player Coach finds ways of doing that. Alex had a go, but his approach was to deal with everyone one on one. Sure, Alex needed to be close to each player, but he also needed to stand back to judge how the whole team played. The team needed benchmarks, a game plan and feedback about per-formance. Alex's failure to do this prevented the team from getting a life of their own and created a dependency culture, as well as emotional strain for him.'

We decided that in Alex's mind developing people and going for results were two different things; he never treated playing and people-managing as integrated until after things had come unstuck. He thought he could leave Rocky, Marcella and the other high achievers to their own devices and without direction while he worked with the weaker players, but this caused him to become out of touch with the business.

We concluded that Alex seemed not to be able to link his discovery of coaching after Richard's departure with his previous Player Manager model of driving for results. His emphasis on mentoring at the expense of business systems and business planning earned him the negative label 'Mother Hen' and gave Tex the ammunition to undermine him.

The situation was not helped by the conflict of culture that was clearly going on at the company, a conflict that was epitomized by the clash between Alex and Tex. The business was giving contradictory signals. For example, Alex told us that the company rewarded hands-on doers rather than high concept types and that 'agency types' tended not to go down well in their industry. This appeared to be borne out by the appointment of Tex, a man who is to coaching and mentoring what Big Brother was to open debate. Yet HR were pursuing a different strategy, encouraging Alex to give coaching and mentoring after Richard left, running indices on people's performance and, in the end, rescuing Alex when the contradictory values clashed. Disjoints between HR and the business divisions are not unusual. The organization in general and Alex in particular were fortunate to have someone in HR with the courage to resist a bully like Tex.

Alex came into our conversation on and off in the days that followed and we reminded ourselves that, aside from his weaknesses, he had also displayed a rare capacity for keeping a team motivated and together. People trusted him and gave him their commitment, not least because he had dedicated himself to improving their game. Later that week we were to discover what Alex himself made of it all when he sent what really was to be his final email to Juniper.

Dear Juniper,

Just had to share with you and other brandage onliners some final thoughts on my recent experience. I know the emphasis in our business is on being creative, but I have come to appreciate that other things are important as well. Believe me I have learned this the hard way and if I can help others avoid the kind of nightmare experience I have just been through then I will have been of service to your readers.

KEEP SIGHT OF THE BIG PICTURE – I let this slip away by never taking time out to plan or articulate to the team where we were going. I became too involved in the detail.

HAVE A FRAMEWORK FOR HOW TO COMPETE – Knowing what the enemy is up to is important. More important still is to use that knowledge to make a plan to win.

FIND THE SYSTEM – I was taking on more and more personally. I was overloaded and did not step back to find a system for involving others in the team. I needed to work smarter not harder.

COACHING IS NOT PARENTING – A lot of one on one contact is valuable but at some time the coach has to back out and let others push the pram. People need enabling but not spoon-feeding.

YOU CAN'T PLEASE EVERYONE – I tried to accommodate everyone, even a real conniving journalist and a bad bad boss. I ended up being too consensual taking input from everyone and trying to massage things when I should have taken time out to formulate my own ideas.

TAKE A STAND – In the end I didn't seem to stand for anything. This made me prey to all sorts of criticism and a hostile takeover bid. I eroded goodwill & devalued my own brand.

FIND PLACES TO SCORE – A player coach needs to have impact to retain other players' respect. This time I am keeping my hand in and on the game.

Anon

We were pleased to hear that between us, Juniper, the lady in HR and Alex himself there had been a good outcome to this Player Coach's challenge:

Dear Anon,
Thanks for the tips. You got there in the end. Keep us posted.

Juniper@Brandage.com

9
The Veteran

Recap. We had met Dun, the Managing Partner of Read and Williams the solicitors, at his imposing office. He told us how he had taken over the firm at a time when the partners were calling for change. He had streamlined the business into profit centres and introduced more professional management into its operations, while retaining some client responsibilities himself. At our first meeting he struck us as a perfect example of someone who had successfully met the challenge for the Veteran Player Manager in 'managing the institution as well as the team whilst keeping both fresh'. We listed out the attributes of the Veteran Player Manager as follows:

Typical Strengths
- *Builds systems and protocols*
- *Hones execution*
- *Identifies goals*
- *Creates acceptable boundaries*
- *Instils effectiveness*
- *Playing skills critical at times*

Possible Shortcomings
- *Wedded to the status quo*
- *Overly detached*
- *Not always charismatic*
- *Demotivates free spirits*
- *Protocols applied too rigidly*
- *Overmanages and underleads*

In this chapter we go back into Read and Williams and discover that life holds challenges even for Veterans like Dun. We work with him as he tries to keep the interests of the institution and the various teams within it aligned. Can Dun win through, or will he join his predecessors on the boardroom wall?

Dun's Story

We were pleasantly surprised to receive a letter from Dun inviting us to act as facilitators at the annual offsite meeting of his law firm's partners. Dun's letter suggested that we meet Carol Chambers, the firm's Chief Operating Officer, 'who will run you through the drill'. We discussed at length whether we wanted to be involved in something that sounded like a cross between equestrian dressage and military square-bashing, but curiosity got the better of us and we arranged to meet Carol.

She was a brisk, upright woman in her early forties who had been, she proudly told us, one of Dun's first recruits when he was appointed Managing Partner. 'This will be the first year that we have used outside moderators, but Dun feels that the format needs freshening up a little. He doesn't want too much departure from the usual procedure, just a few new ideas.'

As we discussed terms with Carol, we asked for permission to approach some of the key people to help us understand the business. She suggested that we talk to Ruth Senior, the Head of the Private Client Department, and Adam Hurst, Head of Corporate Law. She also said that she would be issuing what she described as 'joining instructions' to the offsite. We took these to mean invitations and asked to be included. We arranged to meet Senior and Hurst, but before we could do so received a letter signed by Dun inviting us to the offsite and enclosing the programme, which is shown below.

Disappointed to find that so much had been fixed in advance, we suspected that it was a template from previous years with changes in the dates and a few of the names. We agreed to make the best of things and to find out what the two people nominated by Carol Chambers had to say. We would be listening hard for issues that might be otherwise suppressed by the rigid structure that had been imposed on

**15th Annual Partners' Weekend, De Montford Manor Hotel, Hampshire
Friday 4th–Sunday 6th November**

Friday 4th
Hotel lobby and Orangery
3.30 pm–4 pm Tea and check in
Plenary session, John Adam Room
4 pm–5 pm   Managing Partner's welcome and address
5–6 pm   Review of last year's action points
Bar and William de Villiers Room
6.30 pm   Drinks and dinner
                         Dinner speaker: Sir Justin Prentice QC, 'Is Scale an Issue
                         for the Modern Law Firm?'

Saturday 5th
Hotel restaurant
7–8.15 am   Breakfast
Plenary session, John Adam Room
8.30 am   Introduction, Philip Augar and Joy Palmer
Syndicate sessions
9–10.30 am   Working Parties in Syndicate Rooms
10.30–11 am   Coffee, Orangery
11 am–1 pm   Syndicate reports and discussion
Leisure time
1.30 pm   Coach departs for England versus South Africa rugby
                         match at Twickenham, picnic lunch provided on coach
Bar and William de Villiers Room
7.30 pm   Drinks and dinner

Sunday 6th
Hotel restaurant
8.30–9.15 am   Breakfast
Plenary session, John Adam Room
9.30–11 am   Closing remarks and discussion, Managing Partner

*Dress throughout is smart casual but jacket and tie or their equivalent
must be worn for all meals in the de Villiers room.*

the weekend, a rigidity that we more than half expected to find in the day-to-day management of the firm.

A Visit to Read and Williams

The View from Private Clients

Ruth Senior, we both agreed later, would be the solicitor we would select to deal with any pressing family business. Her air of calm authority instilled great confidence. She was in her fifties, immaculately dressed and coiffured, and made notes with a slim enamel and gold fountain pen on a tiny leather-backed jotting pad. Not that we could imagine Ruth ever forgetting anything.

'So you're the pair chosen to liven up the offsite,' said Ruth with a smile as she poured our tea. 'I hope you don't spoil the fun. A lot of the partners view this as the firm's official holiday weekend, a chance to catch up with those who work out of town and to renew acquaintance with colleagues who, over the years, have become good friends. Of course plenty of business gets done too, but we all feel very comfortable with Dun at the helm and no one really wants to challenge his view. He is wiser than most of the rest of us put together, and not much will go wrong with this firm with Dun as Managing Partner.

'I was here when he took over. He introduced a lot of new ideas, a vision for the future, and a structure for the organization that binds us all together. One of the best things he did was to get us all to focus on profit as a measure of success, not at the expense of client service but as something to go along with it. It transformed the atmosphere, bringing urgency and excitement alongside our traditional values of high-quality, impartial advice. And of course he very kindly asked me to take on my current role, which I have found immensely satisfying. He is an amazing man. Besides running the business, he still handles several key client relationships himself.'

We asked Ruth whether there was anything to trouble the tranquil scene she had just described.

'Well, of course the competition never stands still and there is a lot of change in the air in our industry. We can't afford to fall behind our competitors in what we offer our clients or indeed our staff. But we are aware of these things, they come up at the ManCo, and we try to stay abreast of them.'

At our request, Ruth then elaborated a little on ManCo, particularly how it operated: 'We meet monthly for a whole afternoon to deal with the formal things, but the real business gets done at a dinner held the night before. We all attend – the business heads and the heads of the support functions – and Dun usually raises some issue that is on his mind or that one of us has raised with him. It is a very jolly affair, like a good dinner party, and I find it an excellent place to discuss business issues.'

Ruth did not add much to her advice to keep the offsite running along familiar lines, a view she appeared to hold in respect of the whole business. She left to see a client, and although our suspicions remained about the stiflingly conservative atmosphere, we could see little to get our teeth into as we waited a few minutes for Adam Hurst to join us.

The Corporate Lawyers' View

He arrived a minute or two late looking harassed, but we were soon to learn that he was a walking tornado and probably had to worry a lot to stop himself blowing away. He told us that he had been picked by Dun to join the firm when, as a junior solicitor, his firm was working with Dun's on a large deal.

'I seemed to impress him and he invited me to jump ship. A few years later, when Dun got the top job, I was surprised to be given management responsibilities for the corporate law team which, although small, was very profitable. I've tried to look after the reputation, we've had a bit of luck along the way and we are still regularly involved in many big transactions.

'Dun has continued to have an impact on the business even though he is no longer a full time member of the team. Soon after he became Managing Partner he suggested that certain routine aspects of client service could be standardized, and that helped us cut costs and improve delivery. This was something that was much easier to see from above than from the coal face, but we were all very impressed that he was able to devise and implement such change.

'He is still around to help with client relationships and, although he does less of the actual execution work nowadays, his judgement at crucial moments is invaluable. Which is not to say we don't face perpetual challenges that, quite frankly, seem to get harder and harder to deal with. Thankfully we've got the great man to do our strategic thinking for us, although some of these issues are going to tax even him.'

We asked Adam to outline what these were.

'They are similar to the challenges facing many businesses in the professions. Are we big enough to compete with the best? If not, are we too big and distinguished to be a niche operator? If we are going to compete with the best, can we as a partnership fund our expansion and indeed do we have the management talent to drive that growth? Just look at what is happening in the profession. New York firms are merging with London firms, London firms are expanding on the Continent, the whole legal framework is getting blurred by European legislation and the days of a simple domestic business managed by a few senior partners on behalf of the general partnership are numbered.'

Presumably you talk about these issues, we inquired.

'In a fairly general Dun-like way, yes,' Adam replied. 'But I have to confess we don't seem to be getting very far. In fact, one or two of the middle ranking partners are beginning to rattle the bars of my cage a bit wanting to know what is going on. I don't like to tell them the true answer which is "not very much at all".'

We confirmed that these younger partners would be at the offsite and, after Adam had gone, we phoned Dun to ask for permission to approach them. To our surprise, he said that he was free at the moment and would appreciate an update on preparations.

Dun's in Command

We reported that there might be some issues for the firm simmering below the surface and asked whether Dun thought that the format he had proposed would bring them out.

He leaned back in his chair and smiled: 'We have the highest profit per partner on record at the moment and we didn't get to that position by wasting money hiring consultants when there was nothing to consult on! You are involved precisely because we do face these issues and, by the way, the same goes for Justin Prentice. If his speech on scale and the partnership doesn't make people sit up and think, I shall be very surprised.'

We were learning not to underestimate Dun, who seemed to be the

Veteran Player Manager we had been told about. We had heard how he had brought a more systematic and businesslike approach to the firm, and how his judgement at key moments was 'invaluable'. Furthermore, he seemed to be aware of the key strategic issues. Although reluctant to change the programme ('there is plenty of flexibility in what we already have'), he did give us clearance to ask Hurst for permission to interview Richard Parker, 'one of his young men in a hurry'. Hurst grinned at Dun's respect for protocol, readily agreed that we should meet Parker and introduced us to him later that day.

A Young Man in a Hurry

Parker clearly wanted to unburden himself of some of the things that were on his doubtless fine mind. He launched into an eloquent analysis of the firm's position, speaking slowly at first but building up to a crescendo as his anger mounted. Despite his passion, at no time did he lose the logical flow in his argument.

'I do not share the view that this is a well-run business. It used to be, but the people at the top are too old, too out of touch with clients and unsure of how to cope with the issues of today. Frankly they bore me. I was invited to one of their monthly ManCo dinners to put forward the views of the younger partnership. By the time we had discussed the state of the Test Match, eaten our way through three heavy courses and lit the cigars, it was nearly 10 pm. Who wants to start a serious discussion at that time of night when you have to be back at work a few hours later? They go for rituals and ritual kills off spontaneity, so in the end I said very little. Mind you, I do notice that the issue of scale is on the agenda at the offsite, so maybe my attendance did do some good.'

Parker paused. We were intrigued by his account of what was evidently another of Dun's rituals, and we asked him if there was anything else that he wanted to recall about the dinner.

'Only that the smell of cigar smoke hung about my suit for days, infected the rest of the wardrobe and I had to take the lot off for dry cleaning to get rid of it!'

We sensed that Parker had a lot more that he wanted to say, so we asked him to describe what it was like working at Read and Williams.

'It's what I imagine the Civil Service to be. I'll give you an example of how committees and bureaucracy run this place. I went to school with a chap called Jamie Lemington, eldest son of the Lemington business dynasty. I've been down to stay with them for lots of weekends in Oxfordshire and got to know Jamie's father, Lord Lemington, quite well. Eventually I brought him in to lunch here with Dun and Adam, and shortly afterwards he rang me inviting us to act for them on an offshore tax transaction. This would have been a big piece of business for me and the firm and would have given a clear message to the outside world that we had moved into the modern age, acting for entrepreneurial companies like Lemington's.

'But do you know what happened? Dun's bloody Risk and Reputation Committee turned it down due to a so-called conflict of interest, although none of us could see any conflict at all. I heard a whisper that Dun didn't think it passed the "smell test", but more likely it got in the way of something he wanted to do with one of his so-called clients.'

We asked what it was that was 'so-called' about Dun's clients.

'He tends to think of our clients as his own. He often knows the chief executives or chairmen of our clients, and there is an impression in the firm that this is why we get the business. This causes irritation with my team, as they have often been working their socks off with the slightly more junior people who make the decisions. He is a bit inclined to come waltzing into a transaction halfway through, we waste a great deal of time briefing him and then he goes away and reappears at the closing ceremony! If he is going to get involved, he should do it properly.'

This was a different perspective on Dun to anything we had heard elsewhere, but it confirmed our instincts that the heavy overlay of set-piece procedures at Read and Williams might have caused the firm to have clung to the status quo a bit too long.

We tried to get Parker to elaborate still further but his legally-trained conservative tendencies finally got the better of him: 'I've probably said too much already. But if you want to get a sense of how out of touch this management has become, go to one of their Town Hall meetings. There'll be plenty of room for you, the numbers have been dwindling for a couple of years and the real movers and shakers no longer attend. It is a stage-managed ritual with a few planted questions from Carol Chambers' stooges. The sad thing is Dun really believes that it still does some good.'

After Parker had gone, we stayed in the meeting room at Read and

Williams to collect our thoughts. We were not surprised that Parker resented Dun who, like many Veterans, probably had a natural tendency to overcontrol the free spirits in the firm. We agreed that Dun, whilst impressive and capable of surprising us with his insights, might have become overly attached to the status quo. He had not yet lost widespread support and indeed still enjoyed the respect and devotion of his most senior colleagues, but he would need to freshen up his approach if he was to retain the support of the junior and middle ranking partners. How he responded to the strategic issues facing the firm would probably decide whether he could find a new lease of life as leader.

The Story Unfolds

The Offsite

Day One

The tables in the John Adam Room had been arranged into a horseshoe shape with a large name card at every place and Dun at the head. His review of the year began promptly at 4 pm; after some words of welcome and an explanation of our role in the weekend's proceedings, he began a tour de force of the legal profession at that time.

Although referring to the issues of scale and competition that were on everyone's mind, he focused principally on the firm's performance: record revenues per partner, costs growing more than inflation but by less than the increase in revenues, and a large increase in profits. He referred to notable cases and transactions and mentioned by name those who had performed particular heroics. Ruth's Private Client department was praised as 'an island of stability in a sea of change,' and the heads of the support functions were singled out. After Carol Chambers' review of last year's action points, the session closed punctually at 6 pm and everyone went off to unpack.

When the partners reconvened in the bar, some of them were looking forward to the after-dinner topic and others were struck by the theme of change that had run through Dun's speech. While Richard Parker and a few of his team cornered Joy and asked her what we were doing here, Philip was getting to know some of Ruth's key people. They appeared reluctant to mix with the corporate lawyers and were clearly enjoying being together again out of class, 'as though they were on school outing,' we agreed later that night.

At 7.30 precisely a gong was sounded, a butler announced that dinner was served and everyone filed into the de Villiers Room. After dinner Dun introduced Sir Justin Prentice as a distinguished lawyer, an old friend of the firm and, we were assured, an accomplished after-dinner speaker. We were not to be disappointed.

Prentice paid due homage to the firm, its partners, and to his lifelong friend Dun in particular. He then outlined the changes that firms like this faced, referring to clients' expectations for global coverage, the increased risks in the personal liability of partners for funding expansion, and potential negligence claims. He acknowledged the advantages of independence and partnership, but argued that this would be a model that could apply to niche firms only and that 'businesses like yours will need to decide which way to go.'

When he finished speaking, you could have heard a pin drop. Dun allowed the silence to sink in for a few seconds before thanking Sir Justin for his 'typically incisive and thought-provoking remarks, which I have no doubt will be discussed and dissected in our plenary session tomorrow.' Dun referred to the custom of paying the dinner speaker at the annual offsite with a case of whatever the guest cared to nominate; he assured Prentice that a note of his preferences would be taken before he departed.

We resisted the temptation to join the throng in the bar and sat in the conference office debating what we had just heard and its implications. Dun and Prentice had been at school and Oxford together, their careers had been closely intertwined and Philip had a feeling that Dun was godfather to Prentice's eldest child: 'It just has to be a set-up. That was Dun speaking, not just Prentice, and this whole thing has been arranged in advance. Us coming here, Prentice's speech, all of this is Dun's way of bringing issues out into the open without appearing to be leading the charge himself. But why would he do that, why not just say it himself?'

'To keep the support of Private Clients,' replied Joy, already ahead of him. 'You can't see Ruth or any of her people going along with merger or global expansion, can you? At the same time, Richard Parker and his merry band are not going to hang around while the ManCo wrestle with these issues after they have finished discussing the Test

Match and lit the cigars. Dun doesn't want to line up with either side at this point and he has brought us and Prentice in to get people to show their true colours.'

'In that case,' Philip said, rising, 'we need to "Ask the Audience". I'm off to persuade Dun to introduce a little technology into the weekend's proceedings.'

Day Two

After Prentice's thought-provoking remarks the previous evening, there was an air of quiet expectation in the John Adam Room when we reconvened on the Saturday morning. We explained how the syndicates would run; Joy joined Group A which was to discuss 'Partnership or partnering: some recommendations', and Philip joined Group B to consider 'Global or local: our choice'. Groups C, 'Issues facing the legal profession' which included Dun, and D, 'Involvement in the community' attended by Carol Chambers, were tangential to the main issue and are not discussed here. Carol had arranged the groups to be cross-representative of the age, experience and functions of the partners in the firm. The groups had only ninety minutes to discuss these issues before returning to make a fifteen-minute presentation to the full meeting.

Joy's group, 'Partnership or partnering', spent a lot of time debating whether or not this was the right forum to raise such an issue. A group of Private Client people blamed us for proposing such a discussion and were surprised that Dun had permitted it to go ahead. Richard Parker and a few others from the Corporate Law and Taxation departments grew impatient at the concentration on procedural matters, claiming that it was typical of the firm's obsession with bureaucracy and protocol. At one point Parker almost lost control, jabbing his finger angrily and shouting, 'Clients! We've been talking for nearly an hour and no one has yet mentioned the word! That's what is wrong here. The senior people pay lip service to being interested in clients, but what we actually get is meddling and bureaucracy with no real attention to what the clients want. Our competitors offer a global service, and here we are still needing to get approval for business travel to New York. This place has become all talk and no action.'

Parker's outburst amounted to public criticism of the senior management. Although some of the partners appeared uncomfortable at what had been said, no one actually spoke up to disagree with him and it was clear to Joy that questions about Dun's leadership were at the back of everyone's mind. She decided that this would be best raised privately with Dun and brought the meeting back to consider the equally contentious issue that they were meant to be discussing.

Philip's group, 'Global or local: our choice', held a lengthy debate about ambition and what that meant for Read and Williams. Philip detected a feeling, which no one was quite prepared to say openly, that the senior management had stopped driving the business forward and was content to rest on past glories. Although criticism of the leadership was less explicit than in Group A, doubts were uncomfortably revealed as they debated the best future direction for the firm. In the end this group also split along sectarian lines, with the Private Client people lining up behind a strong national brand and the corporate lawyers arguing for a push into a global marketplace.

When we reconvened, it emerged that Richard Parker had been elected spokesperson of Group A and it was he who gave the first presentation. He tried to put both sides of the question, but it was clear from his tone and body language that he was firmly in favour of merging with another firm:

Presentation A: Partnership or partnering

Slide 1
Advantages of partnership
- ➤ Good image for certain clients
- ➤ Strong internal bonds
- ➤ Encourages long-term thinking
- ➤ Popular with staff, paternalism
- ➤ Continuity
- ➤ Tax advantages

Slide 2
Disadvantages of partnership
- ➤ Risks staleness
- ➤ Discourages change
- ➤ Funding constraints on future growth
- ➤ Gives small-scale impression to big corporates
- ➤ Limited skillset

Slide 3

Issues in partnering

➤ Culture clash?

➤ Management issues

➤ Might alienate traditional clients

➤ Increased burden of corporate governance

➤ Would cause staff and clients to review loyalty

Slide 4

Attractions of partnering

➤ Broadens capital base

➤ Broadens product range

➤ Increases flexibility to attract new staff

➤ Gives positive impression to clients

Parker's presentation was much more balanced and lower key than the impassioned speech he had made in the syndicate room. He set out the pros and cons of the two alternative business models but did not address directly the issue of leadership, and the audience followed his example by asking searching questions in an equally moderate way. People's reluctance to comment on what was obvious to many was, Joy noted later, 'a bit like being at a meeting where no one mentions the fact that there is a rhinoceros in the room.'

The presentation from Group B was given by a fast-rising young partner from the Private Client department, following a similar pattern to Richard Parker's, although this speaker's personal preferences were clearly conservative.

Slide 1

Global means . . .

➤ Large staff

➤ Many locations

➤ Large corporate infrastructure

➤ Opportunity to be in important cases and transactions

➤ Better career opportunities

➤ More resources

Slide 2
Global might also mean . . .
➤ Impersonal
➤ Risk and reputation issues
➤ Loss of special relationship
➤ Less profitability not more

Slide 3
Local means . . .
➤ Knowing your colleagues
➤ Knowing your and others' clients
➤ Predictable costs and revenues

Slide 4
Staying local risks . . .
➤ Standing still while others race ahead
➤ Losing clients that want a global service
➤ Losing staff who want a bigger challenge

Slide 5
Should it be 'Global or Local'
or can we be
'Global and Local'?

The debate on this was more vigorous and touched on the different lifestyles that people within the partnership wanted, some arguing for traditional values and work patterns, others preferring a faster-moving pace. The issue of drive and ambition at the top was not directly discussed but, as with the previous debate, remained an unspoken and uncomfortable subtext.

After the presentations of the remaining two syndicate teams, we brought things to a close and Dun got to his feet. If there was a rhinoceros in the room, he was not going to let on that he had seen it. He reminded everyone that it was a tradition at the partners' weekend for all to join in the Saturday afternoon social activity and that the Saturday evening session would be kept business-free. There would be no exceptions, he stated firmly, to attendance at the rugby match, although it was not compulsory to support England. One of the partners, a South African, was slapped firmly on the back at this point. Dun reminded everyone that the coach would leave promptly at 1.30 pm, that 'a packed lunch and some appropriate refreshment was on board,' and that the rest of the day was for pleasure.

Later That Evening

It was nearly midnight by the time that we got to compare notes about the day and to finalize our plans for tomorrow. We agreed that in addition to the original question of strategic change that we had been brought in to facilitate, we had confirmed two further concerns. These were Dun's leadership style and his role as a player, the latter being of particular interest to the corporate lawyers in the firm. Uncertainty about the firm's future direction had surfaced in part in a direct way, but also indirectly in the form of doubts about Dun's effectiveness. All these matters would need to be addressed at some stage.

An unexpected chance to discuss them with Dun himself came when, shortly after midnight, he joined us in the faculty office. 'There's one hell of a discussion going on in the bar right now,' he said. 'I thought I'd leave them to get on with it. I tried telling them that business was banned until tomorrow and they pointed out that it's after midnight. That's lawyers for you, an answer for everything! How do you think it's going?'

We gave Dun the essence of our thinking: that the partnership was divided about the future direction of the firm and that there were some major management issues bubbling away. Dun was inscrutable and it was impossible to tell whether he was surprised or alarmed about the news, but he asked us to say more.

'There are opposing views about the question of merger, and the partners are lining up along functional lines between Private Clients and Corporate Law,' we told him.

Dun was evidently hearing nothing new, for he merely nodded and asked about the other matters we had referred to: 'By "management issues" do you really mean "leadership issues"?'

Our answer was less than direct. We told him that there were issues of management style that were bothering some of the junior partners who felt that the senior management had lost touch and that the firm had become excessively bureaucratic. We went on to say that this reflected the anti-managerial culture that we had found in other professional services firms overlain with anxiety about the firm's future direction, and that open discussion of the strategic issues would do much to defuse the whole situation.

Dun remained impassive and thought for a moment before answering: 'I agree that if we can settle on the future direction, everyone will be a lot happier. Perhaps we had all become complacent and too set in our ways. Reaching the right strategic decisions won't be easy, but it provides us with an opportunity to reinvigorate the whole firm. It's an opportunity I for one look forward to taking.'

We had intended to be fully involved in the following morning's session and had prepared a comprehensive set of questions to use with an Ask the Audience machine. But after hearing our analysis of the partnership's mood, Dun changed the plan: 'I think I would rather run the whole thing myself, if you don't mind. It's all nicely set up, we've given them a bit of time to think and talk it round amongst themselves, but I think they need to hear a bit more from me.

'Now what I need you to do tonight is to explain to me how your box of tricks works. I think that's going to come in useful. We've got a lot to do tomorrow, and I still want everyone to be home for Sunday afternoon with their families.'

Dun's Closing Speech

Day Three

The conversation over breakfast was dominated by the Sunday papers, which splashed the story of Department of Trade and Industry investigators going into the Lemington Corporation where corporate fraud was suspected. Photographs of Lord Lemington and Jamie and their country house in Oxfordshire, together with allegations that shareholders' funds had been overstated, provided a juicy alternative to speculation about the likely content of Dun's closing remarks to the partnership. However by 9.30 attention had returned to matters closer to home; there was a respectful silence as Dun got to his feet.

'Good morning everyone. Congratulations to you all for getting downstairs on time. At least I assume that you all managed to make it upstairs to your rooms after last night's festivities! For those of you that have been down here all night, please ensure that someone else drives you home!

'In some respects this year's partners' weekend has been true to form. A wide ranging, thought-provoking speech from our guest on Friday night, Sir Justin Prentice, and contributions from many of you that showed the passion and enthusiasm we all feel for the business. I should also like to pay tribute to my secretary, Marilyn, for all of the hard work and careful planning that she has put in over the past few weeks to ensure that this occasion has run smoothly.

'However, you will all be aware that this weekend has also been unusual in many respects. For the first time we have used outside facilitators and that has helped to provoke more outspoken comments than we sometimes receive. It would be disingenuous of me to pretend that this departure from the norm was unconnected with the important issues that have been under discussion this weekend, issues that we will not resolve today. However during the rest of this morning, before we break to spend the few remaining hours of the weekend with our families, I should like to move the debate on still further.

'Some of you will be familiar with the quiz programme *Who Wants to be a Millionaire?*. Contestants can under certain circumstances ask the audience for its collective view and the audience is very rarely wrong. It has occurred to me that if a randomly assembled audience at a television game show usually comes up with the correct answer, a gathering of some of the country's finest legal brains might do even better! Therefore I have decided to apply the same principles to running the firm this weekend!

'On the table in front of each of you is a keypad enabling you to answer some questions that I will put to you over the next half hour. Your answers will be processed by the computer in the corner and displayed in aggregate on the screen behind me. Please be assured that your individual answers are completely anonymous. The aggregate replies cannot be disaggregated and traced back to an individual keypad and, in any case, today there is no seating plan so that there is no record of who is sitting where.

'Four syndicates met yesterday and each produced an impressive summary. The presenters from Groups C and D who considered community- and industry-wide issues will join this week's management committee dinner, when we will consider carefully their proposals before reporting back to the full partnership once we have decided what to do. We as a firm take these issues extremely seriously and they will be given full and deliberate consideration, and we thank the members of those syndicates for their valuable work.

'However, time is short this morning and I wish to give a full airing to the topics that were given to Groups A and B, since these require the contribution of us all and cannot be delegated solely to the management committee. These topics concern the role that this firm will play in a rapidly changing profession. Can we remain at the leading edge of our chosen areas whilst still remaining independent? If we remain independent, can we remain at the leading edge? If we are not at the leading edge, is there still a profitable and meaningful role for us to play in the profession? How would the firm be changed by merger and would we still wish to remain in it? The answers have far-reaching personal and professional implications for all of us, and we will not be reaching a hasty conclusion. What we can do today is to begin the discussion and to form a picture of the partnership's current view. Would you now be kind enough to use your keypads to answer the following questions:

Q. All other things being equal would you rather be here today or at home with your families?
A. Home: 100% Here: 0%

'There are of course circumstances where total anonymity cannot be guaranteed! The next questions are to be answered in groups, first by the corporate lawyers:

Q. Would you rather be a partner in a niche firm or a partner in a leading player?
A. Niche partner: 30% Leading player: 70%

'And now for other members of the firm, the same question:

A. Niche partner: 65% Leading player: 35%

Q. Can your department flourish as a niche?

'Corporates first:

A. Yes: 35% No: 65%

'And now the rest:

A: Yes 75% No: 25%

'To conclude I would like to sound out your views on our chances of success.

Q. Are we flexible and agile enough to respond to the competitive challenges that lie ahead?
A. Yes: 50% No: 50%

'A typical lawyers' answer, "on the one hand, on the other hand"! But seriously, thank you all. None of you will be surprised to learn, and I am certainly not surprised, that the interests of the corporate and Private Client practices are beginning to diverge. The powerful trends to globalism and scale that are increasingly prevalent at the top end of the corporate market, where we have some presence, are much stronger there than in other specialist areas.

'In the corporate world, as Sir Justin and others have stated this weekend, the clients require massive resources from their leading suppliers. Through our excellent relationships built up as a result of expert advice delivered over many years, we have been able to retain many of our existing top corporate clients but we are finding it increasingly hard to win new ones. The corporate law partners are, in my judgement, correct to view scale, and by implication merger, as essential if we are to remain at the top in our specialist areas. Failure to remain at the top will be a dispiriting process for those that remain here. Our best young talent will leave, the best candidates will turn us down, and our clients will steadily marginalize us.

'This process will have consequences for those of you in other areas. Profitability will be seriously affected, morale will suffer as your staff and clients cease to see us as a winning firm and, before long, there is a chance that globalization will begin to make itself felt elsewhere just as it is in corporate work.

'I know that some of you have been critical of my involvement with clients. To those of you who think that I get in the way, I make no apology. It is important to me as an individual and to the firm as a whole that the senior management stays in touch with developments at the sharp end of the business. We have to stay fresh and that means being involved. Others, no doubt, believe that I am not involved enough and criticize the build of overhead and management structures in this firm. But as we have heard this weekend, the world is changing.

We have to adapt to survive. The old world of personal relationships and management that could be done in one's spare time has gone and I, like many others in my position, have to rely on strong support to ensure that the firm runs smoothly.

'You will, I imagine, want to know where I stand on the major issues we face. My view is that if this firm is to survive, we should look very hard at two options. The first is to spin off Corporate Law to a competitor. There is no room for sentiment and the audience is rarely wrong. You have shown me by your answers today that, in your heart of hearts, you know that the corporate law business can only flourish as part of a bigger firm. We should investigate that possibility, which would have the advantage of allowing our other specialists to remain in partnership as a group.

'The second possibility, and to my mind the only credible alternative to spinning off Corporate Law, is to merge with another firm. I simply do not believe that we can carry on as currently structured. Margins will slip, morale will suffer, stress will increase, and the value of what we have will decrease. Some of you will be shocked to hear that I see the choice as being so stark. This is not a view that I have reached hastily or without a good deal of discussion with colleagues on the Management Committee, although not all of them would agree with me.

'This weekend's debate reminds me of another partners' weekend several years ago, when there was also an undercurrent of change. I saw then the stresses and strain that the senior management inflicted upon itself by not bringing these things out into the open and I have no intention of allowing history to repeat itself. If I have been slow to respond to the changes in our industry I am sorry, but my colleagues and I on the Management Committee will not allow them to pass us by. We are in for an interesting year!'

With that Dun sat down and looked around for questions. There was a moment's silence and then a forest of hands went up. Some argued about the issues, others argued about the process, believing that there should have been written warning about the serious matters to be discussed. Acknowledging this, Dun promised to commission a full independent review of the firm's position and to convene a full partners' meeting to consider the options. Few in the room were in any doubt about the likely outcome.

Dun brought the meeting to an orderly conclusion. Most left silently, and only Richard Parker and a few of his colleagues gathered enthusiastically round Dun. Ruth and some other partners were talking quietly in another corner, but the vast majority had checked out before breakfast and were back in their cars making their way up the hotel's tree-lined drive within minutes of the closing address.

One Hundred Days On

Dun was out of the country on business the first time that we went back to Read and Williams, but he had instructed his secretary to set up a full schedule for us. Adam Hurst, we were told, would bring us up to speed with developments.

'Consultants, consultants and more consultants,' was how he summed up the previous three months. 'The week after the offsite we had a ManCo dinner that was a bit different to usual. We got straight on with presentations from the two remaining groups from the offsite, discussed the broader industry and community aspects they had raised and they left after coffee. We then got down to the real business. Dun was a bit sheepish about how far he had gone at the offsite and apologized for not discussing it fully with us in advance. This was very unlike him; he is normally a stickler for doing things by the book, but as he said, certain issues needed raising that went beyond the remit of those of us round the table. We all understood that, and in some ways our respect for him grew. There comes a time when leadership has to replace consensus, and I think even Ruth Senior appreciated that we had reached such a moment.

'Rather than debating the issues there and then, we agreed to get on with appointing consultants to help us review our options. Later we held a beauty contest with four firms presenting and finally chose KEPY. Briefing them has taken up a lot of time – I sometimes think they should be paying us, not the other way round – and then we have had to set up sub-groups involving quite a few of the partners and associates together with a communications programme to keep everyone in touch. And that is in addition to keeping the business up to scratch.'

We asked Hurst how the staff and partners had reacted. He suggested that we speak again to Richard Parker for a view from the radicals. This meeting was difficult to arrange for, as Parker told us when we finally got together, 'Work has taken over my life at the moment. Basically I am running one of KEPY's sub-groups; in addition Adam has given me some of his management responsibilities because he is so busy working with the consultants, and on top of that my biggest client is involved in a contested takeover. There aren't enough hours in the day and I can't really find anyone to whom I could delegate.'

We resisted the temptation to introduce Parker to Roger, our Rookie Player Manager, but asked him for his assessment of the mood of the partners.

'I think a lot of us would now concede that we underestimated Dun. There is no doubt in my mind that the bureaucracy and committee work had, and still has, gone too far and his insistence on meddling with my clients is very irritating. However you have to admire the way he has responded to the pressure for change, even though it was only just in time. Also you can't help but admire his judgement, for example in keeping us out of that Lemington business and in holding the firm together despite the diverging aims of the two big departments.'

For once, Parker had too much on his plate to spend time discussing the firm's problems with us and he soon dashed off.

Exactly on time Ruth Senior arrived, saying that she was equally impressed with developments since the offsite, although as Joy remarked after we had met her, it would take a French polisher to get underneath her professional veneer. 'Of course we are all disappointed that things may have to change. But it is right that we examine our options, and all of us in Private Clients understand that the firm may eventually split into two. However if that occurred, we all hope we would keep the Read and Williams name and that Dun would stay with us.'

Philip asked Ruth whether she felt that the great man had let her down by springing a surprise at the offsite.

'You know, in our heart of hearts, it was not such a surprise. We had discussed these matters at the ManCo, and although it would have been nice to know what Dun was planning, still waters often run deep. No, I don't think any of us should criticize Dun for that.'

Did Dun Meet the Veteran's Challenge?

The challenge for the Veteran is to manage the institution as well as the team whilst keeping both fresh.

Dun himself invited us to lunch a few days later after he had got back from his trip. We were entertained in the boardroom at Read and Williams, an impressive oak-panelled room hung with portraits of Dun's predecessors. 'What sort of hanging do you think I'll get?' asked Dun with a smile. 'Head and shoulders in oils or strung up from the nearest gallows?'

We asked him what he thought he deserved.

'It's probably too early to tell because a lot will depend on the outcome of the strategy review. I did have a sense that I was losing support earlier this year and I put that down to the challenges facing a business like ours. These issues had to be addressed, but it is very hard to judge precisely when to lift the lid. It may be that we were a year too late, but once the lid is off these things there is no going back. I feel it is better to be too late than too early.'

Was Dun surprised at the criticism we had uncovered about the firm's management?

'I was disappointed, but not entirely surprised. After all, the reason we employ people like you is partly to help bring out issues that are bubbling under the surface. I need to know when people have concerns and sometimes they are reluctant to speak directly to their seniors.'

We gently pointed out that there was also criticism of his perform-ance as a player. Behind his back some said he meddled too much, others that he was losing touch with clients; what did Dun think of that?

'It may be that I am so aware of the second criticism that I am guilty of the first, but surely I have a voice in this too. I would not wish to be Managing Partner if it was just dry administration and besides, I think I add something with clients.'

We asked Dun whether he felt stale after five years in the job.

'That's too good a question. After a while one becomes aware of doing things in a certain way and they become comfortable and rou-tine. At what point should they be changed? I suppose when they stop working; and in all honesty, after the record year we have had in financial terms, I do not feel that they have stopped working yet.'

After the lunch we discussed whether Dun had succeeded in meeting the challenge for Veteran Player Managers, a challenge defined as 'managing the institution as well as the team whilst keeping both fresh'. Undoubtedly Dun had been an agent for Read and Williams for several years and had demonstrated many of the positive attributes of Veteran Player Managers. He had built the organization into an effective force, one that for many years had given the partners and staff a good living and a culture they were happy with.

Dun, as with many Veterans, was attached to the status quo and if he had not opened up the barriers to change, Parker and the other young corporate lawyers could have formed an influential dissident group. However, on the key strategic issue, *we and others mistook a conservative style for inflexible thinking*. In reality, Dun was driven by the same business logic as his junior partners and he initiated change at just about the right moment.

Good as we believed Dun's mastery of these strategic issues to be, his conservative style was less impressive. Even in a profession not noted for being progressive, Dun's preference for ritualistic meetings such as the Town Hall debates and for formulaic structures at events like the offsite and the ManCo discouraged spontaneous interaction with his colleagues. Many of these forums had been good in their day but needed freshening up, whereas Dun took comfort from their familiarity.

In doing so much for the institution, Dun had perhaps neglected the other part of the Veteran's challenge: working for the team. Dun's involvement as a player was criticized on the one hand by those who saw it as interference, and on the other by those who thought that he and other senior managers were not doing enough playing and had become just an overhead.

Although Dun may well have been *insensitive in taking so much of the credit for the business*, his senior-level contacts will have done much to improve relationships between Read and Williams and their clients. But people like Richard Parker and other more junior members of his team needed to believe that it was all down to them and Dun should have allowed them that privilege. *Knowing when to let go* is something that all Player Managers have to understand at all levels, but many Veterans have *a tendency to over-control and stifle Play Makers* like Parker.

Finally we discussed the Lemington affair, an intervention that illustrated Dun's *ability to make crucial plays at defining moments* but which left him respected rather than heroic. Philip reflected on Dun's overall leadership attributes. 'To start with, I thought he was like many Veteran Player Managers, a remote, slightly dull, conventional type. He had an air of impressive authority but was not what you might call charismatic. Their reaction to his brilliant decision on Lemington was one of rueful respect rather than adulation. But then he takes a really bold initiative on the firm's future, and you think, well, he really has got something, there is something commanding if not truly inspirational about him after all. It's why he emerged as the genuine article: a Veteran Player Manager.'

IO
The Play Maker

Recap. Vikram is the Play Maker amongst our Player Managers. As a member of the executive at AlphaSolva, a computer services business, he oversees operations and is directly responsible for special projects, termed Big Bets. His ability to transform situations came to the fore during AlphaSolva's Schism of 1994 when he pulled the company round after it had lost many of its key people. As master of the unexpected, the Play Maker's unique contribution is to be able to transform a situation by taking things in a completely different direction. This can jeopardize the Play Maker's support, because others would rather keep things as they are regardless of the state of the game. We summarized the Play Maker's challenge as being 'to lead the team in new directions without disappearing out of sight', describing the attributes as follows:

Typical Strengths
- *Thinks on the edge*
- *Unafraid to challenge authority*
- *Catalyst*
- *Undeterred by adversity*
- *Transforms the game*

Possible Shortcomings
- *Disruptive*
- *Not always responsible or credible*
- *Expensive user of resources*
- *Disconnected from others*
- *Chaotic*

In this chapter we are invited by Vikram to help him 'stir things up'. We meet people from his design team and from the executive team who, despite having tremendous respect for Vikram's talents and history with the company, begin to question their allegiance to him when he becomes overzealous about reconfiguring the business. Will Vikram finally disappear over the edge?

Vikram's Story

A few weeks after meeting Vikram, we received an invitation to join an AlphaSolva webcast. The subject was 'Collaborative Working: The Next Big Idea', and Vikram was to be the host. We connected up with the AlphaSolva web site, followed a sequence of steps that seemed to be taking us through a tunnel of swirling stars and finally reached Vikram's page. He started off the webcast as follows:

In the 1990s companies spent billions on solutions for the connectivity that underpins collaborative working and called it collaborative working as though that provided the answer. Then attention turned to content which in turn has led people to start to understand the intangible processes that add value to content; in short, knowledge sharing. Today we have with us a panel of thought leaders from the field of KM and collaborative working and in a moment they will share their incomparable insights about developments in our field. These present new and unbounded opportunities in the market of enterprise relationship management. Opportunities for what we at AlphaSolva predict will be the 'Age of Sharing' . . .

Vikram continued in a similar vein for some time, telling us how a recent project at AlphaSolva had led to a 'collaborative software' breakthrough. He then brought into the discussion his panel members who, if anything, surpassed him in the number of thoughts and buzz words contained in a single sentence. We tried desperately to stay with the thread of the argument but were still trying to make sense of it all when, just after lunch, Vikram called us.

'Did you get chance to see the webcast this morning?' he asked, explaining that now that the Age of Sharing was a business theme that his clients were buying, there was no excuse for AlphaSolva not practising what it preached. As he had no intention of missing this newest wave, he was proposing some 'human factor' improvements internally. He was already asking questions around the key ideas and suggested that we meet later that week so that, in his words, we could 'keep tabs' on him while he 'shook things up.'

Before we had chance to meet Vikram however, we received another call from AlphaSolva. It was from a man called Andres Hernandez. We learned he had taken over from Vikram in running the Americas, was also a member of the executive team and was over from the US that week: 'I gather Vram spoke to you yesterday and that you will be coming over later this week,' he said. 'When you get here, be sure to pop in and see me.'

The Dark Side

AlphaSolva had offices close to Windsor. We arrived there, jaded and thirsty after a couple of wasted hours sightseeing from the M25. We were already forty minutes late for our scheduled appointment with Vikram but were told by the receptionist that Vikram had had to pop out and had not yet returned.

'Client meeting?' we asked, saving her the effort of offering the usual excuse for Player Managers who are running late or otherwise engaged.

'No I don't think so,' replied the receptionist, innocent of our cynicism. 'To be honest, I don't know where he is.'

To avoid hanging around AlphaSolva's reception area – where tongue rings, tattoos and Teva sandals seemed to be de rigueur – we asked if Andres Hernandez was free. He was, and we were immediately on our way up an Aladdin Sane style coloured staircase to an open workspace with cubicles only in the four corners.

Our hopes of being offered water or coffee quickly faded. As soon as we sat with Andres in one of the cubicles, he narrowed his eyes and said, 'Look, we call Vikram "Vram" for a reason. It stands for Very Random Access Memory. Let's just say Vikram's mind is like the moon. It has a bright side and a dark side, and if he is going to get religion about the Age of Sharing internally then some of us just might want to take his dark side on. I called you in to say that the business is run by the executive and not Vram, so please don't go way out there with him without a safety line back to the ship.'

Bemused as much by the verbal and visual allusions to entertainment from our own age as by anything he had said about Vikram, we needed time to recover. Andres left us at the AlphaSolva demo room and there we waited another thirty minutes for Vikram to return.

'So you are already here, come this way, so good to see you again,' enthused Vikram as he welcomed us into another cubicle which looked very much like the last one, except it was orange instead of purple. 'I see you've met Andres. He is a great supporter of the Age of Sharing. I know he will be right behind everything I envision for collaborative knowledge platforms and multifocal work groups in a soon-to-be one globally integrated team of our designers.' He scarcely needed our encouragement to say more.

'Last time we met, didn't I mention how we had cancelled the regular Big Bet review meetings and now called them for special purposes only? Well, one of the design teams felt we were getting uncompetitive on costs and called a meeting to talk about it. Following that meeting I set up Taskforce Dvorak to investigate best practice everywhere. I told them to come back with some recommendations in a month.

'And boy, they did just that. Project Dvorak reported that even though our organization is flat, we are still compartmentalized when it comes to transferring best practice across projects. They estimated that the cost of reinventing the wheel in every region for solutions that could easily have common system kernels is about $750,000 to $3 million a project. Not only do we take the hit directly on the bottom line, but it is becoming an issue in major bids where a few of our best customers have started grumbling about value.

'The people on Project Dvorak said that if only we could set up some system for knowledge sharing, and make some part of the programme management organization responsible for embedding and reusing the know-how from each system by embedding it in kernels, we could reduce costs by around $10 million by the end of next year. Operational efficiency is my job, and as well as that, a lot of our new business knowledge is generated through Big Bets. It's an exciting challenge.'

'Have these findings and proposals been shared more broadly with anyone else?' enquired Philip, who had so far said nothing while drinking the coffee we had at last been offered.

'Only with Andres in the US and Claudia who looks after Europe and Asia,' replied Vikram. 'They were both completely onside and very encouraging, so I plan to take the idea forward at the XT meeting at the end of the month.'

'XT meeting?' we asked.

'Yes, it's our executive team meeting; we have one every three months. First though, I want to get more input on the idea from the guys.'

'How are you going to do that?' asked Joy.

'By asking some Vram-type questions and seeing how they run with it, of course,' replied Vikram, evidently pleased with the idea that provocation was what he was famous for. 'I thought you might want to observe this so you could watch a Play Maker in action,' he added.

Vikram had clearly taken to heart the label we had suggested to him when we first met and was in an unstoppable mood of excitement about the changes afoot. 'I'm planning to post everything on our intranet tomorrow morning. All the programme managers and designers can look at it and complete a short questionnaire about how things are run around here. We'll hold a web conference at the end of next week. I hope you can participate. The results will speak for themselves and the XT will want to go forward automatically. It will be so good for us all. And this time, unlike the Schism of 1994, the changes won't be precipitated by a crisis.'

On our way back we had plenty of time to reflect, moving forward as we were at about 15 miles an hour.

'Was he like that when we first met him?' asked Philip, still reeling from the torrent of words and ideas. 'He's nearly over the edge.'

Joy had seen this type before. 'He's engaged. It is hard for anyone else to keep up when people like Vikram are running with an idea. The "high" they're on blinds them to the need to manage its impact on others. While they have a vision for where they are heading, for others it is just a blur.'

Cunning – Or Naive?

The ramifications of Project Dvorak, tied to the Age of Sharing, were more significant than Vikram suggested. It seemed to us that under the 'shared' arrangement Vikram was about to propose, the principle about who took decisions about new developments would shift away from the regions. Vikram's unfolding play, his internal Big Bet, implied transfers of power and accountability with political implications that could cause resentment. Despite Vikram's confidence that Andres was onside, we felt that Andres saw only the dark side.

Wanting to alert Vikram to this we tried to get hold of him from the car, only to be told that he was tied up. Our voicemail was not returned and when we called again a couple of days later he was out of the office. In the end his assistant, Kyle, gave us links to the web questions Vikram had sent out to 'all associates' and the web conference that would be held in a couple of days. 'Vikram really wanted to be sure you could take part,' Kyle added.

Before we could look at the questions, Andres phoned. 'I am calling from Washington,' he said, 'where about six of my top guys are up in arms about some questions Vram put out on the intranet. He said he was going to do something like this, but I had no idea he would post it to my guys as well without checking in with me first. Vram thinks we can't see through his game plan, but believe me, people here are saying that the Age of Sharing belongs to the free software movement not AlphaSolva, and they have no intention of working in a bazaar.

'This time Vram is too far out. When I spoke to him an hour ago he said, "Andres, stay with me. I'm a Play Maker and this is really what our business needs." I don't give a damn right now what a Play Maker is, but if you have given him any ideas then you'd better be able to bring him back through the atmosphere with the ship intact.'

Nervously we went to the site where Vikram's questions were posted. We discovered that the bazaar Andres had referred to related to Eric Raymond's essay contrasting the open style bazaar method of developing software in self-organizing teams with the more structured cathedral approach.[1] Vikram had asked everyone to read it ahead of the web conference to stimulate debate around Project Dvorak's ideas for more shared and flexible approaches within AlphaSolva. He had also posted the taskforce's detailed proposal for a new operating structure, which we soon realized was going much further than Vikram had indicated to us in his cubicle.

We couldn't help feeling that developments of this magnitude, which had aroused emotions as intense as those just expressed to us by Andres, were better handled in a less public, less virtual manner than an intranet questionnaire. When we looked at the questions for the associates, it was apparent that Vikram understood very well the cultural changes implied in the proposal. He had asked everybody to indicate which of a series of statements they believed to be true. They could provide supporting examples and additional comments if they wished, and he would host a 'chat' based on the views expressed. He had thanked everyone in advance for their contribution, saying that the executive team were interested to hear all associates' views and would not form an opinion of their own until after that time. The statements appeared on the screen as follows:

Do You Live in the Age of Sharing?
Check the following Statements that ring true to you:
● Winning in global markets demands stable controlled management of AlphaSolva's resources and talent
● The existing regions and departments fragment the knowledge needed to develop solutions to complex business problems
● Flexible and informal project structures will give AlphaSolva designers most freedom for creativity
● People need to know unambiguously who's boss
● Managers at AlphaSolva need to be more collaborative and less controlling
● Networks of knowledge are a remote ideal
● The best managers of people's performance are themselves

We discussed whether Vikram realized what he was about to unleash and Joy summed up our feelings: 'It depends whether he has thought about this politically as well as logically. He is either very cunning or extremely naive. Either way he is likely to be in for more than he has bargained for when he hosts the web conference.'

The Story Unfolds

Out of Sight

The number Vikram had given us enabled the three of us to discuss with each other what was happening on the screen. The web conference, held across three time zones, revealed that out of all possible respondents 80 per cent had completed the web questionnaire, with an even higher take-up from the Americas. Vikram said playfully to us on the phone that the confessional nature of the Oprah generation might explain some of the disparity in the response rate. As Vikram was telling us this, comments began to appear on the left side of the screen.

'Why did no one in the executive take part?' the first comment asked.
'Do as I say and not as I do', appeared a second comment underneath.
'Didn't you read the accompanying email' chastised the third, 'the executive are waiting to hear our views. AlphaSolva is an Open Society!!!'
'Get on with the results' said the fourth comment, and as no other comments appeared Vikram took the 'get on with it' as indicative of the mood.

He showed a series of charts and then moved to a summary of the additional comments. We studied the charts very carefully because we wanted to understand what support there was for Vikram. Further, we wanted to observe just how Vikram responded to any disparity between his views and the body of opinion in the business. We feared that Vikram, like many Play Makers, would move too far too fast ahead of the players whose support he needed, thus risking the credibility of his proposal as well as his personal reputation.

'Mixed' Reactions

The charts showed that Vikram was indeed a long way ahead of the rest, but that the regions were very divided. In Europe there was a lot of support for a more open approach to resource and knowledge sharing. One comment seemed to sum up the mood: 'I have a feeling that we are duplicating a lot of our effort and I am quite happy to share more information about our systems and to trust other people to use that knowledge well. I would also like to think there was a repository of system kernels somewhere that we could replicate as appropriate. It would shorten the delivery cycle on about 60% of our projects without making the overall solution anything less than bespoke.'

In Asia the views seemed fairly balanced and were reasonably made, although the overall commentary was limited. In the US however, opinion was undoubtedly against Vikram and there was a strong preference for retaining as much local control as possible. A number of the comments from the US were quite barbed ('The Age of Sharing: who are you kidding? The Cage of Sharing more like'). Others revealed a deep concern for product quality under the proposed changes: 'Only local project managers who own relationships with the immediate customer stand any chance at all of interpreting solution needs and designing solutions that maximize project delivery to time, quality and cost. If we let go of this tried and tested approach to control, our track record of success will go to the dust.'

After these slides had been shown, a flurry of comments appeared. Vikram said to us on the phone, 'Hmm, more of a mixed reaction than I expected. I wonder what gives with the US crowd? They are usually the first to jump at any kind of idea towards a more global approach. I don't understand why everyone can't see the obvious logic and cost benefits of what is being proposed.' The 'mixed reaction' showed that the mood of the Americans wasn't so much confessional as enraged:

– Vram just tell the executive that you don't have across the board support for this.
– Tell them no project manager in his right mind would operate in this arrangement.
– I don't agree. We could give it a go if the regional heads were onside, the benefits are obvious to see.
– This is one big bet that will fail. Vram you are too way out.
– At AlphaSolva information is still power. We can't even partner within the regions when it comes to forecasting and planning the accounts. No way can we operate with global networked processes.
– Agreed! In my sector we are still in the 'age of watch your back and Not Invented Here'.
– It's a recipe for confusion and chaos Vram. Only you could throw something like this into play.
– Vram it's wacky but not out of play. It is helpful to think about resource sharing this way. We could pilot a knowledge product. It could become the repository for several sectors in Europe.
– I'll watch the European Union then.
– V you don't get that this will kill our culture of freedom. No designer will be able to say that's mine and no designer will feel accountable for problems.
– Jack Dvorak now.

Vikram wound up the web conference, promising participants that they would be hearing from him soon, but stayed on the line to talk to us. Joy wanted to understand how it was that Vikram had so misjudged the opinion of the designers in the US and how he had managed to miss the concern that Andres had made so clear to us. She felt that as we had heard a lot from Vikram, we now needed to broaden the conversation.

'Vikram, let me suggest something,' she said. 'Why don't Philip and I follow up by calling some of the people who were online? We could also speak to some of your colleagues in the executive before you take this information back to them. You don't seem to have enough support to carry Project Dvorak through, and a web conference can't get to the bottom of the resistance that clearly exists. After a few conversations we would all have a fuller grasp of what is going on.'

Vikram wasn't too happy about the suggestion. He felt that whatever people were really thinking should be said in the open directly and should not need a 'third party agent' to draw out. 'I've relied all my life on the Socratic method of enquiry,' Vikram explained, 'and to me this is just a more tangled enquiry than we normally experience. To get through, don't we just need more and better questions, more honest debate?'

'Look, Vikram,' replied Joy as sensitively as she could, given that she was fighting an urge to mention the hemlock of Socrates' final fate, 'Socrates also said, "Wisest is he that knows what he does not know". You don't know and we don't know what all this heat is about, and my guess is that more of the same method of enquiring will simply entrench opinion. It won't help you find out anything new.'

Vikram clearly saw our offer of an intervention as an affront to his open methods but he was also open to the idea that all alternatives should be tested and curious to see if we could add anything. In a manner that was more mischievous than resigned, he said, 'Go for it. If you think you can add something, then add something!'

Feedback on Vikram

Anxious not to lose the moment, we immediately arranged follow-up calls. After speaking with his colleagues, we gave Vikram the feedback in a summary document divided into three sections.

Barriers to Change

- Project Dvorak was too secret squirrel. Why should we be interested in proposals from a 'taskforce' when it didn't even seek our views?
- At no time has anyone sat down and tried to explain what this change would mean for me.
- Whatever Vikram is up to has all been put across in slogans about the Age of Sharing and Orwellian-style presentation on the web. It's thought control not thought leadership. I would have expected better from Vikram than that.
- Instead of all this 'Age of Sharing' management babble, why the hell doesn't Vikram just get his head down on the projects we are trying to bring in on time and to cost? We need bread today not jam tomorrow.
- Vikram has invented a whopping great sledgehammer to crack a tiny nut. The issue is project costs, not social reengineering at AlphaSolva.

Image as a Play Maker

- Vikram always makes the same mistake when he makes his moves. Engineering people is not as simple as engineering software.
- Project Dvorak is a clumsy power play for Vikram to grab much more central control of the design process. It would be a mistake.
- Vikram is always too focused on one big thing at the expense of day-to-day practicalities. Unfairly or otherwise, people feel he does not have the interest of the people or the business at heart.
- When Vram sees the wisdom of the idea, he forgets that he still needs to persuade everyone else. 'Right' rarely proves itself. Less rhetorical questions and more practical realism would help.
- I feel like a pawn on an invisible chessboard. Vikram asks for my ideas but I know his mind is already made up, even if it is unfeasible or lacks support.
- Vikram is so 'in your face' with ideas using all the technological power at our disposal to get 'input'. Yet when I need a simple answer to a customer problem on a project I can't get Vikram even to hit reply on his voicemail. The man is great as long as you don't actually need anything done.

Opportunities for moving forward

- Vikram has upset the US, but here in Europe there is a lot of goodwill. My advice would be to push on the most open door.
- Vram has to physically sit down with his taskforce and a group of people in the US to really share the Dvorak blueprint. If he doesn't, we are in for a turf war.

- Tell Vram to think of the exec as a place to build coalitions, for joint problem solving among everyone.
- Best practice in Asian projects could be easily replicated. I wish we had been asked to showcase this ahead of last week's web conference.

Vikram finished reading and reflected for a while. We asked him whether he might have triggered something that could easily have been avoided.

'You mean I let the cat out of the bag without thinking about where it would run,' he replied. 'I think I can see that. I can also see what to do next.' He looked at us, said, 'Well, thanks for giving me the feedback. It's been highly instructive. I'll let you know how I get on,' and the meeting was suddenly over.

We were a bit taken aback that Vikram didn't feel the need for a broader discussion but he was off in his own thoughts. We knew that he flourished in adversity and, given that we had already gone further than his desire for us simply to 'keep tabs' as observers, we decided to email him some ideas on how to build coalitions but otherwise left him alone.

After Vikram had gone we reflected on his motives. We were inclined to give him more benefit of the doubt than were Andres and the US project managers. We believed that Vikram was driven purely by ideas and an urge to move the business forward. Political considerations and power plays were far from his mind. He was so wrapped up in his thoughts about playing and how to reshape the game that he had neglected the managing part of his role. He was displaying the Play Maker's classic tendencies to be disruptive and had lost sight of others' needs and expectations. Now he was dangerously close to blowing his credibility.

His last internal initiative had occurred when the business faced a crisis and those in senior positions had little left to lose. This time it was different because the business was still going well. With no obvious need for new approaches, Vikram had to manage his intervention carefully, a trait that does not come naturally to many Play Makers.

One Hundred Days On

Our next contact with AlphaSolva came from Kyle, Vikram's assistant, who told us that Vikram would like to meet us again soon. Before then, would we mind speaking to Andres and Claudia, the two other regional heads, and also to four people involved in running design teams and the programme office?

The first person we talked to was Claudia. She was travelling to the US the next morning and offered us an early get-together at the Heathrow Starbucks located in Terminal 4. It was our first contact with her, and we soon wished that we had had the benefit of her perspective from the outset.

A Piece of Her Mind

Holding her latte in one hand and turning her cell phone off with the other, Claudia said: 'Vikram is one of the most creative people I have ever met. He is so good at keeping things open when the rest of us are running out of ideas. He has a knack of asking the unexpected question and usually when we need it. Sure, it slows down immediate progress and that is inconvenient, but it has to be wise to take a step back from time to time and question the assumptions upon which the business is being run. On this Vikram is first class.

'Project Dvorak was one of the few things that ever derailed him. In fact to be honest, I don't think it did derail him psychologically. It was all a big experiment for him, but he lost a lot of support from people to whom he had been a god since he pulled the business back from the brink in 1994. The hardest thing for Vikram to take was that people really began to believe he was doing it for his own ends and not for the benefit of us all. On this, I think he has now done some real learning.'

We were fascinated to know what had happened while we had been away and asked Claudia what had caused Vikram to learn.

'When he came to the XT about Project Dvorak, he made light of the resistance that was building,' Claudia replied.

Hearing this surprised and alarmed us. We remembered our feedback session with Vikram and how he had seemingly taken the point on board that he prematurely let the cat out of the bag. What had happened?

'Vikram started off the meeting by saying that he had a proposal for improving operations,' she continued. 'He said that the people on the executive who would most benefit were onside with the idea, and that although a few people were still warming up to the proposal a bit more discussion would sort things out. By the time Vikram had said all this, Andres was boiling. He muttered something very strange about Vikram and the dark side of the moon and then said that blatant takeover moves like this were doomed. The rest of us were shocked as Andres is not normally given to outbursts but Vikram, well, he was gobsmacked. Apparently he had visited with Andres the week before and everything had been agreed between them, so he couldn't understand the sudden U turn.

'Frankly, I couldn't face the idea of a pissing contest between two very stubborn and independent-minded men, so I offered a way out or a way forward, depending on how you like to look at it. I suggested a pilot across three projects in Europe. It really wasn't that hard. The rest of the XT were still trying to understand the detail of what was being discussed but were silenced by Andres' unusual aggression. When they realized they could postpone understanding for another three months, they all said, "Well done, Claudia," and congratulated me on my pioneering style.

'After the meeting I gave Vikram a piece of my mind. I told him to grow up and start listening. I added, probably without justification, that having to deal with a fortysomething iconoclast in every XT was a bore. Unless he wanted to blow his credibility with the design teams, it was time he got his hands and his head round the social mechanics of introducing new operations. At the time he seemed too shellshocked to take it in. Yet by Monday I realized we would be good business partners on this.'

'So why the conversion?' we asked.

'On Monday Vikram came into my office and showed me a migration plan. He actually mentioned you two by name, saying you had given him a guideline on how to influence and build coalitions. While he had not looked at it until after the outburst at the XT, he thought it might give tips for implementing the pilot.

'This was a turning-point. The pilot has been running for eighty days now and we have an interim report on its progress at the end of its three months. Vram and I have a meeting scheduled for this next week after I get back from the US. By then Andres will be in the loop on progress, and I will have tested his support before we make the next move.'

There's No One Like Macavity

We were left wondering how it was that Vikram had marched into the minefield despite our feedback, but were now due for the other calls. As we hadn't time to get far from the airport before these were due, we had booked a small meeting room in a hotel close to the terminal.

Our first call was with a member of the French team called Marina who was also at an airport, Charles De Gaulle, outside Paris. 'I've only got a few minutes for this,' she shouted, 'I need to get to my gate.'

'We won't need long,' replied Philip. 'We just wondered if you had any comments on Vikram who . . .' But before he had finished Marina cut in, shouting, 'Oh, Vram! Tell him I told you I'm a great fan. He's tops. Just last week we . . .' and then the call was lost.

When we tried calling back we went into Marina's voicemail, so we made our next call to Seth, one of the four current floating members of the executive and Head of the Programme Office. He had, we learned, been a friend of Vikram since the early start-up days. We asked whether he had felt positive or negative about the new operations proposal.

'The thing about Vikram is that he just isn't into any kind of control. It makes him a great mentor and friend, but a dreadful manager. When any other person would say, "Right, what do we need to do to get this done?" Vikram will ask, "Why do we need to do this?" and throw out ideas about what we could be doing instead. I was on the taskforce of Dvorak and I have stayed fairly close to the pilot. I know how deeply hurt he was about Andres. He felt betrayed not by the disagreement but by the fact that Andres saw him as wanting to take control. It couldn't have been further from the truth. As I said, Vikram doesn't know the first thing about control.

'I ask you, which man is more dangerous: Andres, who would take total control of the oxygen in the building if he could, or Vikram, who might one day turn off the supply altogether just to test out what oxygen is really for? I told Vikram years ago he is precisely the sort of person that could accidentally start a war.'

At this stage our picture of Vikram was becoming much clearer, as was the error of judgement he had made. Our remaining calls gave us variations of the same message and also provided much more information about the detail of the pilot in Europe. Everyone agreed it was going well, but as for the wider implications it was still too early to tell.

By now it was time to call Andres. 'Hello,' he said, 'I bet you two are furious with Vikram, aren't you?'

'Why would that be?' we asked.

'Because he ignored your normally very expensive advice. Didn't listen to a word of what you had to say from what I could tell. Just the same old, incorrigible Vikram. Wants to impose the Age of Sharing on the rest of us when he cannot share a single idea. Took a big insult from Claudia to knock some sense into him as well as some straight talk from me. You must have heard it all by now, big plans reduced to a rinky-dink pilot in Europe. Still, I expect it is something we can all "share" and learn from!

'You know the thing that bothered me most was the man's insistence that the cost problem needed a total rebuild. But why not look at resourcing and do something about utilization? If we had a problem with costs, we could have found some very easy wins here. Our projects are usually top heavy with senior designers. It doesn't need to be that expensive. I had been pulling together some data on this that I was about to share with my guys and then . . . Well, you know the rest.'

'But why was Vikram so sure he had your support?' we enquired.

'Don't ask me. What am I supposed to do when, after someone has floated a few ideas with you, they then take your lack of a direct NO WAY NEVER as a sign of a contract in blood? It's too hard to argue with Vikram in any case. You can drown in the rapids of his rhetoric. I never for a moment suspected he would create an online plebiscite without bringing it through the regions first. Who did he think he was, Bill Gates or the President?'

We wanted to know from Andres where things stood between him and Vikram.

'I'll tell you after I have seen Claudia this afternoon,' Andres replied. 'To be honest, it's awkward. We are avoiding each other. I know we are doing some good things with the pilot. There's a link where you can go to check weekly progress and post questions. I don't want my guys to think we are the world's largest island over here, so we have stayed hooked in.'

'So what do you anticipate will happen when it is time for the pilot to report to the executive?' we asked.

'That depends on Vikram, doesn't it,' said Andres before hanging up to take another call.

On the journey back to London, we talked about what we were going to do with the feedback and how best to advise Vikram to tackle the awkwardness with Andres. Philip admitted that he had 'never known anyone harder to read and so I've no idea which approach would work best for him. Should he be up front about it with Andres or should he leave it to Andres to take the initiative?'

'The problem is we are dealing with Macavity,' said Joy. Philip looked blank. Joy had tried him with obtuse allusions to T. S. Eliot before, so she knew she would have to quote in full from 'Macavity, the Mystery Cat':

> *'Macavity, Macavity, there's no one like Macavity,*
> *He's broken every human law, he breaks the law of gravity.*
> *His powers of levitation would make a fakir stare.'*[2]

'OK, OK, I get it,' replied Philip. 'He's hard to pin down. That's true enough. And he doesn't readily heed advice. As we will not be able to pin him down, let's go with the flow and refer only to the feedback or the issue with Andres if we get him engaged.'

Closing the New Schism

Vikram had been keen to see us as soon as possible after we had spoken to his colleagues, so we arranged another meeting in Windsor. Back in the orange cubicle Vikram seemed more animated than usual. We could see from the way he was looking at us that something had captured his attention. 'Emotional agendas,' he said immediately. 'That's the sticky thing. I get it now, whereas before I was convinced the business benefits would be enough.'

'Well, you are not alone with that one, Vikram,' said Philip. 'I was in a presentation once when a division head interrupted the business case I was putting forward by telling me not to confuse him with facts, as his mind was made up.'

Vikram smiled, and Joy reminded him of 'that famous quote from Galbraith. You know the one about changing one's mind. It goes something like "Faced with the choice between changing one's mind and proving there is no need to do so, almost everyone gets busy on the proof."'

'I can now see that my job is to make sure that the proof doesn't get too hardened!' said Vikram, grinning. 'Your hints and some coaching from Claudia have opened my eyes a bit. I just didn't stop to think how Andres would feel, whether the move could be threatening to him or not. I hadn't got myself pencilled in for glory, but if I had asked just a few simple questions or had taken time to really allow Andres to talk while I listened, it would have been obvious that this could be one interpretation. The other thing I have learned is that provocation isn't always the way to bring people with you. In fact it can alienate support, irrespective of whether the questions are the right ones or not. But tell me, what do I need to do about Andres?'

We suggested that he was facing another schism, this time a personal one: 'You can start to close the schism by making a gesture. Make the effort to visit Andres before the executive meeting. Listen to what he is saying. He seems to have some very practical ideas. Try to interweave his ideas with yours, maybe by finding something you can work together on.'

'I'll do it,' Vikram said. 'We haven't missed a beat on the pilot so far and we don't intend to miss a beat in the future. The Age of Sharing includes me too.'

'Vikram,' Joy said as we were leaving, 'you are democratic to a fault. And I mean to a fault.'

Did Vikram Meet the Play Maker's Challenge?

The Play Maker's challenge is to lead the team in new directions without disappearing out of sight.

As we got ready to leave Vikram, we felt that if the Play Maker's challenge was being met, then it was as much to Claudia's credit as his. Her initiative in proposing a pilot in Europe, where there was already considerable support, probably saved Project Dvorak as well as a more damaging breakdown between Andres and Vikram. We touched base with Claudia on our way out and spoke to her about what we had called the Play Maker's Challenge. We asked for her opinion and she made several good points, as follows:

Changing without a crisis.   'The key to Vikram's problems was that, in a sense, there was no challenge for him to meet. Unlike the time of the Schism of 1994, the business was moving forward smoothly and there was no pressing need for a radical shift in operations. At moments like this people believe change creates rather than averts crisis. Yet when I told Vikram that most people fear change, he replied, "But why, when it is so exhilarating?" Someone who is high on their own game can't see that new moves threaten people who thought they knew what was what.

Managing the emotional agenda.   'Vikram saw this as one more design project where logic would win the day. But by ignoring the important factor of how the people affected felt about things, Vikram caused anxiety, suspicion and downright opposition. Win the emotions not just the minds, was something I told him. Do not rely on the power of logic alone to win people over.

'A consequence of people's insecurity about change is that there is a need to make them feel part of the process. Getting them to understand the logic behind them is a part of it, but not the most important part. Vikram probably imagined the first question people would ask to be "What is the specification or plan?" But faced with the prospect of change, most people immediately think of another question: "What does this mean for me?" This fundamental misunderstanding of how people react to new departures nearly cost Vikram and AlphaSolva dear.

Keeping high touch.   'People need time to trust new ideas and work out the impact on them. It is easier to work out where someone is coming from and for people to test each other's understanding when they can see each other. In a place like AlphaSolva we can over-rely on technology and Vikram made communication too complicated. Environments where people feel safe and free to be open are unlikely to be big forums, however democratic. Even if everyone understands what is going on, people are reluctant to voice concerns. A slogan such as the Age of Sharing can add to the distance. Slogans are valuable in launching initiatives, but only if the promise feels real. Vikram has done some great things with customers, but in the marketplace he is working with a defined need. Internally there was no groundswell of opinion for new operations. The sharing idea needed more "high touch" efforts to build goodwill, whereas Vikram relied only on the forces of reason and technology.

Being inclusive. 'Vikram missed this one. Early on he could have gathered input more broadly and tested the water with his views. Instead he believed that his small taskforce was the best way to pull the proposal together. While this added speed and focus, this benefit was outweighed by the consequences of creating an exclusive pocket of new thinking. This thinking was then in danger of being rejected by the very people it was intended to benefit – for no reason other than its failure to include them in the first place.

'Vikram is about as cunning as a cookie, whereas Play Makers need to be more than great originators; they need to be great manipulators as well. For someone like Vikram, the idea of acquiring the skills of manipulation or influence would seem distasteful. But I bet most Player Managers would prefer to be labelled politically astute than politically naive. The difference between the two is the ability to say more than "Here's an idea. What do you think?" or even "Here's an idea and I know it's right." Skilful Play Makers know how to say to others: "This is what I stand for. Please join in," in a way that stimulates support and ownership.

Staying within sight. 'Most people here were happy with the status quo and they resented Vikram's proposal. But he wasn't attuned to this and carried on running with his idea until he was out of sight. He left confusion in his wake. The fact that he went for such a big idea exacerbated this, especially as he missed quick wins to be found closer to home. I imagine that Play Makers that stir things up and provoke change under these circumstances often end up with nicknames like "Vram" or are labelled "blue sky dreamers" and "unrealistic".'

Claudia's summing up was spot on. Vikram found disturbance thrill-ing, so he was surprised that others felt anxiety and resentment at his interventions. His enthusiastic efforts to push through his ideas led to suspicions that he was engaged in a political power play. Everyone but Vikram understood how his ideas could be misinterpreted. However we shared Claudia's view that he was without guile and that people's suspicions were ill founded. He was an imaginative visionary swept up in the force of an idea and, like many Play Makers before him, disappeared into his own logic and out of sight from the team – leaving them wondering where and why he had gone.

11

The Player Again

Recap. In this chapter we revisit two people who had given up their Player Manager roles to return to full time producing. First we talk to Maggi, a classic top player promoted to management in a call centre where success with clients was the key to respect. In the end the dual demands of playing and managing had proved too much, and she was moved back into running accounts. Consequently she left 'a place where the memories were painful and where I felt I had failed' to make a clean start. Next we go back to meet Martin, the maths teacher who knew instinctively that playing was what he did best and took the initiative to get back to his first love. Martin preferred teaching children to running the school. He was glad to be back in a job that allowed him to do that as well as to spend more time with his family. The typical attributes of the Player Again we described as:

Typical Strengths

- Returns as a better player
- Strengthens the team
- Lesson to others – the only way isn't up
- Advocates value of pure playing
- Less stressed individual

Possible Shortcomings

- Leaves it too late
- Re-entry can be difficult
- Loss of face
- Reward issues
- Who does the managing?

After our previous meetings with Maggi and Martin, we concluded that the real challenge for the Player Again, almost perversely, is to 'get out sooner rather than later, regardless of perceived loss of face'. How were they finding life back in the field?

Maggi's Story

Our initial meetings with Martin and Maggi had revealed a marked contrast in their reactions to being Players Again, and we were eager to explore these still further. Maggi was away when we first rang. Her husband told us that she was on a retreat and would return the following week. We spoke to her shortly after she got back and, although we were not certain that she would agree to a meeting after our previous session which she had found so distressing, Maggi seemed quite happy to hear from us this time.

Maggi's Mad

Maggi invited us to join her for lunch at her spa. Philip raised his eyebrows at this, but Joy assured him that it was not unheard of to receive coaching at the spa and that in any case we were meeting her for lunch, not a sauna.

Having trailed halfway across London, we felt dusty and edgy compared to the newly tranquil person we encountered. On arrival we were taken in the direction of the 'Healthy Option' dining room and noticed that Maggi was already seated. She seemed to have streaked her hair blue for the meeting and added three studs to her left ear.

'I'm feeling so much better since I saw you last,' were her first words, and indeed she looked a lot less tense than when she had abruptly curtailed our first encounter. 'I have been away on the most amazing workshop in Greece. It was all about work and meaning and transforming the inner . . .'

'Are you ready to order?' interrupted the person serving our table, leaving us to wonder about the nature of Maggi's internal transformation. We quickly ordered our Healthy Option lunch, where everything remotely wicked and appetizing came 'on the side' or not at all.

'You were saying,' said Philip.

'Oh yes, the workshop,' said Maggi. 'It forced me to do a lot of reflecting about what happened with my boss and Mark, who if you remember was the blue-eyed boy who replaced me . . . well, actually bumped me. You know, I had really just bottled everything up and this was the first time I had had the chance to express my inner rage.'

'Inner rage?' queried Joy.

'Yes, inner rage. It's what you get when something awful happens to you. You try to be professional, take it on the chin and get over it, but underneath you blame yourself and think you are worthless. There's also a feeling that if you weren't so inadequate, things would have worked out OK.

'But deeper down, underneath the brave external face and all the internal punishing self-criticism there is a little part of you screaming with rage. A piece of you that dares not defend itself, a voice that says "That's unfair, no one cared or listened and why did this happen to me?" '

'And you discovered this on the workshop in Greece?' Joy inquired.

'Yes, well no one was going to give me the chance to discover it at work. You know it's very brutal in our business. You're hot or you're not. And when you're not, people shun you. You become an untouchable, so to speak. After Mark was given the client services job, I was expected to revert to programme sales as though nothing had happened. But something had happened, something that in the end made me leave because I felt such a failure. But what I discovered last week at the workshop was that actually I had an alternative. I could have stayed and got mad.'

'Mad?' said Philip. Having just come to terms with discussing workplace problems in a spa, he now found it difficult to envisage professional rehabilitation on a Greek island retreat.

'Yes,' said Maggi, 'mad. Mad at my boss for giving me a job I was unsuited to and for not helping me to adjust in any way at all, mad at Mark for the supercilious way he came in and took over once I started to flounder, mad at my team and clients for not changing the way they thought of me so I was still trying to be all things to all people, and mad at the whole organization for putting in ridiculous new management systems while making zero allowance for the extra load this creates and zero investment in what it would take to do these new things well.'

'So all in all, mad then,' said Philip, glad of the arrival of his salad. Eating somehow reduced the alarm we felt at the intensity of what was now clearly becoming Maggi's outer rage. We took a moment to collect our thoughts.

'Just suppose, Maggi,' said Joy, 'that you did get mad. Imagine that you are still employed there. You are back in the office. Now what would you really say, and to whom?'

Maggi's 'Constructive' Feedback

Maggi, whose lunch had been on the light side of lite, had already finished eating. She reached into her bag, pulled out a small silver-looking container and said, 'It's a good question. What would I say?' She took the top off the container and began rubbing something into her wrists and continued: 'I would have to start with my boss and the "constructive" feedback he gave me on the day that he politely took away my job.'

We gathered from the aroma that was drifting strongly in our direction that Maggi must have rubbed something like lavender balm on her wrists. No doubt this was to balance the yang of the rage with the yin of some calm. Anyway it seemed to do the trick, because as she described her situation, she adopted a more dispassionate tone.

'I don't think I told you last time we met, but what triggered the swap over to Mark was some feedback that my boss had been secretly gathering from my team. It transpires that one of the senior sales reps had always resented my appointment, although I never discovered why. He told my boss from day one that things wouldn't work out. I found out later that instead of supporting me outright, my boss had asked this person to keep tabs; that literally every two weeks, he would feed back to my boss a score of how I was doing based on informal chats with the team.

'Once I started to struggle with keeping my ratings with clients and installing the new sales organizational methods and systems into the team, my scores plummeted. Instead of coming to talk to me about it, my boss decided to get more direct opinion from the team. Obviously the team could smell which way the wind was blowing and that's why the feedback was so negative. I was a good target. Now can you see why I am so mad?'

'What did the feedback say exactly?' we questioned, noticing that

Maggi had not actually told us what she would do differently, but rather was giving us more detail of what had happened in the first place. Maggi breathed in deeply. Despite all that she had learned in Greece and even with the soothing benefits of the lavender balm, she was still finding aspects of this difficult. We soon found out why.

'The feedback was stark and not very balanced, if you ask me. My boss told me that the team thought that I was too highly strung and was making mistakes. That it was difficult to respect me as a manager because I was holding on to the good accounts and not imposing on myself the business disciplines I was imposing on the team. That it was impossible to learn from me because my communication was sharp-edged and came across not so much as advising as chastising. That I would ask for progress reports on work I had barely made clear was necessary. Oh, and that although I had been top of the ratings before the new job had weakened my performance, it was hard to accept me as the leader – I just wasn't one of the team anymore. I just sat and listened. Before I had even really begun to load what it meant my boss launched into the exit speech about . . .'

Maggi paused and then added: 'Well, you know the rest. I was out of my boss's office and back in my cubicle without saying much at all. I was just flooded with all sorts of emotions that I could barely express. I felt everyone out there was looking at me as if I had been part of some sort of witch hunt, so that people were happy to have sealed my fate.'

We asked her who else she had spoken to.

'No one, really. I put in a call to our Head of Human Resources. I felt sure part of this was because I had been thrown in at the deep end with no training or reduction in my existing role. I felt I had been treated harshly.'

'Then what happened?' we asked. 'Well, for one thing the Head of Human Resources never called me back. They say women can't net-work, and it's bloody true in my experience. They never work together with either other women or the men, apart from the ones who directly influence what they are doing and who can help them get on. Our Head of Human Resources had only recently been appointed anyway and she was really struggling herself. The job had about as many teeth as a newborn baby. People call her the Minister of Injustice, the one who has to handle the people who aren't really cutting it at their jobs and has to explain why it's in everyone's interests to keep square pegs out of round holes. I knew she wouldn't get back to me. She probably didn't want to get dragged into something with someone as prominent as my boss.'

At this point we were reminded of Roger, our Rookie Player Manager, who never asked anyone for help. We felt that in many ways Maggi was similar; that in her first Player Manager job she had tried to handle everything in a part proud, part hurt kind of isolation. Certainly there was an air of resignation about her fate. No wonder she was mad: she had accepted everything that had been thrown at her. She had neither put up much of a fight, nor asked herself honestly how much of the feedback might be fair or something that she needed to address. Certainly from her account her chance to address anything had been stolen from her, and we thought that this was contributing to her feelings about the situation.

We had no evidence beyond our interviews with Maggi, and because of her wish for anonymity we were unlikely to get any. All we had was her story and a sense that she was only part way through a difficult transition which might get more difficult before it got easier. We had finished lunch and Maggi seemed relieved when we suggested a break, even though Joy's question about what she might have done differently remained unanswered. We agreed to meet again in an hour, this time in the tea lounge. 'I'm off to the quiet room,' said Maggi, grabbing a couple of books from her bag before putting it over her shoulder and standing up to leave.

Maggi's Confusion

Maggi was a bit of a puzzle to us at this point and we spent the next hour trying to work her out. On the one hand we took her to be a hard-nosed business person focused on her goals and on getting results. She had to be that; otherwise she would not have been the top producer in her group or have been given the management job in the first place. On the other hand, the character we had met twice now had lost all focus beyond a decision to renovate her house and, we assumed, her inner self. Most surprising to us, given her background, was the way that at the time of her demotion she had seemingly accepted lying down something that she felt was deeply unfair.

We decided that she was so traumatized by the moment of truth that she went into shock. The manner of her removal had been sudden and brutal. She had to cope with details of the hurtful feedback as well as the realization that people she had trusted had been secretly checking up and telling on her. It was probably the first time that she had had to face professional failure, and under the circumstances of her betrayal it is not surprising that she froze. Had such a previously feisty spirit been so shellshocked by what had occurred that the result was long-term damage, or would she come through?

'I think several things are going on in her mind at once,' said Joy. 'The overall effect is one of angry confusion. Maggi flip-flops between the situation being everyone's fault and some kind of corporate set-up, and taking it all on her shoulders as her fault for being so bad at her job.'

'But she hasn't said anything about being bad at her job,' said Philip.

'Precisely,' said Joy. 'That's what gives away the fact that she is feeling that she was bad at it.'

'I see,' said Philip, struggling to accept that you could communicate feeling bad about something either by owning up to it or, if you preferred, by saying nothing. To overcome his uncertainty, he tried rephrasing Joy's analysis: 'So you are saying that we could help the confusion by tackling the two sides of the situation separately. On the one hand we have what she feels has been done to her, on the other we have what she feels she has done to herself.'

'That's my take,' said Joy. 'At the moment Maggi is taking it all as a whole and this is proving overwhelming, despite all her efforts at greater wisdom and, well, inner peace.' Philip made some notes on a Healthy Option napkin, which he passed to Joy.

Maggi
– Good producer
– Disliked putting more formal process in
– Own performance started to fall
– Began to feel stressed
– Took things out on team
– No sit down with boss
– No command of team
– Didn't see Mark coming

The situation
- Boss didn't help at outset
- Boss aggravated things throughout
- Team encouraged to go round M with grievances
- Never given chance to improve
- Undermined M with Mark's appointment

'We could add "gave up" to the points about Maggi,' suggested Joy, 'and add something to "The situation" list about "destructive and not constructive" feedback, but we really need to talk more to her before taking things much further.' And with that we headed off to meet her in the tea lounge.

Maggi's Story Unfolds

Healthier Options

Philip's worries that real tea might be the only thing the tea lounge didn't serve were unfounded. He was, however, in the minority with Earl Grey compared to the herb tea drinkers and noticed they now included Joy, who had opted to join Maggi in camomile tea.

Trying Times

'What have you been reading?' we asked Maggi cordially by way of restarting the conversation.

'*How to Get Ahead* and *The Promotion Problem*,' Maggi answered, adding that they were recommended to her by someone at the workshop last week. 'I'm not that far into either of them but I can begin to see what I was up against. Maybe if I had read these first, I would have realized I was onto a loser at the outset. I've learned that organizations operate by an unwritten set of rules and that learning how to navigate through these is what gets you to the top. It looks as though it's how you say things and who you say them to that really counts.'

Joy interrupted her, asking: 'And how have you related this to your situation in your last job, Maggi?'

'That I couldn't have succeeded if I tried.'

'And did you?'

'Did I what?'

'Did you try?'

At this point Maggi looked at us both and said nothing. Philip, sensing that Joy had taken Maggi to an edge, said, 'There are different ways of trying, aren't there? You tried very hard in one sense – no one could have faulted you for the effort you put in or the hours that you worked – but you didn't try at all in another sense because you didn't try anything different. Trying to find another way of dealing with the problems you encountered might have been more successful than trying to live with them.'

Maggi was still considering what we were saying and Joy felt that she needed some help in relating this to practical things she had done. 'While you were away reading, Maggi, we noted down a few of the things you have been telling us,' said Joy, unfolding the Healthy Option napkin for Maggi to look at.

She studied the 'Maggi' list carefully. 'Well, at least you think I was a good producer,' she said finally, her inner calm clearly wrestling with her outer rage.

'No doubt about that,' Joy told her, 'otherwise you wouldn't have been offered the job in the first place. We are certain, given the right circumstances, you could be a first-rate manager too. The problem was that there were some things in the mix of all this, about you and about the situation, that made this opportunity not quite right for you. Before we talk about this, though, take a look at the second list, the one headed up "The situation."'

Maggi did so, and there was clearly another battle going on between calm and rage. Rage won. 'Bastards,' she said.

'Maybe they were,' Joy continued, 'but we all have to deal with people like that, either by working with them or getting them moved out of our lives. Is Philip's second bullet point, the one that says you disliked the formal process that you were required to implement, relevant here?'

Maggi looked uncomfortable and was quiet for so long that we thought she was not going to answer. Suddenly she said: 'There wasn't a single day while I was in management that I felt I was in the right job,' and we sensed the truth. 'I loved working with clients, using my knowledge and my relationship skills to do great business. All those account plans, forecasts and other processes that were being imple-mented; well, to be honest, they left me cold. Obviously I couldn't argue that they weren't needed for the business because they were, but they weren't something I needed. And this must have come across to the team.'

All Wrong from the Outset

Maggi had already realized that it had been unwise for her to have taken on a job with which she felt no sympathy, so we avoided stating what was obvious to all of us. Instead, we asked what went through her mind when she was first approached about doing it.

'When my boss offered me the job I felt . . . well, I felt I should want it. This was it – me in management, in a stretch role with a chance to show I could lead the team. But it was all wrong from the outset and only went downhill from there.'

'One of the things we have learned in our research is about the circumstances in which players become Player Managers,' Joy told her. 'These appointments are very often made at a time that suits the business not the individual, and many times what appears to be the best solution for the business in the short term may not be right for the person involved.

'Being offered a managerial position, especially for the first time, is a very critical career moment. Emotions are high: pride at being offered a promotion, triumph at beating rivals for the position, and excitement at facing a new challenge. To think coolly and clearly at such times is hard, but important.

'You could have asked your boss what the right skills for the job on offer were and then compared them with your own strengths. If you had doubts and wanted to buy thinking time, requesting a personal profiling exercise might have helped. Anything that can show a more objective assessment of your strengths and shortcomings can save a lot of anguish in the long run.'

Saying No

Maggi was looking at us as though we had stepped off another planet, despite the 'opening' effect of her journey to Greece. She said impatiently, 'Those self-awareness things are easier said than done in the real world. I was at work, not in therapy for heaven's sake! Showing doubt sends negative messages.'

We were left wondering where the new Maggi had suddenly gone when she added, 'OK, so I was afraid of giving the impression of not being up for it and losing the opportunity to progress.'

'That would have been a risk, but it might not have been the biggest risk,' said Joy. 'It is unlikely that your boss would have withdrawn the offer so soon after making it. You were selected in the first place because you were considered right for the job, and I doubt whether asking for some help in making a decision would have undone all your excellent reputation. Anyway, unless you went through the analysis we suggested, on what basis were you making a decision?'

Maggi thought for a moment before replying: 'It's like I said, I just didn't feel I could turn down an obvious promotion. Now what you are telling me is that I should have explored the proposition more carefully. I guess that's fair: "Accept in haste, repent at leisure". If I had questioned my boss at the beginning and throughout about what was expected of me, many of the issues that surfaced later on would have been out on the table, and I would have had a chance of staying on the front foot. The real risk wasn't the risk of being passed over, but rather of being pressured into taking the wrong job.'

Philip looked hard at Maggi. 'There is one key question to ask yourself before accepting a new job,' he said. 'Is it right for me? And if the fit is wrong for whatever reason – lifestyle, mismatch between your aims and those of the organization or simply a belief that the organization has got your skills wrong – then just say No!'

Maggi had clearly not previously considered that saying 'no' was an option and she looked relieved at what Philip had just told her. 'I can see now why it says "Healthy Options" on your piece of paper. I had much more of a choice than I realized. But once I was in the job, had I missed my chance to decide whether or not to step up or were there further options for me?'

'Let's move on to the time when you had been doing the job for a while and, as Philip's list says, you were beginning to feel stressed,' said Joy. 'I would guess that you felt that this situation was of your own making and that you had to deal with it yourself. You probably told yourself that everything would work out fine, just as it had in the rest of your career. Player Managers often muddle along, convincing themselves things are fine and ignoring vital signs that something just isn't working. But if it's not working, taking time out to separate out the pieces might have helped. This is often the time to talk it through with someone else. But in your case you never opened these issues up.'

'Not with anyone at all,' admitted Maggi ruefully.

'Indeed,' Joy continued. 'When things are going wrong, at the very moment when we most need help, we get reluctant to reveal our weakness. This reluctance is understandable but usually misplaced, because most people are flattered when asked for advice and are more than willing to lend a hand.'

Coming Full Circle

Maggi was looking miserable, staring blankly at the floor. We felt that now it was the realization of the missed opportunity as much as the painful memories that were hurting. 'But it's so difficult to think it out when you are feeling so low,' she almost whispered, the rage having blown itself out.

Faced by Maggi's despair, Joy said quietly, 'We all face situations where others are in control, but even at such times we nearly always have choices. When we take responsibility for our choices and accept the risks of going for what we want, anxiety often subsides. The process of doing something to take command of your own destiny is invigorating in itself, and nearly always produces a better outcome.'

Maggi now looked as though she had gone full circle. 'OK, I take all that. I never gave myself a chance because I just did the next obvious thing and then internalized it all. But having said that, not one single person, neither my boss nor anyone else, ever offered me one jot of support.'

Philip picked up the Healthy Option napkin one last time and redrew attention to his second list, 'The situation': 'You are probably expecting me to say that you never showed them that you needed help, so how would they know that you wanted it. But quite honestly, Maggi, from what you have told us, we should be sitting down with your boss as well as you. He never got right behind you and supported you fully. In fact it was worse than that. He undermined you by sanctioning a secret reporting line that seriously damaged your credibility.'

Then Maggi smiled. Now, for the first time since we had met her, she seemed to have broken free from those pressures and memories that had so troubled her. The anger and bitterness had vanished, and there was little sign, or need, of lavender balm 'calm'. As she reflected on our afternoon, she said, 'You know there probably were things I could have done differently once I was in that situation and I can see now that I could have prevented it coming to a crisis. But in the end I'm happiest out of it. More tea, anyone?'

Maggi One Hundred Days On

After we left Maggi at ease with herself somewhere between a Greek island and a health spa, we wondered what she would do with her life once the house she was renovating was complete. We felt that talking through her situation with us had helped her realize that there are always more choices available than first appears. We speculated that she might go back into business and perhaps even return to another high-profile sales role, but when we finally heard about her plans we were in for a surprise.

We received an advert in our inbox letting people know about a new venture Maggi had gone into with a partner, who we discovered later was the woman Maggi had met on the workshop in Greece. Maggi was now involved in selling for this woman's aromatherapy wholesale business on a part time basis.

She called us later in the week and we discovered that the job gave her the balance she needed. She was back talking to clients and selling, something for which she had a natural talent. This was in contrast to the woman she had joined forces with, whose strengths were in product management and business administration.

'The great thing about this,' Maggi told us, 'is that I can do it from my house. I have had an amazing restyling job done in the basement, which is now my office, and I am completely networked to all of our clients and suppliers. You must come and look at it some time. On the original plan the basement refit was all set to be a home spa, but a couple of weeks after talking to you I wondered why I needed so much space for a spa of my own. I figured it was a kind of therapy or even some kind of escape from a terrible imbalance, not so much in my circumstances but in me.

'Soon after that, a few of us who had been to the workshop in Greece got together, and the woman who had lent me the books was in a terrible state of anxiety about her business. It transpired she could face everything except picking up the phone and dealing with clients and prospects. Well, you can imagine the rest. I would be lying if I said that I was over what happened, but now I can face it without feeling so hopelessly angry and without the conviction that I failed. It doesn't matter so much, because I feel secure again knowing what I am good at. Don't ask me if I have any regrets, because you know the answer would be that I wish I had got out sooner rather than hanging in there to the bitter end.'

Pleased to hear that things were turning the corner for Maggi, we were ready to pull our thoughts together about how she had dealt with her Player Again challenge. We decided to wait, however, until we had spoken to Martin, our other Player Again.

Martin's Story

As we went back to meet Martin at his house, Maggi remained very much on our minds. We had gained an insight into why she had accepted the Player Manager's job in the first place, and into her failure to get out of it once things first began to go wrong. But why, when the situation deteriorated as badly as it did, did it apparently never cross her mind that a voluntary return to Playing Again was a credible option? Her experience made the contrast with Martin's decision even more interesting, and we wanted to understand what made him so different. By now it was well past the summer holidays, and we wondered if Martin might be displaying more Maggi-like symptoms now that school was no longer out.

Martin's Mad

Martin opened the door, ushered us inside and invited us to take a seat in the kitchen so that he could chat to us while he made the tea. Without needing to ask, we were confident that Martin, like Philip, drank only tea that was real.

'So how is your research going?' asked Martin. 'Met any good characters for your book? I was thinking of giving your number to my brother last week. He is a bad case of something, although I am not sure what. You have probably met loads of people like my brother by now, and I doubt you could knock any more sense into him than I could. The fact that he is a compulsive workaholic doesn't stop him from giving me advice, though.'

Martin's Brother

Martin was our last case study. We did not really want to open up a new line of enquiry but could not resist asking Martin what kind of advice he got from his brother.

'He was always urging me to take the head's job,' Martin answered, 'saying that if I had to be in a profession as undignified as teaching, then the least I could do was rescue my position by aiming for the top. "Martin," he told me, "do you understand what it means now that you have been to the governors and stood down, with the result that they have appointed that woman? You'll never be given another shot."

'He seems to believe that I have inadvertently arrested my own development – as though I don't think about my actions. He thinks that I operate in some quaint naïve little corner that the rest of the world has left behind. He seems to imply that if I were a grown-up I would wake up and run away from my life in shame. Yes, that's it, shame. My brother feels I should be ashamed of myself. But why would I want the head's job in the second place when I had turned it down in the first place?'

We asked Martin to compare himself with his brother.

'I've never been like him. I have never thought of success as a pursuit, something you have to chase after where there is a prize at the end. For me it's very simple. Success is something that ensues when you are engaged in the thing that you love, it's part of a creative process, the value of which can only emerge from the creation. That's why I have always loved maths. It's the language through which I work, create and communicate. My brother wouldn't understand that for a second. He thinks I am mad.'

It seemed that everyone was mad these days, though if it was infectious we would rather we caught Martin's madness than Maggi's. Martin's position seemed one to be envied, not reviled. Our appetites were whetted; we wanted to know more about the brother and enquired what he did.

'He is in media of some kind. Originally he was in advertising. He was supposed to be the creative one in the family, with a Fellini-style outlook and aspirations. But when I listen to his accounts of what work he is actually up to, I have to say it doesn't sound very creative at all. This is a pity really, because he is always working, even when he is home. I swear I spend more time with his kids than he does, yet he thinks I'm the loser in the family. He's the one that needs a wake-up call, not me.'

Next we asked Martin whether it was possible that he and his brother were both equally fulfilled but that their needs were different.

'It's funny you should mention that,' he said. 'I told my brother about an article I was reading last week that explained why people in occupations like mine find fulfilment despite all the obvious demands of the job and, by his standards, our low social status. Apparently there is an emotional high that comes from doing something creative and nurturing, even if it is hard work. It is supposed to be a bit like a runner's high. I don't know if it is true or not, but it probably explains why I look younger than my brother even though I'm the eldest.

'Is he fulfilled? I doubt it. He and his wife have certain benchmarks against which they measure success – type of house, car, holiday – and they have attained them all. In that sense they have fulfilled their goals. But does that make them fulfilled as people? Not by my definition, because of what they have to put up with to get it. My brother is an extreme case, no doubt. Most of us probably have more balance in our lives than he does, and if it starts to disappear then we do something about it.'

Martin's Friends

Philip wondered whether Martin knew of any other people like him who had tried management, decided it was not for them and done something about it.

'Not many in teaching, although I know of plenty who have never left the classroom because they enjoy it and are turned off by administration or management. But I can think of a couple of examples of people in other professions who have stepped back from management.'

Honest Standards

We asked Martin to tell us more. What, if anything, did his two examples have in common? Had their return to being Players Again been smooth like Martin's or traumatic like Maggi's?

'One is a close friend who is a doctor and whose story might interest you. He was a specialist in burns treatments for many years. Then three years ago he ducked out. Went into cosmetic surgery of all things. It took us a while to work it out. He had grown weary of being on call all hours, of patching people up when he was so tired that he was barely able to concentrate.

'Naturally we all suspected him of wanting to make a fast buck. But the real motive behind it was his kids. He just wanted to be on a more normal schedule for them. Burns he can go back to later. Being there for his kids he only gets one shot at. We all stopped teasing him about the switch when we saw that.'

'Martin,' Joy interrupted, 'you said a moment ago that if balance starts to disappear from our lives then most of us do something about it. Do you really think that's true? Or are you and the doctor just isolated cases?'

Martin looked at Joy as though she was struggling with the obvious, then he smiled and said, 'Those of us who are honest with ourselves do. Now if you want to ask me how many people are honest with themselves, well, that's an entirely different question.'

At this point we were reminded of Maggi and her reluctant acknowledgement of how she had accepted a job that was wrong from the outset. It seemed that Martin and the doctor had not had this struggle.

'So when it came to the choice for you, Martin,' said Philip, 'was it difficult to be honest with yourself?'

'I have never not been honest with myself, so it wasn't like I had to make an exception in this case. But there is a point here that is important. It ties back to the thing that makes my brother so frustrated with me. It's about what is expected of you if you adopt other people's standards, and what you expect from yourself if you set your own standards.

'Obviously we feel best when those two sets of standards correspond. Ultimately, finding some correspondence between the two is the only way we stay out of the mad house. But when we join an institution we are usually signing up to other people's standards, and it takes a certain amount of will and courage to hang on to any standards of our own that don't correspond with the standards of the institution.

'This brings me to my second case. I have a private pupil in the evenings, a girl who I am helping with algebra and calculus. Her father used to be a management consultant and he nearly burned himself out trying to reconcile two sets of standards. He told me that he had left a large consulting firm to join a niche player that was founded by some big name gurus from the US. They were trying to build a practice in Europe, and in the early months this meant taking work from any-where. One of the US guys sold a job in South Africa and gave it to my pupil's father, asking him to be there for several months. But his second daughter had just been born, so that he was travelling back at weekends. He was flying coach as the project wasn't really making money, and doing this every week was proving exhausting. So he tried to find someone to share the load. No one else would do any travelling, and he was considered "less than fully committed" for raising the issue. In the end he felt he was killing himself for a bunch of partners who cared about nothing but the project, and when his new child didn't recognize him one weekend, he quit.

'He felt that he had been entirely committed by doing an unreason-able amount of travelling at a difficult time for him personally. When this wasn't recognized, his real commitment became clearer. It was to his family and to his own well-being, so he ignored the pressure to comply to the firm's standards and followed his own instead. He told me his new policy towards work was "NTR", and when I asked him what that meant, he said, "Non Treadmill Revenue". A lot of people in the firm apparently just shunned him after he left. Personally I admire what he did and I couldn't agree more about the treadmill, or "dreadmill" as I think of it.'

Who Does the Managing?

As we listened to Martin describing the cold shoulder that was given to someone who had rejected the prevailing values, we wondered how people had reacted at school once it became known what he was going to do. 'What did the people around you say?' we asked. 'There must have been people in the institution who thought, "Oh, he's not really like us after all", or "Now he has let the side down". How did they take it?'

'There's more than one way to look at this,' he replied. 'On the one hand there are a group of people who admire me for what I have done, for sticking out for teaching as the most valuable part of what goes on in a school. They think that what I have done somehow validates their own role as a teacher. For them I have been an overt advocate of teaching as the core of our profession. The Head of English said, "Well, it's a poke in the eye for the bean counters and I should think you have teed off the governors, but it sends a great signal about what lies at the heart of the institution." He then quoted some poetry at me, something like, "What is this world if full of care, we have no time to stand and stare". I can't say I have got much more time even now for standing and staring, but I think I got the point he was alluding to.

'On the other hand, there is another group who regard me differently. They don't think I am foolish like my brother does. Instead they think I have been selfish. I could tell the governors felt I was letting the side down and Patricia, who became Head in my place, told me it was the typical behaviour of someone refusing to grow up and do what was necessary. After all, someone's got to do the managing. I stood up to that standard or expectation if you like and said, "No, sorry, it's not for me." But just think if everyone did that. Then where would we be?'

Martin had posed a good question. He seemed to be implying that unless Player Managers are given more recognition and some help in learning to balance an impossible workload, more and more of them will give up, either by burning out or taking the rational self-interested course that he himself had followed. We realized that his question was not entirely hypothetical, for during our research we had heard of institutions in the public sector that were finding it difficult to fill managerial positions as many professionals opted to remain in production roles. This was the flipside of Martin's story: if too many people become Players Again, who will do the managing?

Did Maggi and Martin Meet the Player Again Challenge?

The challenge for the Player Again is to get out sooner rather than later, regardless of perceived loss of face.

After we had said goodbye to Martin, we discussed the different routes that he and Maggi had taken back to Playing Again. Martin had done it with dignity and, apart from the expression of some frustration by the new head of the school and some sniping from those who had different values, with minimal criticism from colleagues. His family, if they listened to the brother, might have seen Martin as a failure, but Martin had the inner certainty to stand up to that. Martin had, we agreed, 'got out sooner not later, regardless of perceived loss of face,' and had clearly met the Player Again challenge as we had originally specified it.

The key for him was his definition of success as being a state of mind rather than a form of external recognition. He knew what he enjoyed doing, he had a sufficiently independent mind to stick to it, and he had enough self-confidence to recognize that promotion, for him, was no kind of advancement.

The contrast with Maggi in her Player Manager role could not have been sharper. She ignored all the warning signs that were there from day one. Because she did not really identify with the account manage-ment system that she was meant to be installing, the odds were loaded against her from the outset. She took the role because she feared that she would be looked down on if she declined it and because she saw it as 'progress'. But no fate could have been worse than the undermining and politics that she endured or the humiliation that she felt in the manner of her downfall. In the end she arrived at a similar place to Martin via the Greek islands and a health spa, but it took a while before she finally came to terms with what had happened.

After a few months we wondered whether Maggi's journey to recovery was still on course and we took up the invitation to see her office in the basement of her house. It was indeed the nice set-up she had described and Maggi was happy to be there, back in sales, working in a player-only role that she felt comfortable with and in an organization whose aims she supported. Martin had given us permission to show her his story, and we offered it to Maggi as something that was likely to help her still further as she came to terms with the past. She asked for some time to study it, and a couple of weeks later sent us the following notes which summarized the lessons she had so painfully learnt.

With the benefit of hindsight

Look before you leap. The emotional turmoil I felt on being offered the Player Manager Head of Sales role – triumph, fear and elation all mixed together – was no platform from which to make a rational decision. I committed myself too soon as a consequence of not taking a cold hard look at the offer.

You can say no. I accepted a role that deep down I knew was wrong for me because I thought my employer and peers would think less of me for showing lack of ambition. I never tested it out, but if I had said 'no', or like Martin asked to step down once I knew it was wrong for me, my employers might have said, 'Fine, carry on playing, your client ratings are just great.' Even if they had been hard-nosed, at least I would have had the satisfaction of controlling my own destiny.

Make your own definition of success. Fulfilment can come in lots of different ways and should be measured against your own not someone else's standards. My main lesson from Martin's story is that in future I must set my own agenda.

Step down sooner rather than be pushed later. I was drowning not waving, and I should have realized that earlier and signalled it more clearly. That way I would have had options.

Be true to yourself. I was a half-hearted supporter of the account management system I was implementing. I was acting out a lie. Unless you can identify with the standards of your organization, get out fast!

Take pride as a player. In my new job I am proud of what I bring to the business as a pure and committed player. I know that it is me, that I am good at it and that my skills blend in well with those of the others that work here. What more could I ask from a job?

Maggi seemed to have come to terms with her Player Manager experience and had finally gained from it. She and Martin were Players Again and comfortable with it. As Maggi herself had put it, what more could anyone ask from a job?

I2

Roundtable

Crisis Points

We hadn't stayed in touch with our Player Managers after completing our original research, but we occasionally wondered whether there had been any lasting effects of the changes that each had made. A piece in a magazine about AMSS entitled 'Fancy That' prompted us to make enquiries. The feature showed a picture of Nicola with Jean Marie and applauded the 'fast and fancy footwork so admired by our leading edge readers' displayed by Nicola and her company in acting 'swiftly and intelligently to acquire the much fancied AMSS'. It went on to describe AMSS as 'a hotbed of talent with a niche franchise that competitors would envy', and that 'someone will be kicking themselves for letting this gem slip from their grasp'. Nicola at least, we concluded, had kept on track and on top of her challenge. If the picture of a smiling Jean Marie was anything to go by, the 'difficult' label that had attached to her was now erased from the corporate memory. Fancy that.

The article about Nicola reminded us that she had come to a crisis point in facing her challenge, one that had led to an angry late night call to Joy, and we realized that each person in our team had faced a similarly defining moment. Roger the Rookie had left his job abruptly after becoming isolated and overwhelmed, and history had almost repeated itself following feedback he received at his new job. Alex, the Player Coach, had also met history when, after he had remodelled his approach following the resignation of Richard, he was faced with the need to do so again to meet a crisis of confidence from Rocky, Marcella and the bad boss Tex. For Veteran Dun, after steering the business for so many years dissent had started to penetrate his previously

unassailable position at the helm, persuading him to bring in consultants and begin a new wave of change. At AlphaSolva, Vikram's crisis
point came in an angry executive team meeting around a second schism
in the business, this time created by his Play Making. Martin was too
grounded to be swept off course by the Player Again challenge, but
Maggi's crisis came as she was tipped into silent rage on being brutally
removed from her role.

The only character that had not been to the brink was our wholly
fictional ideal, Amanda Sage. The Player Manager's challenge is largely
about heading off crisis points, and we decided to introduce our Player
Managers to Amanda to help us all understand how. We set up a
roundtable discussion to give us an opportunity to see how our Player
Managers now viewed their challenge, to catch up with their progress,
and to enable them to match themselves against an ideal.

Introducing Amanda

To stimulate the roundtable debate, we wrote to the participants
explaining that although every person and every situation was different, we had developed a framework that categorized the different
kinds of Player Managers. We included a copy of the attributes and
challenges we had defined for each type and asked them to compare
these to their own experience. This was accompanied by a condensed
version of the 'discussion' we had with Amanda in Chapter Four,
supplemented with comments about what she thought of Player Managers who were less than perfect.

Amanda's Story

I have been a Player Manager for many years now and I liken it to spinning
plates. I am constantly juggling different parts of my job to keep these plates
up in the air. If I stop or my team stops, the plates will come crashing down.
A couple of years back it struck me that better management was a critical
success factor for competing. Player Managers are akin to Janus, the Roman
god of gates and doors. Janus had two heads according to his depiction in
myth, one to look forward and one to look back. He could keep his eye on
both sides of the gate by constantly looking in two directions at once. For a
Player Manager, on one side of the gate is the pressure to produce personally;
on the other side is management of the performance of the team and the

business. The challenge is to be a leader, someone who can influence other people and the things they can achieve.

I am a guardian at the gate like Janus, because the way I work with the resources entrusted to me can add value or destroy it. I am responsible for value in three areas. First is our short-term performance, the delivery of results to plan. Second is our growth, the numbers in our mid-term plan. The third area is sustainability. I am expected to deliver the plan that will help us win in the long haul and the team of talent for ensuring that we get there.

My personal playing is a piece of this but not the priority, which is to use the six levers I have developed to maintain the guardianship of the gate. My first lever is to define and state the *end game,* and the second is its translation into a real time *game plan.* Each team member knows what is expected of them, because the third lever is to set clear *benchmarks* of performance and the fourth is to put in place *team enablers,* things that enable the benchmark to be achieved and the game to be won. The fifth lever is *feedback,* making it available to everyone and ensuring that there is a strong tie between feedback, performance and rewards. The sixth is seeking people's *commitment,* by giving everyone the chance to achieve something out of the ordinary and by setting a personal example.

None of this is easy. It requires a number of attributes that most Player Managers don't have when they start out and some never learn. I think these attributes are:

- Vision
- Self-belief
- Love of the game
- Will to succeed
- Disciplined approach
- Judgement in difficult situations
- Command of the team
- Flexibility
- Staying power
- Balancing personal and team performance

I have met Player Managers who not only lack these attributes but also seem hell-bent on not acquiring them. It is unbelievable but somehow permissible for Player Managers to lack self-organization and discipline, to be pessimistic and feel put upon with regard to their load rather than being optimistic and pragmatic about the constant juggling involved. Some Player Managers are so wrapped up in the stardom of their playing or in hiding their managerial incompetence behind it that they haven't really grasped that they are now in charge of the performance of a team, that when things become messy and demanding, as they invariably do when people are involved, it is their handling of the situation that makes all the difference. That said, others are so caught up in the difference they make that they fail to notice if no one is really behind them, that commitment and allegiance have gone. Finally there are those who just weren't meant to make any kind of difference as a Player Manager, and I wonder why they took the job in the first place.

The assault of work on a Player Manager is endless. It takes more than empowerment and enlightenment and involvement and any other '-ment' you can think of to survive. Janus was permanently on guard. Yet he was also the god of new beginnings. In my view, Player Managers can only stay on their own game through this onslaught if what they are doing involves meeting challenges and learning by experience. The key is to be professional and realistic and make sure it stays fun.

The roundtable would show how Amanda's six levers were relevant to our Player Managers.

Player Manager Roundtable

The purpose of this roundtable is to find out what good Player Managers can do to overcome the challenges of their dual role. In preparation, please read the attached extracts and think about their relevance to you. On the day of the roundtable we will ask:

How typical are you?

There will be several Player Managers attending and each will be asked to speak for a few minutes comparing themselves and their own experiences to one of six different types. We will be explaining more on the day, but in advance please:

- Study the strengths and shortcomings of the type that you have been asked to consider.
- See how you measure up to these attributes.
- Read through the challenge that faces the type you are dealing with.
- Apply your own experience as a Player Manager to that challenge.

How do you compare to Amanda?

We will be providing a framework to collect your responses and pull the entire discussion together, but in preparation you might like to think about:

- Your first reactions to the extract from Amanda Sage. What stands out?
- How do your experiences compare? Are your challenges similar or different?
- What do you most/least identify with in her style?
- Would or did Amanda's levers help you?

Levers for Player Managers Defined

There are no rules that can guarantee success as a Player Manager, but here are brief definitions of Amanda Sage's six levers.

Know and state the end game

- An understanding of the goals of the team or organization. Letting people know what these are is as important as choosing the right goals.

Have a game plan

- A credible and comprehensible plan for how to pull off the end game. People only relate to goals if they know how to achieve them. The plan is likely to require constant communication and adaptation.

Set the benchmarks

- The standard that lets people know what is expected so that they can apply themselves to the right target. Whether the benchmark is quantified (for example milestones towards the endgame) or a qualitative standard (for example, 'treat all customers as though they are special') the team needs to know the Player Manager's expectations.

Enable the team

- Anything that helps the team perform to the benchmarks and follow the game plan as they move towards their end game. The end game, the game plan and the benchmarks have to leave people thinking, 'Yes, I can imagine how we could achieve that'. A Player Manager then enables this by giving resources, leadership and discretion.

Use feedback

- Any information that lets people know how they are doing and how to improve. Without feedback people are performing blind – including the Player Manager. Feedback ties the end game, the game plan and benchmarks together through constant evaluation of progress.

Build commitment

- Commitment flows from applying the preceding five levers well. But it is also a direct lever pulled by the energy of the Player Manager's own personal example.

The Roundtable

We chose a small hotel just outside London for our meeting, deliberately wanting to avoid the aura of grander conference settings. Everyone gathered in an anteroom and as our team chatted slightly uneasily, we were anxious for some insight into their initial reactions to Amanda's material.

Dun, who looked like a first-class traveller who had been bumped into economy by our choice of venue, remarked that Amanda seemed almost too good to be true. Alex said he would like to meet Amanda and handed Joy three tickets to a cocktail evening where we could make the introduction. Maggi expressed disappointment when she learned that Amanda wasn't going to be there in person, saying that in all her corporate experience she had never known that kind of boss, and could she put Amanda in touch with the organizer of her programme in Greece.

Nicola felt sure Amanda was a woman of some spirit who, while a tad 'touchy-feely' towards the team, clearly had an instinct for chasing down lax professional standards. Martin said he was glad he wasn't married to Amanda as he would find it all too exhausting and Vikram, typically, just asked a question. He wanted to know where Amanda worked, how we had met her and how come she had it all worked out. We sidestepped his question by saying he would find out later and drew everyone into the main meeting room.

The Warm Up

The Sentence that Leapt Out

To break the ice we asked everyone to say a few words about themselves and to give their initial reactions to Amanda's extract. We also
wanted to know which particular sentence had stood out for each of
them.

Roger, who had so far just quietly been drinking his coffee, was the
first to speak: 'I thought she sounded like a very smooth operator who
would keep her head, well both heads, in difficult circumstances. The
sentence that leapt out at me though was: *"The assault of work on a
Player Manager is endless"*. This is true, and the only way to survive
it is not to feel that you personally have to spin all those plates. Amanda
is right when she says *"The challenge is to be a leader, someone who
can influence other people and the things they can achieve"*. So that is
what stands out most for me.'

Everyone nodded, and then Nicola commented: 'The onslaught just
gets worse and the ability to focus on where you need to make your
plays for optimal impact as well as powering up on levers for the team
is the only way to make headway.

'The sentence that I fastened onto was different though,' she continued. 'It was: *"My personal playing is a piece of this but not the
priority"*. I thought my playing was the main act. I ran out onto the
field kicking and pretty much just expected everyone to watch and
start kicking like me. So I am interested in what Amanda says about
using *"the six levers I have developed to maintain the guardianship of
the gate"*.'

Dun was next to speak. 'All of our industries have just come through
an unprecedented period of growth and expansion, which I agree has
placed even greater demands on practitioners, or Player Managers as
you call them. At our firm we feel that competition will intensify
further and that growth will slow significantly. So the sentence that
particularly caught my eye was: *"It struck me that better management
was a critical success factor for competing"*. I agree with that and
so, like Nicola, I want to know more about the levers for better
management.'

Now it was Maggi's turn: 'I must be one of those Player Managers
Amanda refers to as not "meant to make any kind of difference as a

Player Manager",' she declared. 'What leapt out at me was the last part of that sentence: "*I wonder why they took the job in the first place*". She is not the only one wondering that. Later I hope we can tie that to what Nicola and Dun have said about better management and levers.'

Then Martin added: 'I suppose I am echoing Maggi when I say that the sentence that most resonated with me was: "*The key is to be professional and realistic and make sure it stays fun*". New beginnings are often a big part of that.'

Alex, who had been listening intently to everyone, said: 'I noticed something different. It's doubtless habitual, but I focused on the list of attributes and scored myself against them. I can see why I hadn't quite got the mix right. What struck me, the sentence with my name on it if you like, was: "*I am expected to deliver the plan that will help us win in the long haul and the team of talent for ensuring that we get there*". That's the elusive mix I was chasing.'

Vikram smiled at Alex: 'Elusive mixes are hard recipes to make so I doubt that today we will come out with a single formula for success. In fact the sentence for me wasn't in the descriptive extract at all. It was in the specification, the page of lever definitions. It says: "*There are no rules that can guarantee success*". What then is the rule for helping us with that?'

Food for Thought

Joy had noticed that Vikram's comment had given everyone food for thought and it seemed to her an appropriate point to summarize the proceedings thus far: 'If I have followed what has been said, then we are all expressing interest in Amanda's levers for improved Player Manager performance and we want to find out more about them. This is because we think that the onslaught of demands is only going to intensify, that Player Managers will indeed be the guardians at the gate of this onslaught, and that anything that creates leverage will be of value.

'Additionally there is interest in Amanda's style and in the attributes Player Managers need for success in juggling the dual demands of the role. Around that, there is a view that some of us may not have those attributes and we are either learning them or moving on to new beginnings. Finally we have a more fundamental question: with something so variable, complex and individual as Player Managing, can there ever be any kind of formula for success? The first part of our agenda, "How typical are you?", will help us explore that.'

As each person took their turn, the list of their attributes and the definition of their challenge could be read from an overview of all the profiles and challenges that appeared on the laptops placed around the table.

Through Their Own Eyes

Roger

Roger began by recounting how he had met us, gave a synopsis of his first efforts at Player Managing and explained that he was just at the start of a new challenge. 'Taking command without doing it all personally is just one of the challenges that the Player Manager faces. I wouldn't say that it is necessarily the most difficult; it's just the first one I encountered. If I don't crack it, then I don't suppose I will ever find out much about the others! The first time that I tried it, most of the shortcomings on the screen kicked in and nearly brought me down.

'Was that down to my organization or me? I was thrown in at the deep end with no preparation and no real clarity about the role that I was meant to be carrying out. I knew what I was meant to be responsible for, but others in the team and the organization had a different agenda. This definitely undermined me and drove me to behave according to type. I don't deny that quite a few of the Rookie's attributes applied to me.

'Being "task not people oriented" was a big shortcoming. I focused on getting things done without really thinking about how this impacted on others and what the long-term consequences of this would be. In part this ties in with some of my strengths: I am expert at the playing part, I want to succeed and will work all hours to achieve that. I wanted the job badly. Yes, I was keen to step up and I was prepared to tolerate a big workload to make a success of it.

'But the job was too big for one person. I tried to shoulder everything but quickly spiralled down. It always seemed easier to do things myself rather than explain them to others, so I delegated less and less and I found myself getting more and more isolated from the team. I couldn't admit that problems existed so I left – only to repeat the whole scenario again. I am on my third go but I am getting it together at last.'

Table 4: Player Manager Profiles

Attributes and Challenges

Rookie

To step up and take command without doing it all personally

Strengths
- Never done it before
- Keen to step up
- Gets things done
- Determined to succeed
- Technically expert
- Works long hours

Shortcomings
- 'Task' not 'people' oriented
- Fails to delegate
- Feels responsible for everything
- Relies on 'expert' status
- Doesn't seek feedback
- Prone to denial

Player's Player

To replicate their own success in others

Strengths
- Sets the pace
- Creates a climate of 'excellence'
- Inspirational
- Serves as role model
- Mentors star players
- Earns respect and admiration

Shortcomings
- Can overextend and divide the team
- Secrets of greatness often tacit
- Intolerant
- Less of a mentor to the average player
- Vulnerable to loss of momentum

Player Coach

To develop talent without losing sight of the bigger picture

Strengths
- Knows the players and how they play
- Develops and motivates others
- Generates team spirit
- Secures trust and commitment
- Improves everyone's game

Shortcomings
- Gets distracted from player role
- Loses sight of the end game
- Gets stuck in one-to-one meetings
- Doesn't build infrastructure
- Overprotective

Veteran

To manage the institution as well as the team whilst keeping both fresh

Strengths
- Builds systems and protocols
- Hones execution
- Identifies goals
- Creates acceptable boundaries
- Instils effectiveness
- Playing skills critical at times

Shortcomings
- Wedded to status quo
- Overly detached
- Not always charismatic
- Demotivates free spirits
- Protocols applied too rigidly
- Overmanages and underleads

Play Maker
To lead the team in new directions without disappearing out of sight

Strengths
- Thinks on the edge
- Unafraid to challenge authority
- Catalyst
- Undeterred by adversity
- Transforms the game

Shortcomings
- Disruptive
- Not always responsible or credible
- Expensive user of resources
- Disconnected from others
- Chaotic

Player Again
To get out sooner rather than later, regardless of perceived loss of face

Strengths
- Returns as a better player
- Strengthens the team
- Lesson to others – only way isn't up
- Advocates value of pure playing
- Less stressed individual

Shortcomings
- Leaves it too late
- Re-entry can be difficult
- Loss of face
- Reward issues
- Who does the managing?

We allowed a pause for a few questions and comments and the general sense in the room was one of sympathy for Roger. Maggi and Alex wanted to know more about the boss and Roger expanded on Dr B's 'deep end' school of management. Maggi's rage symptoms recurred when Roger explained how at least two other people thought that they too had his job, but she dealt with it without recourse to lavender balm. Alex said something about ties and headhunters that no one else caught, and we thanked Roger for his honesty. This had set a good benchmark for the rest; now for Nicola.

Nicola

Nicola came alive on taking her turn. Using the tricks of a top communicator, she made good connections all round. She had studied her brief and it paid off, because she never paused to refresh her memory about the attributes and challenges and never even glanced at the laptop screen. She told a colourful version of her late night crisis point, and her moment of truth amidst the wedding guests at a London hotel. Within two minutes everyone was engaged with her as a person and eager to hear how she measured up to her challenge.

'This will sound arrogant, but my problem was that it came too easily to me. I was born to sell, and until it was nearly too late I never passed on my talent to others. I was obsessed about my personal productivity and drew vain comfort from being able to outsell everyone else. I expected all of them to perform as well as I did, but as for giving any help apart from saying "Follow me!" – which is about as useful as a ski instructor saying the same to a novice at the top of a black run – I never did. Looking back, I was far too intolerant of anyone who couldn't yet ski and I never took the time to help them out beyond saying, "Look, do it like me."

'The upshot is there on the screens under "Shortcomings". With a factionalized team and average players feeling left out the instant that momentum slowed, I hit a wall. It was the worst thing that happened to me; and the best. Call it a wake-up call or whatever, but to feel good about myself again I had to change. Now I take pride in the achievements of others, in the whole team and organization, and not just in my personal production. After that my strengths came into their own, so I believe that I now generate "respect and admiration" from everyone, not just from an exclusive club of the top people in my team.'

For a moment we expected applause – and by the look of rapture on his face Alex would have been in the lead – but there was a long silence that we allowed to develop.

Martin broke the silence: 'You got religion then?'

'Not religion, Martin,' she replied, 'just a sense of what managing is really about.'

Alex

We disturbed Alex's rapture, calling on him to speak. Nicola was a tough act to follow.

'I think of myself as the guy that always got it half right, albeit a different half at any one time and, until recently at least, never both halves together. The halves that I am talking about are the two parts of the Player Coach's challenge, developing talent and the bigger picture. I originally focused hard on staying in command – too hard, maybe. Then I got a wake-up call from someone who left because I neglected him and I re-assessed my approach. I repositioned my role with a big focus on the first half of the Player Coach challenge, developing talent, and guess what? I did it badly, spending so much time "down in the weeds" as I was told, that I nearly lost the game.

'A lot of my problems stem from the way I developed people, especially once I found that I was rather good at bringing them on. I have good instincts for getting to know people and how they perform. People trusted me and became committed to me as their leader. We had terrific team spirit.

'The rub was that I became too absorbed with my little development group. It took my eye off nearly everything else. My playing virtually ground to a halt and I spent too much time in one to ones. It would have been better for me to step back, but I just didn't let go. In the end I came through, but not without sterling advice. Now I see Player Managing as a blend.'

Alex was personable, and people warmed to him even though we feared Nicola hadn't found him a match. Dun made a statesmanlike comment and Martin said that there would be a career for Alex in teaching if he could handle the pay cut. As there seemed little interest in debating Alex's story further, we asked Vikram to come on next in the hope that he would stir things up. In that, we were not to be disappointed.

Vikram

Vikram wore the half amused, half confused smile that we had seen before at moments when he was on a roll. He looked straight at us: 'I've absorbed and thought about everything in this data pack, and to be honest I'm still struggling with the notion that a Player Manager can do anything as tightly defined as "to lead the team in a new direction". I don't mean to disagree with everyone here, but I have to question whether or not "direction" is the answer. Isn't there a rule in systems theory that says complex adaptive systems cannot be directed, they can only be disturbed?[1] And isn't an organization such a system? And if the rule is true, then aren't we just kidding ourselves with all this talk about direction? None of us can predict what will happen, so how can we set out to influence it?

'And,' Vikram continued, 'if organizations are beyond influence, isn't that the time to start thinking about new options, to really start inventing a new model? Instead of asking if we need more management or better management or more qualified Player Management, we could ask instead what comes after management. Do we really need management at all?'

We had glanced at each other nervously when we caught the emphatic tone of Vikram's 'And', but relaxed on sensing that Vikram had spotted that he was moving out on his own with this one. To his credit he checked in with the group, looking round and asking: 'Does anyone see what I mean?'

'I do,' said Maggi, who we noticed was back on coffee, albeit the decaffeinated kind. 'I see it absolutely. It was one reason I was so resistant to some business processes that my company was intent on introducing. I felt the real purpose of these processes was tighter management control at the expense of the discretion of my team and me. In my opinion the sales rep at the sharp end is the best person to call the shots. We pick up the vibes about what is going on with clients and that is the only intelligence that counts. Personally, I do not need managing. In turn, I didn't want to impose it on others or get bogged down in the administration of managing my team just to report data upwards to people who still wore suits.'

'But surely someone has to pull the whole thing together?' queried Nicola, sounding slightly stricken as though her recent learning about team leverage was threatened. 'The Player Manager's job is to make sure the whole is bigger than the parts and that requires direction and integration of effort, doesn't it?'

'Maybe you are right,' said Vikram, appeasingly. 'But it is a very Newtonian view. Before we all continue applying it, it's worth looking at whether its assumptions are still valid.' Vikram was doing his best to keep people with him, but so far Nicola was not persuaded.

'Look,' Nicola said, baring her famous smile, 'as far as I know, Newton was right and apples do still fall down from trees. We have just acquired a new company and we are looking for synergies and efficiencies. I can't just leave it to integrate itself, can I? Otherwise we will never get our money back.'

Dun had been silent so far, but now he stepped in: 'I have a feeling that games are being played with us here. What you are doing is what it says there on the screen: you are pushing us to the edge. Whether it's thinking on the edge or challenging authority, you can see that you have had just what it says: a catalytic effect on others.'

'Isn't there something else about the Play Maker's role?' interrupted Martin. 'Isn't there something about not "disappearing out of sight"? Don't Play Makers, just like teachers, have to pace themselves to the needs of the class?'

Dun turned to Joy. 'It seems to me that my friend's intervention today illustrates the second part of the Play Makers' attributes – their shortcomings. Words like "disruptive", "not always responsible", "disconnected" and "chaotic" encapsulate these shortcomings perfectly. It seems to me that there's a world of difference between transforming the game and destroying it.'

'But,' said Vikram, with a definitive 'but', 'how can you transform something without destroying it? What is left of the caterpillar when the butterfly emerges?'

'Come again?' said Alex.

Time for a Break

We were in desperate need of a break, so we ignored Alex's query to take advantage of what could be interpreted as a rhetorical question from Vikram. We suggested everyone let the debate sink in. The arrival at that moment of coffee, real tea, herb tea and pastries gave us the chance to allow a more informal debate to develop. Dun formed a group with Roger, Alex and Nicola. Maggi and Vikram seemed to have found each other and Martin breezed over to us.

'Worried then?' he said. 'It reminds me of a parent–teachers evening I once held when they all blamed the head and started talking about parent rule.'

We asked him what he did.

'Told them that we weren't here to boil the ocean and got back to business.' It sounded like good advice to us and we eased people back into the meeting room to hear from Dun.

Dun

'I've more in common with Vikram here than any of you might imagine. I too never really believed in management. I regarded it as a waste of talent and inferior to practice. I dealt with clients, worked with a team and played my part in running the partnership when called upon. But where Vikram and I differ is that I saw what happens when organizations are not managed and ours began to slow down. In our profession, running a firm is like riding a bike: you are either going forward or falling off, and I felt a sense of duty to get in the saddle and start pedalling when invited to do so by my partners.

'To begin with, the challenge was like the one that you see on the screen. I had to move from concentrating primarily on the team to considering the interests of the institution as a whole. That was harder than it sounds, because as a Player Manager I was still involved with the team and I felt a strong bond with them. There were times also when they seemed to need me, whether it was my judgement or my contacts, and I know that in the early days, other departments felt that I spent too much time with them.

'I learned to resist my natural tendencies to go back to the team, focusing instead on bringing some method to our operations. Without boring you with the details, most of what I did involved the introduction of processes, things to make us more efficient and more professional. I also put a scorecard in place so that we could understand how we were doing on our dual goals of profitability and integrity to the law and clients. The key words on the screen are "systems and protocols", "execution" and "effectiveness". I suppose the fact that people were prepared to live with this meant that I did also create "acceptable boundaries".

'For quite a while these "strengths", if I may borrow your description, carried me along and concealed my weaknesses. People came to think I was a bit grey and others found me inflexible; a stickler for the rules. Yet they put up with that while we were going forward. And then things changed – not us, we carried on in the same old way – but in our industry. New influences came to bear and people told me that I was stuck in the past. Once that started I detected less of a desire for them to see me in the deals: "he is trying to interfere again" seemed to be the mood. I caught wind of this soon enough to adapt, but it was a shock. It was as though I had become such an agent for the institution that I had lost touch with the teams.'

There was silence after Dun had finished. Though in some ways the most eminent person present, he had bared his soul to a roomful of strangers. Vikram broke the silence with a gesture. He extended his hand to Dun.

With that, the tension that had been building subsided, and while this lasted we turned to Maggi and then Martin.

Maggi and Martin

Maggi started by disclosing that she had been ousted from her job. 'I got just about everything wrong in the challenge that there was to get wrong. I got out later rather than sooner with maximum loss of face. My friends tell me it was a spectacular fall from grace. But we can all laugh about it now because it was the best thing that ever happened to me. It took me back to what I was good at, but the journey was painful and the way that I went about it was all wrong.

'I regret not listening to my misgivings about managing and sticking to selling. Realizing that has helped me in my new career; I am now a better player and can give something to others by being in the right role, by being happy in what I do. Partly this relates to being a partner in a small, open organization, but also it's to do with being true to myself. I got there in the end.'

Maggi's story aroused a good deal of respect and, we thought, high levels of self-scrutiny amongst all but Martin. We joked that before everyone left to start new careers as pure players, Martin would tell us how he came to terms with his challenge.

'Whether or not I have lost face depends on who you talk to. Some people that I am close to view me as a failure; someone who couldn't hack it and who got out before it got to him. Others just assume that I got fired. I got tired of hearing the joke: "What's it like to be back at the chalk face?" Only those who know me understand it was my choice, though the important thing is that I know that myself.

'If I look at the strengths Players Again are meant to have, most of them apply to me. I am a better teacher for having had a spell away from it, and I think that others see me as an example of how the only way forwards need not be up. I am certainly much happier and, I suppose, less stressed as a result.

'There are two shortcomings to the way that I have chosen to go. One is financial. I took a significant salary reduction when I stepped down and private coaching has filled only part of the gap so far. We have a struggle to make ends meet. The other issue is "who does the managing". I don't know the answer to that, although I took something from the earlier debate. I don't like to think I burden others by saying "not me" because, weighing up the pros and cons, what I did was the right thing.'

It was time to sum up the contributions from our seven Player

Managers. In doing so we drew out the connection between the attributes and the challenges. In most of their cases our Player Managers had reached their crisis points by not adapting the skills that had won them promotion in the first place. When their strengths were overplayed, their shortcomings were revealed and they often became their own worst enemies. The interplay between these strengths and shortcomings was what determined whether the challenge was met. We promised to return to the questions Vikram had raised about the future of management, but for the moment it was time to move on to the second part of our agenda: 'How do you compare to Amanda?'

We asked everyone to focus on Amanda's three objectives and her six levers for achieving them. We were interested to examine how each Player Manager's attributes determined the levers that they pulled and how, in turn, this affected the outcome of their challenge.

Every Picture Tells a Story

We refreshed everyone once more on Amanda's three objectives of short-term results, mid-term growth, and long-term sustainability and asked them to look back over the definitions of her six levers. We explained that we would relate these to both the time when we had first met and also to the situation that they found themselves in now. We called those 'Time One' and 'Time Two'.

In a file they could share from the laptops in front of them we asked everyone to complete two columns about their use of the six levers. The instruction on the screen read:

Simply indicate for each lever displayed in the left hand column both for time one and for time two whether or not this is something you had in place or applied. Time One (T1) is when we first met you and Time Two (T2) is now.

When their input was complete, we went round again asking everyone to explain their responses.

Levers Pulled	Rookie Player	Players' Player	Player Coach	Veteran	Play Maker	Player Again	Player Again
	Roger	Nicola	Alex	Dun	Vikram	Maggi	Martin
End Game							
T1	X	✓	↓	✓		X	✓
T2	X	✓✓	↑	✓	☺	✓	✓
Game Plan							
T1	X	✓	↓	✓		X	✓
T2	X/✓	✓✓	↑	✓	☺	✓	✓
Benchmarks							
T1	X	✓	↓	✓	😐	X	✓
T2	✓	✓	↑	✓	☺	✓	✓
Enablers							
T1	X	✓	↓	✓	☹	X	✓
T2	✓	✓	↑	✓	☺	✓	✓
Feedback							
T1	X	✓	↑	X	☺	X	✓
T2	✓	✓✓	↑	✓	☺	✓	✓
Commitment							
T1	X	✓	↓	✓	☺>☹	X	✓
T2	TBA	✓✓	↑	✓	😐>☺	✓	✓

Roger's Four

Roger began by saying that he had never been one for overcomplicated matrices and management grids, and that when it came to communicating a point he had learned to do without such technical props. He acknowledged however that 'perhaps I am only saying that because I get so few ticks.' Everyone looked at the screen to see that across all of the levers he had only assigned himself ticks in four out of a possible twelve boxes on his use of the levers at Time One and Time Two.

Roger said straightforwardly: 'This is how my style compares to Amanda's. Although I am now in my third Player Manager job I am still a rookie, having learned the hard way what this job is all about. Notice I don't have an end game, even now. True, I have only been back at my old company for a few months but my style still errs towards being tactical. I am just really learning to handle the people thing in a way that enables the team to be more productive. I used to be accused of being a bit isolated and not delegating. It was no wonder I couldn't delegate with confidence because I hadn't taken time to specify a game plan. I didn't trust my team to deliver the results the way I thought things should be done, but as I hadn't given them any benchmarks, how could they?

'As for enablers, well, that is where I feel I have now put some good things in place. A few simple methods and frameworks help everybody work together more smoothly. Now that I see my job is to help other people get results, I am much less defensive when people come forward with suggestions. Apparently I started out with the feedback skills of a clam, and when I did give feedback people felt it was like being with a teacher giving instructions. I was trying to manage everything from the mindset of a player, not a Player Manager.

'I was barely in command of myself, never mind the team. Looking back, I was almost paranoid. But that changed once I realized how poorly I was influencing. I tried to earn respect for what I was already respected for and did nothing about the levers that would have helped me take command. I see from reading Amanda's extract that I could be more strategic still. I need an end game and a game plan. On commitment – well, it's too early to tell. If I can't put a tick in that box within six months, I will have failed. My stock is up though, because a lot of people didn't seem to trust the man I replaced.'

Nicola's Sixteen

It was Nicola's turn next: 'Unlike Roger, who I am sure is just being terribly modest, I have given myself sixteen ticks out of a possible twelve. So before everyone starts thinking I am one of those Player Managers Amanda criticizes for being wrapped up in their own star-dom, let me explain.

'In bond sales, nobody really thinks long term. We are very short-term focused, and if anything I amplified that thinking. I always had an end game and that is why that box is ticked; it was for us to be number one and the game plan, which is also ticked, was for me to be the best producer with everyone following my lead. As I said earlier this was immature, and while seemingly great for me was actually damaging the team.

'I hadn't quite understood the commercial advantages of team leverage, of the idea that if you use 10% of your energy to raise everyone else's game by 10%, it can bring in more money than if you gave that 10% of your own energy to playing. The result of this was that although our results were still good, we were getting a bit stuck. I was putting our future growth at risk because the game plan wasn't spelled out. We were just living off momentum.

'I was always keen to enable the team and I made sure we had a climate where we all went out regularly to share stories and successes. But if by "enablers" we are talking about resources and systems, then if anything I was allergic to spending on them. Benchmarks I also tick myself for. If "benchmark" is another word for "standards", then I am a real stickler for keeping them high. But I got feedback that the standards I used were a bit too absolute and narrow. My feedback was unmistakable but apparently too subjective. I put it over more by a look than candid and helpful conversation. Likewise with commitment. I had it all right, but only from those in the club; those outside the club felt more resentment than commitment.

'Actually I had all the levers in place, but in a very unsophisticated fashion and not for everyone. The way I was pulling on them was divisive and corroding motivation. Like Roger, I hadn't found my stride at the next level of Player Managing.

'So why all those double ticks now? Today I do have strategic command of all the players and of the whole game, and I understand that my production is just a part of it. I am using those levers to develop strategy, not just to reinforce my position. As for commitment I was about to say, "Just ask the team, they'll tell you". But I once came horribly unstuck on that one. Let's just say this time I am confident, but hopefully not complacent.'

Alex's Arrows

Alex started off by saying, so affably that no one could possibly have minded, 'Well Nicola, you are a product of your industry scoring sixteen out of twelve. I knew that we marketing people couldn't be alone in using that kind of maths.' Then he turned to his own column on the laptop: 'I have used arrows not ticks, because an arrow is an image about direction. Initially I had no direction, then I went all over the place, and now I hope that I have straightened out. Positioning is something I am supposed to know something about, but I positioned myself very badly. I'll spare you the details, but let's just say that in the absence of a map or a compass I found myself horribly lost in a forest with wolves; well, one wolf at least.'

This time the group were intrigued, but Alex, reluctant to give more details, continued with his account.

'I am a bit like Nicola. I thought I had quite a few of these levers in place but I wasn't using them in a balanced or integrated way. This started to show up horribly. My end game was to increase our share of the market by developing a winning team of talent and our portfolio of brands. My original game plan was to set plans with all the people in the team and to let a couple of my best people take over some of my playing. I had given everyone individual benchmarks and also enablers, but I hadn't given the team any system for working together. Therefore I had inadvertently disabled rather than enabled the team. I was off my own game and sidetracked by politics, and some team members began to doubt my commitment to their cause. In the end it was me who needed feedback, not them.

'Now we have some systems and processes in place, together with regular team briefings about where we are all against plan. It might sound as though I have even more to do now that I am back playing and managing the business more systematically but actually, now that I am not trying to be all things to everyone, it feels like less. At last I am in a good position, although I will watch the market on that.'

Dun Takes a Stand

'Call me a Veteran if you like, but the point of Player Managing is to get the game under control and keep it that way. My principal goal, or end game, was – and is – to run our firm well. I blend the requirements of the organization, which involves significant issues of regulation and compliance in our industry, with the professional needs of our people in the field – including myself as an individual practitioner.

'I have uncertainties to deal with all the time. This can involve conflicts of interest between sectional interests and group-wide considerations, for example between the conservative instincts of Read and Williams' private clients and the needs of the overall business to change in response to industry trends in the corporate sector. To handle these conflicts we need a game plan. There is also risk of conflict between more conservative instincts towards the status quo and the need to keep the business fresh, as expressed by our younger element. On this I have recently found myself challenged, so I have discovered the value of team enablers as I was pushed by, well, by Play Makers like Vikram here.

'My challenge was to enable their need for creative freedom without letting go of the reins of our firm. It is a hard balance to strike, but easier when one can take a view that has a team as well as an institutional perspective. When these conflicts start, the effectiveness of one's mechanisms for collecting feedback becomes crucial. It is important to listen and, even more, to know when to respond. You cannot be too democratic about this, otherwise the very basis of your election to leader in the first place begins to corrode. I like to believe that I got the balance right between listening and acting on the feedback, and on taking a stand when I felt strongly about something. Oddly enough, it's the times that one is brave enough to take a stand that builds real commitment.'

Vikram's Smiley Faces

It was Vikram's turn, and we were a little bit tense. So far, everyone had followed the question on levers and the more fundamental questions were all nicely parked. If anyone was about to un-park them, it would be Vikram. At the right moment we would welcome it, but that moment wasn't now. Vikram clearly had no sense of this: 'This might sound odd coming from a programmer and systems designer like me, but my whole approach to Player Managing is "no diagrams".[2]

'It follows from what I said earlier. As we can't direct or determine things, then the idea that Player Managers can put in frameworks that neatly control people's performance, like puppet masters pulling on the strings of puppets, is bullshit.'

Alex cut in. 'Then why have you put all those different faces up on the screen which imply that it isn't?'

'In my industry we use these symbols a lot, as does anyone on the web,' responded Vikram. 'It's a code for emotional tone. Although I had seen loads of these in my time, I had never really appreciated their significance. They remind us that people have feelings.

'I have learned that feelings are an important ingredient of complexity. I may not have the power to direct circumstances, but I am an agent in the system; I can trigger change by an intervention. While unable to control the outcome, I can discover something about the effect of the intervention by studying people's emotional reaction. This, I have learned, is often the real energy behind the intellectual positions people take. It is the clue to what they really care about. I still believe that the best way to win in business is to outthink the competition; scale is useless without the best ideas. But I also realize that the best ideas can end up in the recycle bin if you don't take emotional agendas into account.'

'Call me simple if you like, and believe me you wouldn't be the first, but aren't you saying that you do want to influence things then?' queried Martin.

Vikram smiled at Martin's question. 'People don't like confusion. Chaos might be the soup we are all swimming around in, but nobody wants to live like that. So we have our end games and our game plans to minimize confusion on the way. If you look at my faces on the screen, you will see that I believe that by not having an end game and game plan at Time One, I left people nonplussed. People could see that the familiar specification was changing because I had meddled with the system, but while I was happy to wait and see what changes fell out, everyone else felt disabled. Luckily I had a lot of commitment to draw on, and most people trusted me enough to give me the rope to hang myself with. And of course, I nearly did.

'So now I do have an end game, which is to disturb things in a way that doesn't unduly disturb others. To leave them smiling, in fact. My game plan is to handle things in a way that doesn't overly destabilize the people running the business. I have learned that benchmarks and enablers are the accepted code and that they need to be transparent and shared. In my case, people wanted to set up a controlled study and see the effects of that before making any bigger commitment to changes being proposed. That is what they wanted and that is what we did.'

Maggi Runs Free

Part of the way through Vikram's exposition, Dun had begun tapping his pen on his leather-bound pad. So fierce had it become that Roger, Alex, and perhaps the others as well, had noticed. However, as Vikram spoke Maggi's interest was clearly mounting with an intensity matched only by the movement of Dun's pen.

We didn't know exactly how many months it had been since Maggi had been pushed to her crisis point, but we knew that this was going to be the moment when she pushed right back. It was her moment for the protest she should have made earlier, the time when she hadn't tried with her boss. Run for it, Maggi, we thought, but as we did it struck us that her real target was not in the room, so the surrogate would be 'the rule of law', aka Dun.

Maggi breathed in deeply and began. 'Since giving up my Player Manager role, I have been wrestling with the notions we are today calling "playing" and "managing". I even studied business theory, but much of it assumes that we can't be grown-ups, that we are somehow incapable of sitting down to define, organize and execute our own work. The real issue here isn't about chaos or control as the way forward, it is about the way we treat each other at work. The crux of this, and I think it is the crux of the levers too, is authority. It is about everyone's attitude to power.

'While you were all debating the "no diagram" thing, I adjusted my Time Two scores. I originally scored myself very few ticks, because I have no team and assumed that I wasn't pulling these levers at all. Yet I am. In the start-up I'm now involved with, we manage ourselves with these all the time and we don't get hung up about it either. It is now crashingly obvious. Not only do professionals like me not need managing, in the end we cannot be managed. In the end the debate on authority becomes academic.'

'Say again?' requested Roger.

Maggi obliged. 'We cannot be managed because our know-how is so specialized and complex. Moreover, the circumstances in which we need to apply that know-how are too dynamic to wait for a decision from someone who doesn't know what we are talking about anyway. Do you get it? The puppets know more than their masters.'

'Only up to a point,' said Dun thoughtfully, 'and then only in certain organizations or professions. It is simply not true to say that all situations are so fluid that only the people on the job can understand them. Experience and teamwork are vital to solving problems in many professions, and I am not just talking about the law. Do you think that hospitals or financial institutions or precision manufacturing could function properly without a framework or a process to decide resource allocation? Would you like to go in for heart surgery knowing that the operation would be performed by a team that reached its own decisions on the hoof? Is that the way you would like them to respond to a crisis when instant judgements and leadership are required? Would you like your pension fund to be managed by a single fund manager doing his or her own thing, with no reference to an asset allocation framework or others' experience of market cycles?

'I am afraid,' Dun continued, looking first at Vikram and then at Maggi, 'that what's good for the software industry or even retail start-ups does not necessarily have any wider application. It's not about no diagrams and puppets and masters, it's about structured management of complex problems. And that requires people like us to do some managing.'

There was an uneasy silence after Dun had finished. We took advantage of the quiet and moved the meeting on.

Martin's Perfect Sum

Martin, who had said little so far, was the only one left to go through the list of levers. Before he started, Nicola joked, 'I suppose you are going to conscript the workforce into some kind of knowledge-based co-op as well, aren't you?'

Feeling unjustly sentenced ahead of his trial, Martin said, deliberately, 'If I was, I doubt very much that you would be coming with me, eh Nicola?' He was ready to take the floor.

'If I have followed our lively conversation so far, then what is under debate at this stage is no longer the levers but rather who should be pulling them. Everyone agrees that these six levers can be very usefully applied, and if you look at the marks all down my list you will see that I have found them positively useful too. So much so, in fact, that I have achieved a perfect score. Twelve boxes, twelve ticks. But others who know me could have been equally entitled to give me twelve crosses. So what makes my marking stand up against theirs?

'The levers are always there to be pulled. What differs is the behaviour of the people pulling them. It's the attributes that we talked about earlier that influence when and how they are pulled. In my case I pull all the levers, regardless of what I am doing. Others don't pull any levers even when they are responsible for managing. Some would say I walked away from the levers altogether. But I didn't; I still pull them all, but in class with my students. The name of the game has changed, that's all. I am no longer managing the institution like Dun, and the people that still are would score me zero. Whatever circumstances we find ourselves in, the levers are there and it is our choice whether to pull them or not. We cannot walk away from that. We can't predict what happens to us as Vikram says. But it is always our choice how we react. There is nothing random about that.'

Martin had neatly tied the profiles of our various types to the levers and we were grateful for that. Player Managers, pure managers and pure players all have to meet challenges with their personal portfolio of strengths and shortcomings. Amanda's levers can improve climate and performance, but the decision to use them is a matter of personal choice, and even then they do not represent a formula for guaranteed success. We were indeed back where Maggi said we should be: with real people doing real work.

One Hundred Minutes Later

Philip was to take our guests for lunch while Joy prepared a summary of the morning events which she would give when everyone returned.

She couldn't quite work out how to close on the fundamental issue about the future of management that remained awkwardly hanging in the air. In organization theory, it was a familiar old chestnut. But how did it relate to Player Managers who had to look both ways as they struggled to manage while they worked? In the end she followed the example of those around her, relating the issue to real people doing real work, supplemented with another old chestnut: sport.

'You have shown us that each Player Manager's style is personal, as are their circumstances,' she said. 'We can all see, I am sure, that Vikram would be as unlikely to succeed at Read and Williams as Dun would at AlphaSolva. You and the jobs that you do are testimony to the law of infinite variety. Everyone has their own story and the types that we described cannot catch all of these subtleties.

'However, following our discussion it appears to most of us that success is not random. Whether intuitively or systematically applied there are things, or levers, that Player Managers can get hold of to raise their own and others' performance. These levers will be applied in different ways by different people according to their attributes and the situations in which they find themselves. They form the basis of the successful producer-manager, because they provide a method of using the whole team's resources to get better results whilst leaving the Player Manager with enough capacity to carry on with personal production. That kind of leverage is the only means known to us for Player Managers to cope with the problems – for example mistakes, overwork, stress, burnout – that are always present whenever managing and producing are combined.

'We originally took our idea for the Player Manager from sport, and as we have worked with you and got to know you we can tell that Player Managers in work are all, in their way, competing. And like any athlete who strives to excel in his or her particular discipline, Player Managers in work have to be thinking constantly about how to raise their game.

'In certain sports it has become popular for the head coach or team manager to develop a playbook – a whole book of pre-planned moves. As with Player Managers in business, some leave their plays more open and freewheeling. Others define plays more tightly, training their teams to follow numbered routines.

'What stands out is that both of these types of play have proved successful. And on occasion both have failed. What is common to the success is a game plan that outwits the other side, played by a well-chosen team with the willingness and means to adapt when things change.

'There is no universal solution, no single right way or wrong way. Whether you are juggling balls or plates, some will get dropped. What we have to do as Player Managers is to work out how many we need in the air to keep the crowd happy and the juggler in a job.'

The Fictive Hero

Everyone said their goodbyes with the strained effusiveness of people who had shared an intense experience but would very likely never see each other again.

'Oh no!' said Philip on the way back into the room. 'We forgot to tell them the most important thing.'

'What do you mean?' Joy questioned, not quite following.

'We forgot to tell them that Amanda Sage isn't real.'

Joy was silent for a moment. Then she remarked pensively: 'What is it that Wallace Stevens says in that long poem about the Supreme Fiction? "How simply the fictive hero becomes the real".[3] I'd say Amanda Sage was real enough.'

PART THREE

Double Jeopardy

13

The Invisible Manager

No Distinction

In J. K. Rowling's new classics, the budding wizard Harry Potter is given a cloak of invisibility.[1] To judge from the way that mainstream management literature has stared right through them, we wonder whether Player Managers have also been wearing an invisibility cloak for much of their existence.

If, however, The Player Manager has become The Invisible Manager, then it is through an easily explained disconnect rather than through the use of a magical cloak. This disconnect lies in the general perceptions that 'producing' and 'managing' are distinct and separate activities, and that the latter is more worthy of attention than the former in enquiries into how organizations work.

The failure of the majority of observers to recognize the importance of Player Managers or even to identify them as a distinct group requires explanation, given the important role that they now perform. That role sees Player Managers in industry struggling to bridge the gap between the rhetoric and the reality of empowerment in flattened hierarchies, in the public and private professions coping with growth and complexity whilst keeping up appearances as hotshot producers, and in the knowledge economy trying to do their jobs as they keep up with rapid change. Across all economic sectors, important management responsibilities are in the hands of people who have to look both ways into managing while they work: the invisible – but very real – Player Managers.

The lack of recognition of Player Managers as a group arises for different reasons in different sectors. In industry this lack of recognition is rooted in the 1950s when management, after being progressively defined as a discipline through the first half of the century, was elevated above production in the business hierarchy. Management was now a subject to be studied, to be written about and for which postgraduate qualifications like an MBA could be obtained. Work, on the other hand, was the thing that needed to be done, not studied. Even though technical work itself became more complex, specialized and recognized by the growth of its own professional bodies, in these years management was the primary lever for increasing its productive value.

Once management became a specialization in its own right, it became all too easy to miss the overlaps between managing and producing. Consequently models for management, even in the new flattened and empowered world, bear the legacy of scientific management and focus primarily on the managing part, less on the playing part, and rarely on the problems of combining the two. This merely reflects practice. Once 'general' management became an occupation for technical specialists to aspire to in the second half of the twentieth century, organizations carved the separate career paths for managers and producers that are still evident today. The disconnect became established.

In the public and private sector professions the Player Manager disconnect arises the other way round. Specialists in this area consider 'playing' to be more significant than 'managing'. Seeing technical professional skills as the primary source of value, they view management as a necessary, but unwelcome intrusion rather than as a primary lever of productivity, as evident in the anti-managerial culture we have described. Heroes in the professions are those in the front line: the star barristers, the rainmakers in corporate finance, the creatives in advertising and the consultants in medicine. It's the cases they win, the deals they pull off, the ads they write, the lives that they save that are glorified, and the managing gets scant attention. Indeed, it is striking in the literature about the professions how until recently little had been written about the people that manage them.[2]

In the New Economy, as more people became involved in knowledge work the shortcomings of general management became more apparent. Handling the unexpected in innovative ways was the key to competitive advantage, and the interdependencies between good business decisions and creative production become obvious. In practice, the barriers between producing and managing were dissolving; many businesses found themselves too unresponsive to keep up. Yet even the very recent theories designed to address these problems, including models of adaptive leadership, 'third phase organizations',[3] emergence and ideas about 'new management'[4] treat 'managing' as a distinct activity. Inadvertently or otherwise, these models imply that managing remains separate.

In looking right through Player Managers, outside commentators are doing no more than reflecting the way that Player Managers are regarded within the workplace. Few businesses see the whole equation by fully recognizing the increasingly interwoven nature of producing and managing, even though many of their most important people are juggling both roles. The failure of their employers to recognize this explains why so many of the Player Managers that we encountered are overloaded with work and are underprepared for the responsibilities that they carry. Their employers have not registered the challenge that the duality of the role brings. Like another invisible character, this time the less harmless Jack Griffin in H. G. Wells' established classic *The Invisible Man*, they 'make no distinction'.

We Started with a Few Murders . . .

'We'll start with a few murders. Small men. Great men. Just to show we make no distinction,' announced Claude Rains in the movie *The Invisible Man*.[5] As we have reviewed the experience of Player Managers during the last twenty years, we conclude that as a consequence of this lack of distinction the body count has been high. This period included a decade of restructuring and downsizing during the reengineering of the eighties, a decade of growth following the 1991–2 recession and the millennium bust. It saw the transition of many western economies away from manufacturing to services and the underlying structural changes associated with the information age. These events, and the concomitant replacement of traditional unskilled jobs with more skilled knowledge workers and the enlargement of the middle classes, have been as significant for management as the nineteenth century Industrial Revolution was for labour.

Beginning with major job losses affecting managers and workers alike, metaphorical but not literal murder occurred throughout the western world, although the language of empowerment often cloaked this. In the nineties, as the demand for talent intensified and companies competed with one another for the best people, a different language was spoken. Talk about developing human capital became de rigueur as the century turned and, at least until the recession of 2001, there were some real signs that talk was being matched with action. Coaching and mentoring programmes became more common and, in the professional services sector at least, companies began to provide lifestyle support programmes for employees too busy at work to get home to let in the plumber.[6] Balancing the demands of work and the life outside it became a politically correct issue, evident in the chairing of a business breakfast at 10 Downing Street by the British Prime Minister Tony Blair, to launch 'Employers for Work-Life Balance'.[7] Throughout business and the professions, the rhetoric of long-term commitment and the re-establishment of partnership values revived. The dark days of downsizing seemed a distant shadow.

A key question for us, as we surveyed our evidence from Player Managers out in the field, was whether this new attitude to human capital was real enough to affect the great numbers of people actually doing the Player Manager's job. We wanted to know whether organizations had responded to changes in the nature of work because they believed that human capital was the differentiating factor in superior performance, or whether the talk about developing people was a tactical device created to snare the best talent during the economic boom.

Our preliminary conclusions on this are not positive. Although growing numbers of those we met had been affected by 'people platforms' of one kind or another, few considered that their employers showed any real understanding of the problems that they faced as Player Managers. While we came across many Player Managers who are happy in what they do, this is very often in spite of, not because of, the organizations in which they work. These Player Managers, described in Chapter Three as the Believers, consisted of natural competitors who were better equipped than most to flourish in a hostile climate; others who either got on with things or for whom work was serious but would not be allowed to get in the way of life in the fullest sense; and only one group – those living Aristotle's 'Good Life' – who were at one with their organizations. We found very little evidence of employers' initiatives causing people to feel that their jobs had become more manageable or that their personal development was of real concern.

Another large group of Player Managers were not happy at work, and we described these in Chapter Three as being Under Pressure. Whilst not holding their organizations entirely responsible for this, in many cases the employers' attitude to human capital is a factor in the pressure. The language of good human resources management – 'our people are our most important asset' for example – is hackneyed. Most organizations actually behave in a different fashion. Overloading naturally high-achieving Player Managers while failing to provide adequate support is a recipe for burnout, and there is evidence that this is increasing.[8]

Our scepticism about how deeply the new attitudes had penetrated was confirmed by events at the beginning of the new century as the recession tightened. The spectre of downsizing returned and all sectors quickly applied measures to 'rightsize'. When the earnings season approached, companies acted pre-emptively at the first hint of trouble: 'Today's job cuts are not solely about large, sick companies trying to save themselves, as was often the case in the early 90s (think IBM and Sears). They are about healthy companies hoping to reduce costs and shore up earnings by chopping headcount (think Goldman Sachs and AOL Time Warner). They are about trying to pre-empt tough times instead of reacting to them. These layoffs are radical preventive first aid.'[9]

Some lessons had evidently been learned. Even as companies rapidly laid off the 'talent' they had so heavily courted, there was widespread recognition that the cease-fire in the war for talent would be short. For those with scarce skills, layoffs came in the form of sabbaticals, leave with reduced pay, and time off for further study. This was old economy cost cutting with a new economy twist,[10] a sugar-coated downsizing. But despite the changed rhetoric in the intervening years, in 2001, just as ten and twenty years before, companies turned on their 'greatest asset' at the first hint of trouble. The idea of the shareholders accepting lower returns hardly crossed anyone's mind.

The Only Game in Town

Businesses that downsize to protect profits are not run by bad people, even if to the Player Managers who get caught up in this they appear callous. Everyone is just following the rules of the game as they are laid down. These rules give credence to free market competition as a necessary stimulus to business efficiency and entrepreneurialism. Deregulating capitalism from protectionism and excessive red tape while exposing all sectors to open market competition has created unparalleled prosperity in the West, it is argued.

The experience of Eastern Europe and the failure of communism is used as evidence that there is no viable alternative to capitalism as a means of production. Capitalism, therefore, must be allowed to run an unfettered course. This, it is believed, is the best way to create a rising tide of prosperity that will benefit everyone.

With capitalism as the only game in town, the rules have been set by reference to shareholder value, and there is no doubt where the impetus is coming from in the latest round of downsizing: 'Often they are reacting to angry investors. Never has Wall Street put so much pressure on companies. Share prices have become highly sensitive to even the tiniest earnings shortfall; investors will pummel a stock at the first hint of disappointment and job cuts are seldom far behind.'[11] Shareholder pressure for the removal of chief executives of companies whose results disappoint has led to a number of high profile 'resignations', casualties that act as a very powerful inducement for chief executives to be seen to be 'doing' something if results seem likely to fall below expectations.[12]

It is hard to blame senior management for protecting short-term profits by cutting back on jobs and long-term development expenditure. Managers are judged by the results of today, and frequently there are no alternatives if they themselves are to survive. This will not change while shareholder value is the central tenet of most organizations, and many would argue that it shouldn't. Shareholders are accountable to pension fund trustees, trustees are accountable to pension fund members and pension fund members need their pensions to be funded. They need to be invested in shares that go up, in shares that will create 'value' for them.

Yet for all of the discussion of stakeholders' interests,[13] no significant progress has been made towards running organizations in the interests of all stakeholders. Customers and employees consistently play second fiddle to the shareholders' needs as organizations are driven relentlessly towards securing the maximum short-term return. Private companies might be expected to show a more paternalistic approach, public sector organizations might be expected to pay more heed to their 'customers'. But everywhere the notions of 'shareholder value' and 'market forces' have become dominant, encapsulating the primacy of the short term. However, there is plenty of evidence that sustained shareholder value requires growth, not cost cutting: 'The debate pitting Wall Street (downsizing is good and pushes up share prices) against Main Street (layoffs hurt real people) is phony. A look at companies that have created the top stockholder returns over the past decade – such as Coca-Cola, Amgen and Applied Materials – indicates that the engine for these gains has been growth, not cost-cutting layoffs.'[14] Achieving that growth requires long-term programmes and a sustained investment in people as well as in products.[15]

Yet most organizations seem to regard the long term as merely the outcome of the serial short term as they focus mainly on immediate results. As we have shown in this book, it is often the Player Managers who have to deliver these sought-after performance gains. They are at the front line guarding the gate, attempting to both keep up the numbers and secure growth as they reconcile the multiple interests of customers, employees and shareholders. No wonder they are under pressure.

We do not expect any kind of fundamental shift in business objectives away from shareholder value. Capitalism powered by market forces is here for the foreseeable future. If there is to be any revision to the shareholder value regime, it is most likely to come through a realization that in the long run the interests of all stakeholders are identical. Particularly – but not exclusively – in the knowledge economy, a committed and motivated workforce is a key factor in providing the competitive edge that creates long-term shareholder value. The work of Jim Collins and others has demonstrated that it is the development of a corporate culture going far beyond short-term profit goals that distinguishes many of the companies that deliver shareholder value on a sustained basis.[16]

This longer-term focus requires the development of human capital in a way that could help to make the job of the Player Manager more manageable, and there are some signs of change. The story of Ricardo Semler and his Brazilian company, Semco, which he transformed through consultative democracy[17] is again attracting attention. In the UK and US many businesses have adopted flexible working practices as a means of attracting and retaining staff. Influential figures such as Peter Ellwood, the chief executive of Lloyds TSB which ever since the 1980s has been in the vanguard of the shareholder value movement, have spoken of the need to nurture human capital: 'By putting work–life balance at the heart of their corporate culture, organizations can improve morale, reduce absenteeism and employee turnover and increase productivity.'[18]

However, such initiatives are at the periphery of life in the workplace and there is not much evidence that increased resources are being put into management development beyond the bare minimum to provide for the needs of the day. The problem is that there is less and less reason for anyone to care about any particular company's future – not even the CEO, whose average period in office in large companies is only a few years. If that is so, then Player Managers will have to wait a long time for any fundamental change to emerge; in the meantime, they will have to survive by coping as best they can.

Double Jeopardy

What are the options for organizations in an age where short-termism rules supreme? One obvious course is just to carry on muddling through. That means expecting Player Managers to take the strain, overburdened and underprepared as they are. Many employers will allow this because the damage caused by this approach is never immediately apparent, emerging only in a high burnout rate amongst key employees. Player Managers who find themselves working for organizations like this will, we hope, find some survival strategies in the stories that we have outlined in this book.

If muddling through remains the most common choice, how much better if the Player Manager model were more carefully applied. This means giving them distinct recognition in more organizations, and in the literature, as well as appropriate enablers such as training and support tailored to the demands of the role. It is the antithesis of the 'deep end' school of management and it is more expensive in the short run. But as Player Managers would perform better if prepared for their dual role, it would be money well spent. This will be important when the next upturn comes, as organizations once more set about strengthening, rhetorically at least, their human capital.

There are other options. One is to reinstate the full time manager, returning in effect to the many-layered command and control hierarchies. There are some circumstances where this might work, for example where greater output might justify the additional layer of cost, or with those employees who prefer to be told what to do and to whom to report. However, for many others rigid hierarchy and the loss of the freedom to influence would be unacceptable. It is difficult to imagine that skilled knowledge workers and other professionally trained people who have grown up in a world that at least speaks the language of empowerment and flat structures will be happy to salute the flag. Nor would harking back to the good old days of command and control work for many modern organizations. They require matrix management allied to complex information systems and business processes to cope with diverse geographies and products across dynamic, competitive markets.

An alternative option for 'new age capitalism' is to extend the Player Manager concept to a model that involves all players in a team sharing the managing. This option twins the concept of empowerment with the much-posited ideas associated with network organizations[19] that a number of mainstream observers are finding increasingly relevant: 'Within the next twenty or thirty years we may well see the disappearance of conventional management and reporting structures, replaced by interdependent networks engaged in transactional relationships.'[20] The idea is to create even more agile and adaptive organizations, with self-managing teams acting quickly to share knowledge and solve problems as they emerge.

Player Managing as currently practised is a step down the road to self-managing teams and there are many steps in between. When authentically tied to empowerment however, all-player teams provide a model to explore for the future. For employers to become comfortable with such a distributed model of management and to be confident that leverage would still be attained requires conventional wisdoms about authority and leadership to be redefined.[21] We are far from discarding old wisdom, even though involving people in the running of the organizations in which they work may prove to be the best route to building the commitment that produces long-term gains for all stakeholders. Player Managing is at the heart of this model and many Player Managers are just waiting for the call.

We doubt whether the call will come to many very soon. Organizations seem set to continue to respond to the ten-year economic cycle, hiring voraciously and speaking of 'empowerment' and 'developing people' in the upswing, laying them off to protect short-term profits in the downswing. To stay on top of this and to survive themselves, few business leaders are likely to invite options where they relinquish the reins of control. But in industries where human capital is the only genuine competitive edge, more organizations will realize that how they conduct themselves, be the 'swing' up or down, will fundamentally affect their ability to attract and retain talent long term. That might mean the shareholders accepting lower short-term returns, but in the long run it will lead to a more sustainable business model that benefits people as well as the bottom line.

The most likely trigger for change will be supply-side pressures. In the US for example, by 2008 there will be 6.2 million more jobs than people to fill them according to government projections.[22] This will create competition for staff and choices for employees. Those with skills, especially those with rounded Player Managing skills, might become free agents like major league sportsmen, selling and reselling themselves to the highest bidder. Others may choose not to work as full time employees at all unless the advantages of a permanent position clearly outweigh the risks of self-employment. In a perverse twist of current practice, market forces might finally persuade organizations that human capital really is their greatest asset and that it needs as much care and maintenance as traditional tangible assets.

* * *

After nearly a generation of transformation and empowerment, organizations still treat their human capital expediently. Player Managers in this scenario are but the foot soldiers of postmodern work. The hope is that even with shareholder value as the objective of most organizations, more sophisticated and less short-term ways of attaining it could emerge. In the meantime, Player Managers would do well to assume that they are in double jeopardy. Not only are they themselves invisible, like young wizard Harry Potter, but they are also the targets of the more pernicious Invisible Man: 'We'll start with a few murders. Small men. Great men. Just to show we make no distinction.' It is time for more Player Managers, men and women, to make their own distinction.

Notes

Chapter 1

1 Drucker, Peter, *The Practice of Management*, Butterworth Heinemann, 1955, 1969 reprint, pp. 156–7 and 382

2 Galbraith, John Kenneth, *The Affluent Society*, 2nd edn, Hamish Hamilton, 1969, p. 159

3 Sampson, Anthony, *Company Man: The Rise and Fall of Corporate Life*, HarperCollins, 1996, pp. 96–8

4 In the period 1968 to 1980 actual employment growth for management and executives in the US was 43% – almost twice as high as the Bureau of Labor Statistics had projected for the period.

5 'If Japan Can . . . Why Can't We?', *NBC News White Paper*, www.does. org/masterli/q76.html

6 Owen, Geoffrey, *From Empire to Europe*, HarperCollins, 2000, p. 246

7 In 1986 and 1987, three reports identified faults in the UK system of management development: Mangham and Silver 1986, Constable and McCormick 1987 and Handy 1987. The Council for Management Education and Development was formed and in 1988 the controversial Management Charter Initiative was launched. Supported at the time by the Confederation of British Industry, the initiative proposed the establishment of a Chartered Institute of Management, with an associated qualification to be administered by the British Institute of Management.

8 Micklethwait, John, and Wooldridge, Adrian, 'Peter Drucker: The Guru's Guru', *The McKinsey Quarterly* 1996, Issue 3, p. 144. Drucker, Peter, *Adventures of a Bystander*, Heinemann, 1979, p. 273

9 Yankelovich, D., and Immerwahr, J., *Putting the Work Ethic to Work*, New York Public Agenda Foundation, 1983

10 Maslow, Abraham, 'A Theory of Human Motivation', *Psychological Review* 50, 1943, p. 370 and *Eupsychian Management: A Journal*, Irwin, 1965

11 Herzberg, Frederick, Mausner, Bernard, and Snyderman, Barbara B., *The Motivation to Work*, John Wiley, 1959

12 Kanter, Rosabeth Moss, *The Change Masters*, Simon & Schuster, 1985

13 Palmer, Joy, 'The Human Organization', *Journal of Knowledge Management*, Vol. 1, No. 4, June 1998, pp. 294–307 and De Geus, Arie, *The Living Company: Habits for Survival in a Turbulent Business Environment*, Harvard Business School Press, 1997

14 Stewart, Thomas A., *Intellectual Capital: The New Wealth of Organizations*, Bantam Books, 1998; Leadbeater, Charles, *Living on Thin Air: The New Economy*, Viking, 1999; Sveiby, Karl Erik, *The New Organizational Wealth: Managing and Measuring Knowledge Based Assets*, Berrett-Koehler, 1997

15 Heifetz, Ronald A., and Laurie, Donald L., 'The Work of Leadership', *Harvard Business Review*, January-February 1997, pp. 124–134, reprint 97106

16 Brown, Shona L., and Eisenhart, Kathleen M., *Competing on the Edge: Strategy as Structured Chaos*, HBS Press, 1998; Pascale, Richard T., Milleman, Mark, and Gioja, Linda, *Surfing the Edge of Chaos*, Crown Business, 2000; Birkinshaw, Julian, and Hagstrom, Peter (eds.), *The Flexible Firm*, Oxford University Press, 2000

17 Dopson, S., and Stewart, R., 'What is Happening to Middle Management', *British Journal of Management*, 1990, 1, pp. 3–16

18 Mintzberg, Henry, *The Structuring of Organizations*, Prentice-Hall, 1979, pp. 348–379

19 Brock, David, Powell, Michael, and Hinings, C. R., *Restructuring the Professional Organization*, Routledge, 1999

20 Sampson, op. cit.; Scarbrough, Harry, 'The Unmaking of Management?' *Human Relations*, 1998, Vol. 51, Issue 6, pp. 691–716

21 Drucker, Peter, 'The Coming of the New Organization', *Harvard Business Review*, January-February 1988, pp. 45–53. Drucker is generally credited with coining the term 'knowledge worker'.

22 Donkin, Richard, *Blood Sweat & Tears*, Texere, 2001, p. 278

23 Lorsch, Jay W., and Mathias, Peter F., 'When Professionals Have To Manage', *Harvard Business Review*, July-August 1987, pp. 78–83

24 Scarbrough, op. cit.

25 Open University, 'The Effective Manager', Book 9, 1996, p. 35, refers to 'The player-manager syndrome'. McKenna, Patrick J., and Maister, David H., *First Among Equals*, Free Press, forthcoming 2002, refers to the player coach.

Chapter 2

1 Kennedy, Allan, *The End of Shareholder Value*, Perseus Publishing, 2000
2 Rappaport, Alfred (ed.), *Information for Decision Making: Quantitative and Behavioral Dimensions*, Prentice Hall, 1970, and *Creating Shareholder Value: The New Standard for Business Performance*, Free Press, 1986
3 The movement was encouraged by aggressive and powerful institutional investors such as TIAA-CREF and CalPERs in the US.
4 Kennedy, op. cit., pp. 64–6
5 Owen, Geoffrey, *From Empire to Europe*, HarperCollins, 2000, p. 359
6 Sampson, Anthony, *Company Man: The Rise and Fall of Corporate Life*, HarperCollins, 1996, pp. 184–5
7 Rogers, David, *The Big Four British Banks*, Macmillan Press, 1999, pp. 59–60
8 'The Good Times Keep On Rollin', *Economist*, 25 October 1997
9 Owen, op. cit., chapters 4–13
10 Geroski, P. A., and Gregg, P., *Coping With Recession: UK Company Performance in Adversity*, CUP, 1997, pp. 4–6
11 Statistical Abstracts of the US
12 Owen, op. cit., p. 359
13 Stewart III, G. Bennett, *The Quest for Value: The EVA™ Management Guide*, HarperCollins, New York, 1991
14 *Business Week*, 28 February 2000
15 *HR Focus*, June 2000, copyright Institute of Management and Administration
16 'Buy Now While Stocks Last', *Economist*, 17 July 1999
17 Hammer, Michael, and Champny, James, *Reengineering the Corporation: A Manifesto for Business Revolution*, HarperCollins, 1993
18 Interview with former executive from the IT industry, 2001
19 Norm Brodsky in *Inc*, Vol. 22, Issue 10, pp. 37–38, July 2000
20 Max Horlick in *Employee Benefit Plan Review*, May 2000, Vol. 54, Issue 11, p. 50ff
21 Brodsky, op. cit.
22 Bureau of Labor Statistics, 'Assessing Projections of Management Jobs', Monthly Labor Review June 16, 1999, available from www.bls.com and www.dol.com
23 Caronna, Carol A., and Scott, W. Richard, in Brock, David M., Powell, Michael J., and Hinings, C. R., *Restructuring the Professional Organization*, Routledge, 1999, p. 78

24 Thatcher, Margaret, *The Downing Street Years*, HarperCollins, 1993, p. 47

25 ibid., p. 616

26 Enthoven, Alain C., *Health Affairs*, May-June 2000, Vol. 19, Issue 3, pp. 102–119

27 Thatcher, op. cit., p. 598

28 Kitchener, Martin in Brock et al, op. cit., p. 184. Le Grand, Julian, *Health Affairs*, May-June 1999, Vol. 18, Issue 3, pp. 27–39. Administrative costs rose from 8% of the NHS's total to 11% between 1991–2 and 1995–6, and between 1990 and 1995 the numbers of administrative and clerical staff grew by 15% and general senior managers by 133%.

29 Enthoven, op. cit.

30 Report from International Financial Services, London, *Financial Times*, 12 May 2001

31 'Lawyers Get Down to Business', *The McKinsey Quarterly*, Spring 2001, p. 45. See also the *National Law Journal*'s survey of New York's top 100 law firms in 2000. Those with more than 500 lawyers grew staff numbers by an average of 14%, while those with less than 200 grew by under 3%.

32 Brock et al, op. cit., p. 6

33 Greenwood, R., Hinings, C. R., and Brown, J., 'P-2 Form Strategic Management', *Academy of Management Journal*, 1990, 33(4), pp. 725–755

34 Hinings et al in Brock et al, op. cit., p. 131

35 Brock et al, op. cit., p. 2

36 ibid., p. 8

37 Thurow, Lester, *The Zero Sum Society*, Basic Books, 1980

38 In the 1960s and 1970s about 25% of the difference in average stock price earnings could be attributed to changes in reported earnings. By the early 1990s this had dropped to less than 10%. *The New Economy Index*, www.neweconomyindex.org

39 Average annual growth in the US economy has been calculated at 4.1% 1995–2000 (2.8%, 1973–1995) and business and consumer spending on IT accounted for 30% of this. *Business Week*, 27 August 2001.

40 ibid.

41 The US firm Cognetics Inc. recently estimated that the mainly New Economy companies listed on Nasdaq created more than one in six new jobs in the US.

42 Erik Brynjolfsson of MIT discovered a correlation between IT investment and smaller firms. The average US company is now about one third smaller than 25 years previously, both in terms of sales and number of employees. *The New Economy Index*, www.neweconomyindex.org

43 Research at the University of Texas by Donald Hicks revealed that the longevity of Texas businesses in the 1990s had dropped by half since 1970. For more on 'The Law of Churn', see Kelly, Kevin, 'New Rules for the New Economy', *Wired*, September 1997

44 Cellan-Jones, Rory, *dot.bomb: The Rise & Fall of Dot.Com Britain*, Aurum Press, 2001, p. 190

45 From the AT&T Divestiture, *A Memorial to the Bell System*, www.navy relics.com

46 www.Dell.com

47 See, for example, Kelly, Kevin, *New Rules for the New Economy: Ten Radical Strategies for a Connected World*, Harvard Business School Press, 1998

48 Daniels, Cora, 'The Man in the Tan Khaki Pants, Wall Street Unbuttoned', *Fortune*, 1 May 2000

49 Palmer, Joy, 'The Human Organization', *Journal of Knowledge Management*, Vol. 1, No. 4, June 1998, pp. 294–307

50 Pam Jones, Joy Palmer, Carole Osterweil and Diana Whitehead, 'The Changing World of Performance', *Mastering Management, Financial Times*, 2 August 1996

51 MacRae, Don, 'Six Secrets of Successful E-Leaders', *Business Week*, September 6, 2001

52 'Nine Myths about the New Economy', *The New Economy Index*, www.neweconomyindex.org/9myths.html

53 'Introduction to Open Source', *Open Source Initiative*, http://www.open source.org

54 'Netscape Announces Plans to Make Next-Generation Communicator Source Code Available Free on the Net: Bold Move to Harness Creative Power of Thousands of Internet Developers; Company Makes Netscape Navigator And Communicator 4.0 Immediately Free for All Users, Seeding Market for Enterprise and Netcenter Businesses'. Netscape Communications Corp., January 22, 1998, http://www.netscape.com, view by date

55 Raymond, Eric S., *The Cathedral and the Bazaar*, O'Reilly and Associates, October 1999, also at www.tuxedo.org

56 ibid.

57 www.opensource.org, op. cit.

58 www.infoworld.com

59 Halal, William E., *The New Management*, Berrett-Koehler, 1996

60 FP Mastering, part 5, July 2001, www.nationalpost.com

61 The premium in the stock market in first day dealings in the US averaged 69% in 1999 and 56% in 2000.

62 Stross, Randall E., 'Requiem for Webvan, Business and Technology', *US News*, 30 July 2001

63 *New York Times*, 4 August 2001

64 'Vigilance in the Face of Layoff Rage', *Management, New York Times*, August 2001

65 Ribon, Pamela, and Roy, Kari Ann, interviewed for 'The Start Up has come to a Complete Stop', *Austin American Statesman*, August 2001

66 Harder, Ben, 'Career Outlook: This Year it's back to Banking', *US News*, 2001, www.usnews.com

67 Mazar, M., 'The New Workplace is Dead, Right?', *Trendscope.net*, September 2001

68 Alan Greenspan speech to Senate banking committee in July 2001, from 'The New Economy: How Real is it?' *Business Week*, 27 August 2001

69 Jones, V. D., *Downsizing the Federal Government: The Management of Public Sector Workforce Reductions*, M. E. Sharpe, 1998

Chapter 3

1 Ginzberg, E., and Vojta, G. J., 'The Service Sector of the US Economy', *Scientific American*, March 1981, 244(3), pp. 31–9

2 George Litwin and Richard Stringer first defined the concept of 'organization climate' to include six key factors that influence the feel of the workplace to those working in it. O. G. Klemp developed it further, issuing both a Technical Manual and a Climate Questionnaire through McBer and Company in the mid 1970s. Harvard Professor David McClelland and his colleagues, also in association with McBer, refined the climate concept in their research on motivation during the 1980s. See also Richard Boyatzis and McBer's work, *The Competent Manager: A Model for Effective Performance*, John Wiley and Sons, 1981. For a recent definition and quick questionnaire see Jones, Palmer, Osterweil and Whitehead, *Delivering Exceptional Performance: Aligning the Potential of Organisations, Teams and Individuals*, FT Management and Ashridge, 1996, chapter 4, 'The New Contract', pp. 144–150. For the links between emotional intelligence, leadership style and climate, see Daniel Goleman, 'Leadership That Gets Results, *Harvard Business Review*, March-April 2000, pp. 78–90.

3 Harris, Harry, *Vialli: A Diary of his Season*, Orion, 1999, p. 1

4 JFK at the June 11 1962 Yale University commencement, extracted from 'John F Kennedy and The End of Ideology', www.english.upenn.edu

5 *Economist*, 8 July 2000

6 Goleman, op. cit., p. 80

7 ibid.

8 Tom Davenport interview with Joy Palmer, Boston, MA, January 1999. Also see Davenport, Thomas H., 'The Fad that Forgot People', *Fast Company*, November 1995, Issue 01, p. 70

9 Augar, Philip, *The Death of Gentlemanly Capitalism*, Penguin Press, 2000, p. 314

10 Thatcher, Margaret, *The Downing Street Years*, HarperCollins, 1993, p. 47

Chapter 5

1 John McDonough interview with Shelly Lazarus, 'Creating an Environment "where people can do great work" ', *Advertising Age*, 21 September 1998, Vol. 69, Issue 38

2 Hedda, Maryann, and Douglas, Charlie, 'Star Man', *Executive Talent*, October 2000

3 Nocera, J., *Fortune* cover story, 5 March 2001

4 Machiavelli, Niccolo, *The Prince*, Everyman's Library, 1992

Chapter 10

1 Raymond, Eric S., *The Cathedral and the Bazaar*, O'Reilly and Associates, October 1999, also at www.tuxedo.org

2 Eliot, T. S., *Old Possum's Book of Practical Cats*, in *The Complete Poems and Plays*, Faber and Faber Ltd, Book Club Associates edition, 1975, p. 226

Chapter 12

1 Holland, John H., *Hidden Order: How Adaptation Builds Complexity*, Perseus Press, 1996

2 The expression 'no diagrams' was taken from Keesling, G., Offensive Co-ordinator Earlham College, *Run and Shoot – An Offensive Philosophy*, www.coachhelp.com

3 Stevens, W., 'Notes Toward a Supreme Fiction' in *Selected Poems*, Faber and Faber Ltd, 1953

Chapter 13

1 Rowling, J. K., *Harry Potter and The Chamber of Secrets*, Bloomsbury Publishing, 1998

2 Notable exceptions include Maister, David H., Green, Charles H., and Galford, Robert M., *The Trusted Advisor*, The Free Press, 2000 and Kubr, Milan, *Management Consulting, A Guide to the Profession*, International Labour Office, 1996

3 Ghoshal, Sumantra, and Bartlett, Christopher A., *The Individualized Corporation*, Heinemann, 1998, pp. 265–270

4 Halal, William E., *The New Management*, Berrett-Koehler, 1998

5 Claude Rains, *The Invisible Man*, Universal Pictures, 1933

6 *Sunday Times*, 15 July 2001, reported such a programme at UBS.

7 Department for Education and Employment press release, 9 March 2000

8 Other research supports this. For example, *Management Today* annual survey cited in *Financial Times*, 28 May 2001 and Institute of Chartered Accountants report, *Financial Times*, 21 March 2001.

9 'White collar blues', *Fortune*, Vol. 144, Issue 2, 23 July 2001

10 Clark, Kim, 'You're laid off! Kind of. Firms look beyond pink slips', *US News*, 2 July 2001

11 *Fortune*, 23 July 2001

12 From amongst many examples, *Financial Times*, week commencing 14 Jan 2002

13 Hutton, Will, *The State We're In*, Vintage, 1996

14 Egan, Jack, 'On money, those !!$%&?! CEO salaries', *US News*, www.us news.com

15 Collins, James C., and Porras, Jerry I., *Built to Last*, HarperCollins, 1994; Kennedy, Allan, *The End of Shareholder Value*, Perseus Publishing, 2000

16 Collins and Porras, ibid. and Collins, James C., *Good to Great*, Harper-Collins, 2001

17 Semler, Ricardo, *Maverick: The Success Story Behind the World's Most Unusual Workplace*, reprint edn, 1995, Warner Books

18 Department for Education and Employment, op. cit.

19 See, for example, Mulgan, Geoff, *Connexity: How to Live in a Connected World*, HBS Press, 1998; Castells, Manuel, *The Power of Identity: The Information Age – Economy, Society and Culture*, Blackwell, 1997 and *The Rise of the Network Society*, Blackwell, 2000; Palmer, Joy, and Richards, Ian, 'Get Knetted: Network Behaviour in the New Economy', *Journal of Knowledge Management*, Vol. 3, No. 3, 1999, pp. 191–202

20 Donkin, Richard, *Blood Sweat & Tears*, Texere Publishing, 2001, p. 281

21 Palmer, Joy, 'Heaven and Hell: Surviving Self-Organizing Teams', *Journal of High Performance Teams*, Vol. 3, No. 4, August 1998, p. 10
22 Ann Kates Smith, Joellen Perry, Sage Dillon and Tim Smart, 'Charting Your Own Course', *US News*, November 6, 2000

Index

PENGUIN ONLINE

READ MORE IN PENGUIN

In every corner of the world, on every subject under the sun, Penguin represents quality and variety – the very best in publishing today.

For complete information about books available from Penguin – including Puffins, Penguin Classics and Arkana – and how to order them, write to us at the appropriate address below. Please note that for copyright reasons the selection of books varies from country to country.

In the United Kingdom: Please write to *Dept. EP, Penguin Books Ltd, Bath Road, Harmondsworth, West Drayton, Middlesex UB7 0DA*

In the United States: Please write to *Consumer Services, Penguin Putnam Inc., 405 Murray Hill Parkway, East Rutherford, New Jersey 07073-2136.* VISA and MasterCard holders call 1-800-631-8571 to order Penguin titles

In Canada: Please write to *Penguin Books Canada Ltd, 10 Alcorn Avenue, Suite 300, Toronto, Ontario M4V 3B2*

In Australia: Please write to *Penguin Books Australia Ltd, 487 Maroondah Highway, Ringwood, Victoria 3134*

In New Zealand: Please write to *Penguin Books (NZ) Ltd, Private Bag 102902, North Shore Mail Centre, Auckland 10*

In India: Please write to *Penguin Books India Pvt Ltd, 11 Community Centre, Panchsheel Park, New Delhi 110017*

In the Netherlands: Please write to *Penguin Books Netherlands bv, Postbus 3507, NL-1001 AH Amsterdam*

In Germany: Please write to *Penguin Books Deutschland GmbH, Metzlerstrasse 26, 60594 Frankfurt am Main*

In Spain: Please write to *Penguin Books S. A., Bravo Murillo 19, 1°B, 28015 Madrid*

In Italy: Please write to *Penguin Italia s.r.l., Via Vittorio Emanuele 45/a, 20094 Corsico, Milano*

In France: Please write to *Penguin France, 12, Rue Prosper Ferradou, 31700 Blagnac*

In Japan: Please write to *Penguin Books Japan Ltd, Iidabashi KM-Bldg, 2-23-9 Koraku, Bunkyo-Ku, Tokyo 112-0004*

In South Africa: Please write to *Penguin Books South Africa (Pty) Ltd, P.O. Box 751093, Gardenview, 2047 Johannesburg*